Boost

The Science of Recharging Yourself in an Age of Unrelenting Demands

Boost

The Science of Recharging Yourself in an Age of Unrelenting Demands

by

Jamie Gruman and Deirdre Healey
University of Guelph, Ontario, Canada

INFORMATION AGE PUBLISHING, INC.
Charlotte, NC • www.infoagepub.com

Library of Congress Cataloging-in-Publication Data

CIP record for this book is available from the Library of Congress
http://www.loc.gov

ISBNs: 978-1-64113-302-9 (Paperback)

         978-1-64113-303-6 (Hardcover)

         978-1-64113-304-3 (ebook)

CONTENTS

FOREWORD

Shawn Achor
New York Times bestselling author of
Big Potential and The Happiness Advantage

Any honest psychology researcher, philosopher, pastor, or leadership guru will tell you in private … perhaps over drinks … that there is a vast difference between knowing what to do and doing it. We know exercise is good. We know getting enough sleep is crucial. We know forgiveness is healing. We know gratitude stops pessimism. We know that we need others when we are down. Yet we clearly don't always do what we know we should—which I think makes it worse. In the past, perhaps only the wisest knew how much they failed to live up to their potential, but with the advent of the information age, no one can be stunned that exercise and sleep are good and smoking and workaholism are bad. **The vast gap between information and action I have found to be not a lack of knowledge or desire, but a lack of energy or motivation in that moment.** Which is why Deirdre and Jamie's book is of utmost importance right now.

We live in the most hyperconnected period of any age, yet when we get more texts of negative news alerts than we do from family members in a day, we suffer. We live in a world with more information and knowledge at our fingertips than at any point in human civilization, and yet when we fill every free moment with distraction, we suffer. The key is not avoiding technology or eschewing social media, it's about getting a boost that allows us to continue to progress in a positive direction.

Boost: The Science of Recharging Yourself in an Age of Unrelenting Demands, pp. xi–xii
Copyright © 2018 by Information Age Publishing

In my work, I define happiness not as pleasure which is short-lived and requires more and more effort to maintain in order to sustain the same return on your investment. Rather, I use the ancient Greek definition—*happiness is the joy you feel striving for your potential*. This is what Deirdre and Jamie are attempting to return to the forefront of our priorities. How can we redirect energy toward positive change and momentum using strategic catalysts in our lives that propel us toward our potential?

Boost has deep implications for everyone—from our overworked students, to our resource depleted medical providers, to our overwrought academics, to our harried managers. Within 10 pages you will see that this book is immaculately researched with tons of citations. But as every researcher eventually learns, research is much less valuable if it is never replicated and lived. Which is why YOU are the most important part of this book. Literally a single behavioral change—a change to your social media habits, a change to your sleep patterns, a refocusing of your energy over the course of the day, a change to the way you interact with others—will give your brain the positive feedback loop required to take another step, then another. This book offers a recipe for a better life, and you are the chef.

We seek boosts in all the wrong places. We go out of our way to get caffeine, we continually check e-mail to get a dopamine boost, we check with social media to see if we can get the boost of a "like" to our vacation photo with the cool filter, then we end the day with alcohol to try to boost our mood or social drive. Real boosting is about breaking that pattern and finding the things that actually fuel our pursuits and our potential.

Now that I'm a father to two beautiful children, I find that I have less time to waste. They make me want to be a better person. They make me want to live longer. They don't allow me to wallow in wasted time. So, for me and you, Boost is not just about *our* success, but the happiness, well-being and success of everyone around us at work as well as at home. In this world of constant distraction and information overload it's hard to know what to focus on to maximize our unique potential and promote the best lives we can. But Jamie and Deirdre are here to cut through the clutter and give you the Boost that makes you fully YOU, and your life fully LIVED. Enjoy!

PREFACE

This is a book about recovery. Not recovery from drugs, alcohol, or surgery, but recovery from the numerous and relentless demands we face in handling our everyday obligations. These demands take a toll on us. Regardless of whether they come from paid employment, caring for young children, looking after elderly parents, or trying to get through graduate school, our daily obligations weigh heavily on us. They deplete our energy. They drain us of motivation. They leave us feeling weary and exhausted. If you tend to feel worn out and want to know how to replenish yourself, this book is for you.

We should be able to recover from our daily obligations during our downtime. But many of us don't. In this book we will explain why downtime is inadequate for helping us recharge our batteries, and present you with an effective alternative. Recent scientific developments from around the globe have shed light on the processes that reverse the draining effects of our obligations and help us successfully recover in our leisure time. Not only that, research also reveals that when effective recovery occurs it not only recharges our batteries, but makes us feel happier, makes us healthier, and makes us better at handling the demands that drained us in the first place. We call this *boosting* to reflect the multipronged benefits of successful recovery. In this book we draw on the most cutting-edge science to explain how to transform our ineffective downtime into valuable *uptime*. Uptime is the time away from our obligations that successfully satisfies the factors that lead us to feel replenished, recharged, recovered, and gives us a *boost*.

Chapter 1 presents an overview of boosting and provides you with a simple framework, called the ReNU model, that will help you understand the recovery process and be able to select leisure time activities that will give you the biggest boost. Chapter 2 discusses the boosting benefits of nature and offers suggestions on how to leverage these benefits in your own life. Chapter 3 discusses how our electronic devices prevent recovery and offers numerous suggestions about how to cut the virtual cord to foster replenishment. Chapter 4 explains the value of sleep and presents a 15-point plan to ensure that you enjoy restful slumber. Chapter 5 discusses how volunteering gives us a boost. It turns out that recovery does not always involve passive activities. Active pursuits such as volunteering are an effective way to recharge our batteries. Chapter 6 discusses meditation, which involves the regulation of attention, and explains how even small amounts of attention regulation can help to promote recovery. Chapter 7 discusses relationships and explains who within your network is most likely to help you feel replenished. Chapter 8 discusses the boosting power of exercise and how physical activity not only makes you healthy, but also makes you feel happy and enhances your performance. Chapter 9 presents the research on hobbies and will help you select hobbies that are most effective at helping you recover. Chapter 10 explains why only some vacations help us boost and offers suggestions about how to make the boosting benefits of vacations last as long as possible.

This book is the culmination of 5 years of effort. We're so pleased to be able to share with you the research on recovery, in addition to our own ideas and recommendations, and hope that the book has a significant impact on your ability to overcome fatigue, recharge your batteries, and improve the quality of your life. We'd love to hear your feedback about the book. If you'd like to share your thoughts with us please feel free to e-mail Jamie at jgruman@uoguelph.ca. Happy boosting.

ACKNOWLEDGMENTS

There are a number of people we'd like to thank for their help in producing this book. We'd like to thank John Stuart for believing in the project and finding the book a home. Thanks to all of the people who agreed to be interviewed for the anecdotes that open the chapters, and Dr. Jessica de Bloom, Dr. Ad Vingerhoets, and Dr. Gerhard Strauss-Blasche for offering their insights for the vacations chapter. We'd also like to thank Dr. Kimberly Cote from Brock University, Dr. Nathan Perkins and Dr. Justine Tishinsky from the University of Guelph, Dr. Martin Gibala from McMaster University, and (future Dr.) Matthew Stork from the University of British Columbia for answering our questions about numerous topics, offering suggestions for information to include in various chapters, and/or for reading specific chapters to assure the accuracy of the information we reported. Of course, we assume full responsibility for any inaccuracies that may remain. We'd also like to thank two of Jamie's students, Sydni Gulko and Brianna Kupiec for reviewing and offering feedback on the "Cutting the Virtual Cord" chapter to ensure that it speaks to a younger generation. Finally, we'd like to thank our families for their support, proofreading services, and allowing us to sequester ourselves for the inordinate amount of time it takes to research and write a book.

CHAPTER 1

ReNU

The Missing R in "R&R"

You are exhausted. You are driving home from work after a long day filled with back-to-back meetings. The demanding schedule has drained you, but it's not over yet. You still have to pick up your children from daycare, make dinner and tidy up the kitchen mess before putting your kids to bed and responding to the e-mails you know are lingering in your inbox. You are wondering how you are going to find the energy to not only make it through the evening, but also squeeze in some quality family time and be well-rested for the next day when you have to do it all over again. In order to meet the continuous demands of life and experience enjoyment while we are doing it, we need to fit in time for refueling.

Whether our primary roles are as employees putting in 9 hours or more at the office every day with work often spilling into our evenings at home, or as caregivers for young children or elderly parents going non-stop managing homes and families, or as students under the constant pressure to excel, the stressful and taxing circumstances we all face on a daily basis lead us to feel depleted, exhausted, and in need of rejuvenation.

This is why harnessing our leisure time and using it to its fullest is vital to seizing the most out of life. The mere availability of leisure time does not automatically make us feel recovered (Pereira & Elfering, 2014). Properly used however, our leisure time can fully recharge our batteries, enabling us to reach our full potential, and maintain happy and healthy lives. Recent scientific advances from around the world have shed light on the factors

Boost: The Science of Recharging Yourself in an Age of Unrelenting Demands, pp. 1–16

that allow you to get the most out of your leisure time. In this book you will learn about these factors, so you can recover most effectively from the demands placed upon you. We refer to the process of recovering during your leisure time as *boosting*. You need to boost if you want to be successful in your roles and restore your energy and vitality. So how do you get a boost? It's as easy as tweaking the way you spend your leisure time. Fortunately, for people whose batteries are already drained, there is no work involved. Boosting is simply a matter of making smart choices about the sorts of activities you engage in. It's just like when you go to a buffet at a restaurant. If you want to eat healthy, you simply make smart choices about the food you select. The same goes for boosting. This book will show you how to make smart choices and teach you about the basis for selecting activities, so you can feel rejuvenated and be at your best.

THE NEED TO BOOST

Our daily obligations take a toll on us. During the week we need to invest physical resources, like energy, and mental resources, like concentration, to get our work done (Meijman & Mulder, 1998). As a result, our resources get depleted. We feel tired, drained, and in need of recovery (Sluiter, van der Beek, & Frings-Dresen, 1999). But we can do better than just recover from our demanding lives. Science has shown that when people use their leisure time effectively they not only feel recovered (Binnewies, Sonnentag, & Mojza, 2010), they also enjoy higher levels of psychological well-being (Sonnentag, 2001), physical health (Hunter & Wu, 2016), and improved performance (Binnewies, Sonnentag, & Mojza, 2009). This is what we mean by boosting—you achieve three highly desirable outcomes at the same time! You feel better psychologically, physically, and you get better at your tasks (see the right side of Figure 1.1).

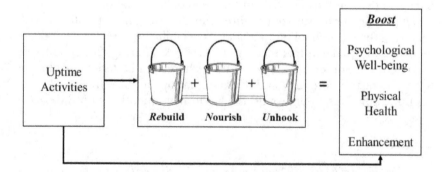

Figure 1.1.   The ReNU Model.

THE BIRTH OF BOOSTING

The stress caused by work and other obligations causes physiological reactions. In response to stress, the body's autonomic nervous system and hypothalamo-pituitary-adrenal axis are activated. These helpful reactions, called *allostasis* (McEwen, 1998), allow the body to adapt to the pressures and stressors it faces on a daily basis. Normally, these biological reactions are short-lived, and the body returns to its baseline state fairly quickly. However, sometimes these adaptive reactions fail to turn off after the stressor disappears. For example, when we experience persistent, regular stress it can cause these biological responses to endure. This creates what is called *allostatic load* (McEwen, 1998), which is when there is wear and tear on the body as a result of being in a constant state of overactivation. As you might expect, allostatic load is bad for you. A persistent state of overactivation can lead to long-term health problems such as heart disease, hypertension, diabetes, cancer, infections, colitis, asthma, cognitive impairment, and depression. It can be difficult for people to turn off the biological reactions caused by the stress of their obligations. This helps to explain why employees with high job strain suffer from more psychological disorders (Stansfeld & Candy, 2006) and are at double the risk of dying from cardiovascular disease (Kivimäki et al., 2002). However, not everyone who experiences strain from work or other obligations suffers from long-term health consequences. Why not?

For many years it was believed that stress-related biological reactions were the direct cause of long-term health problems. However, as just noted, these biological reactions tend to turn off quickly when the things that are causing us stress disappear. Therefore, a new mechanism was needed to explain the relationship between stress and ill health (Pereira & Elfering, 2014). In 2006, researchers from the Netherlands and Germany suggested that one overlooked driving force behind the negative impact of stress on health was incomplete recovery (Guerts & Sonnentag, 2006). The researchers argued that if people are able to recover effectively from the stress of their obligations during their leisure time, the long-term effects of stress would be reduced or eliminated. This focus on recovery as the important missing element in the explanation between the inconsistent relationship between stress and long-term health, and the research it stimulated, was the origin of the boosting concept. If you make the right choices during your leisure time you can avoid allostatic load and get a boost, which includes sidestepping long-term health problems. Let's consider how to make that happen.

THE SECRET TO BOOSTING:
TURN DOWNTIME INTO UPTIME

To get a boost you need to transform your downtime into *uptime*. According to the Merriam Webster Online Dictionary, downtime is simply inactive time, moments when you're not working or busy. If you consider this definition it is easy to understand why the concept of downtime doesn't give you any useful ideas of what to do when you're not working or busy that might allow your batteries to recharge. Simply being inactive is not very instructive. Nor is it a guarantee that you will replenish yourself. Unlike downtime, uptime effectively satisfies the specific factors that lead to replenishment and gives you a boost, and the components of uptime provide specific guidance on how to do this. Research on recovery has revealed that getting a boost is not primarily about the activities you engage in, *but the attributes underlying those activities* (Sonnentag & Fritz, 2007). We can think of these attributes as buckets you need to fill. If the activities you participate in during your leisure time allow you to fill these buckets you are effectively transforming your downtime into uptime, and getting the boost you desire. As shown in Figure 1.1, there are three buckets you want to top up.

The First Bucket: Rebuild

The *rebuild* bucket involves replenishing the resources that get depleted by your weekly obligations. People have two kinds of personal resources they regularly use—physical and psychological. Physical resources are resources such as physical energy and stamina that get used up when we engage in physical activities like emptying boxes out of 18-wheelers, cleaning up after kids, or sprinting from room to room taking care of patients in a hospital. Psychological resources are resources such as concentration, emotional regulation, and self-control that we draw on when doing more cerebral or emotional work like auditing financial statements, comforting an ailing parent, or keeping a smile on your face when dealing with unreasonable customers. Research shows that in the same way physical resources get exhausted, psychological resources, like self-control, also get depleted when they are used (Hagger, Wood, Stiff, & Chatzisarantis, 2010).

To transform your downtime into uptime you need to rebuild the resources that get used up because of your daily obligations. Rebuilding resources means you want to engage in uptime activities that draw on different resources and give your already depleted resources a break. For example, a lawyer who argues court cases all week, and then on the weekend coaches his daughter's softball team and argues with parents about who the starting pitcher should be, is not filling his rebuild bucket.

This is because in his leisure time he is drawing on the same resources he uses to get his work done during the week. As a result, his resources can't replenish themselves. To rebuild, you want to engage in uptime activities that draw on resources that are different, or opposite, from those you use in your obligation time. So instead of coaching his daughter's softball team, this lawyer might want to consider another weekend activity, such as building houses for homeless people, where he can draw on his sense of community and give his argumentative side a break. This will fill his rebuild bucket because he will stop drawing on his "work" resources and give those resources a chance to replenish themselves and return to baseline levels.

Filling the rebuild bucket gives you a boost. Research shows that employees who are able to rebuild resources on the weekend because their Saturdays and Sundays involve few hassles, end up feeling less burned out on Monday morning (Fritz & Sonnentag, 2005). Feeling recovered can even build resources. In one study, employees who reported feeling well rested and recovered during their leisure time had higher levels of confidence, a psychological resource, at work (Binnewies et al., 2009). And this increased confidence led to higher job performance. This is just one example of how boosting can make you better at your tasks.

The Second Bucket: Nourish

The *nourish* bucket is about satisfying our human needs. Like resources, human needs come in two forms, physical needs, and psychological needs. The difference between the nourish bucket and the rebuild bucket is that whereas rebuilding resources is *nice* to do, nourishing needs is *necessary* if we are to thrive (Ryan & Deci, 2000). We all have a physical need for food and water. If we don't eat and drink, we don't live very long. Satisfying such needs is not optional. Failing to satisfy physical needs doesn't always have such dire consequences, but when we don't satisfy them we can't live to our full potential. For example, failing to satisfy the need for sleep or the need for exercise won't kill you. At least not immediately. But not sleeping well and not exercising enough will make you feel worse, make you less healthy, and make you less effective at your tasks than if you sleep well and exercise regularly (Coulson, McKenna, & Field, 2008; Hamilton, Nelson, Stevens, & Kitzman, 2007). They're requirements for good living, and they have boosting effects.

In addition to physical needs, people also have psychological needs that have to be fulfilled if they are to thrive (Ryan & Deci, 2000). Boosting focuses on the three needs that have been the subject of the most research in psychology and management (Deci & Ryan, 2000). The *need for relatedness* is the need to feel close and connected to other people. For example, when you spend quality time with friends, family and lovers, your need for relatedness is satisfied. The *need for autonomy* is the need to feel as though your activities and experiences are freely chosen. When you get to pick what to do on vacation with your spouse, this need is satisfied. The *need for competence* is the need to feel effective by mastering challenges. When you watch a YouTube video and figure out how to fix the defective light in your kitchen, you are satisfying your need for competence.

Satisfying your psychological needs is a key part of boosting. Research shows that people who satisfy their need for competence by mastering a skill or challenge on the weekend come back to work on Monday morning feeling more recovered (Binnewies et al., 2010). Employees who satisfy their need for relatedness by participating in more social activity on the weekend end up feeling less burned out on Monday (Fritz & Sonnentag, 2005). And employees who spend their coffee breaks satisfying their need for autonomy by participating in activities they prefer, come back from those breaks feeling less exhausted and reporting fewer physical complaints, such as headaches and eyestrain (Hunter & Wu, 2014). Filling the nourish bucket gives you a boost.

The Third Bucket: Unhook

The *unhook* bucket has two components. The first component is something you're already familiar with—relaxation. Relaxation is the defining feature of downtime, which you've been practicing your whole life. Relaxing is what we do when we are not working or busy and it's what most people think of when they think about getting away from their obligations. However, on its own relaxation is not enough to give you a boost.

Although getting a little R&R is insufficient for boosting, it is nonetheless an important ingredient in successful recovery. Relaxing is valuable partly because it is simply enjoyable, and pleasurable experiences contribute to the psychological well-being which is part of boosting. It is also important because relaxation can allow our resources to rebuild, and because during relaxing episodes we may nourish some of our needs. However, although relaxation *can* allow this to happen, it does not necessarily *cause* this to happen, which is partly why on its own relaxation is inadequate to secure a boost. In fact, some research has shown that relaxation has a weaker relationship with boosting than some of the components of the other buckets, like satisfying psychological needs (Sonnentag & Fritz, 2007). Nonetheless, as you might expect, research shows that people who are able to relax more in their leisure time end up feeling more recovered than those who relax less (Binnewies et al., 2010). For that reason, it is an important ingredient to keep in the mix.

The second component of the unhook bucket is called psychological detachment and involves mentally turning off from your obligations (Sonnentag, 2012). If you leave work but keep thinking about the presentation you have to deliver next week, you're not psychologically detaching. If you go for a walk to give yourself a break from studying for the graduate school entrance exam you need to ace but continue contemplating answers to the practice exam questions while you stroll through the woods, you're not psychologically detaching. If you go on vacation with your spouse but call grandma at home five times a day to make sure the kids are ok, you're not psychologically detaching. It's not enough to *physically* get away from your obligations; You also need to *mentally* get away.

Psychologically detaching is likely most important for people who find their obligations particularly stressful. These are the folks who most need to reduce their allostatic load, which is intensified by continuing to think about your obligations when you leave them behind. Unfortunately, research shows that people who face the greatest stressors during their obligations have the greatest difficulty mentally shutting off when they escape them (Sonnentag, 2012). Also, not psychologically detaching during your uptime can interfere with your ability to fill the other buckets. For example, when people don't mentally turn off when away from their obligations they don't fill their nourish bucket as much because the quality of their sleep takes a nosedive (Cropley, Derk-Jan, & Stanley, 2006).

Research shows that people who psychologically detach in their uptime get a boost. In a study of five organizations in Germany researchers found that employees who reported the most psychological detachment on the weekend also reported feeling the highest level of recovery the following week (Binnewies et al., 2010). Feeling recovered, in turn, led to higher job performance, and made work seem like it required less effort. Similarly, research shows that people who mentally turn off from their obligations while at home in the evening feel happier and less depleted at bedtime (Sonnentag, 2012). And these positive effects of psychological detachment that occur in the evening last until the next morning when people return to their obligations, which helps to explain why filling the unhook bucket gives us a boost (Sonnentag, 2012).

Together, the three buckets and the boost they produce are called the *ReNU model* (ReNU is an acronym for *Re*build, *N*ourish, and *U*nhook). Because "rest and relaxation" is not enough to recharge your batteries, ReNU can be thought of as the missing R in "R&R," and is the recipe for turning your downtime into uptime.

Typically, boosting occurs when you fill the three ReNU buckets, and we'll draw on the ReNU model throughout the book to help you understand how various activities help you get a boost. We want to note that sometimes, as depicted in Figure 1.1., activities produce a boost directly.

For example, exercise can promote boosting by satisfying our psychological needs and filling the nourish bucket, but it can also help us boost as a result of its direct effect on physical health. Also, although not depicted in Figure 1.1., some boosting elements can fill the ReNU buckets. For example, positive emotions, which are part of psychological well-being, can help us build resources and fill the rebuild bucket. That said, focusing on filling the ReNU buckets is the best way to build your understanding of how to promote recovery from your obligations.

WHICH BUCKET SHOULD I FILL?

In some ways, it doesn't matter which bucket you focus on trying to fill. As you can see in Figure 1.1, the buckets are connected, so as you start filling one the others will start to fill up also. So, if you focus on filling the unhook bucket by psychologically detaching in the evening, you'll also likely rebuild resources. For example, in the study discussed earlier in which employees satisfied their need for autonomy on their coffee breaks by participating in activities they prefer, the researchers also found that those employees ended up having higher levels of resources such as concentration after their breaks (Hunter & Wu, 2016). These employees just focused on filling their nourish buckets but their rebuild buckets filled up too.

Although the buckets are connected, you are most likely to completely fill the one you focus on. Therefore, the bucket you choose to focus on filling should be the one you feel is most depleted. And remember, it's not the activities you engage in that matter, but the underlying attributes of those activities. One implication of this little detail is that activities that often give you a boost can sometimes drain you, and vice versa. For example, hanging out with friends can be an effective way to satisfy your need for relatedness, but a study of airline personnel found that when flight attendants socialized after work, they ended up feeling depressed (Sonnentag & Natter, 2004). This is because after socializing and inter-acting with customers and colleagues all shift, the last thing the flight attendants needed was more socializing. The need for relatedness part of their nourish bucket was already full. To get a boost they needed to focus on filling other ReNU buckets, or other parts of the nourish bucket. In this same study the researchers found that flight attendants who engaged in physical activity instead of social activity ended up in a much better mood.

ANY FREE TIME IS AN OPPORTUNITY TO BOOST

If you ask people what they do in their downtime they tend to tell you what activities they participate in on the weekend. Weekends are, of course, a great opportunity to recharge and refresh. However, *any* free time you have in which you are away from your obligations can be an opportunity to get a boost. Research shows that boosting can occur during long periods of leisure such as weekends (Fritz & Sonnentag, 2005), and vacations (Strauss-Blasche, Reithofer, Schobersberger, Ekmekcioglu, & Marktl, 2005), but it can also occur during shorter periods, such as evenings at home (Sonnentag, Binnewies & Mojza, 2008), lunch hours or coffee breaks (Trougakos, Hideg, Cheng, & Beal, 2014). Even a 5-minute escape from your obligations can be of value. You don't need to wait for a vacation or the weekend to roll around before getting a boost. If you are feeling depleted, you can boost right now. We'll show you how to do this, and provide you with a number of examples, throughout the book.

Although most of the research related to boosting involves employees in the workforce, anyone can get a boost. For example, short breaks increase the well-being of families caring for children with disabilities (Robertson et al., 2011). The negative effects of stress on the health of people caring for relatives with Alzheimer's disease is reduced when they nourish their need for competence (Mausbach et al., 2007). And when children spend their leisure time engaged in sports as opposed to passive pursuits they have higher levels of happiness (Holder, Coleman, & Sehn, 2009). Transforming downtime into uptime is important for everyone.

In the remainder of this book we'll discuss the science behind a variety of activities that fill the ReNU buckets and let you boost. Remember that making smart choices about how to spend your uptime is not about the activities you choose. Rather, it's about whether those activities help you fill the ReNU buckets.

THE TRANSFORMATIVE POWER OF BOOSTING

John Tillerson is a cherubic man with the sort of sunny disposition you'd think characterizes Santa's elves. John has been involved in career counseling for over 20 years and runs his own firm helping people find their ideal jobs. He recently had a new client who was complaining that she was "burned out," "couldn't do her job anymore," was "really tired" and had to find new work. The predicament for John was that when he asked the client to describe the work she did, she lit up. Her back straightened. Her eyes sparkled, and she became excited. John suspected that his client's problems had more to do with her inability to recover from the piles of work she had than with the job itself. So, on a hunch he e-mailed her a link to the TED talk on boosting delivered by the lead author of this book (available at https://www.youtube.com/watch?v=u-U7fzS06ns). He did this simply as a means of starting a conversation about recovery. However, a few minutes after sending the e-mail the client replied asking to speak with him immediately. When they spoke on the phone she told him "Thank you. I don't need to see you anymore. I now know what I need. I need to boost."

John did end up seeing the client one more time and helped her develop a set of leisure activities that would best give her a boost, which included dusting off the old guitar she used to enjoy playing. The client did not change jobs, but when John followed up with her a few weeks later she reported that she felt better than she had in years and that she had "reclaimed her life." She didn't need a new job. She just needed to know how to better recover from the one she had.

SUMMARY

Our obligations take a toll on us physically and mentally. In order to counteract the allostatic load caused by the demands and stress of our obligations, we need to effectively recover in our leisure time. However, downtime is insufficient to ensure that recovery occurs. To successfully recover we need to transform our downtime into uptime by filling the three ReNU buckets. Doing so gives us a boost, which recharges our batteries, promotes our psychological well-being, physical health, and enhances our performance. This is the key to fostering replenishment, beating exhaustion, and being at our best.

UPTIME ACTION PLAN

Throughout the rest of this book we'll discuss how various activities help fill the ReNU buckets that can give you a boost. However, if you'd like to start boosting right away, the *Uptime Action Plan* presented below offers a quick and easy way to begin to transform your downtime into uptime immediately. We'll add to the Uptime Action Plan at the end of every chapter. For now, consider these ideas:

Step 1. Think about your evenings and weekends and list the leisure activities you participate in the most during these periods. Write them down in the spaces below. You don't need to list every activity you engage in, such as brushing your teeth before bed, only those activities you engage in to unwind, such as playing video games, or that take up most of your time during your leisure time, such as watching television or taking care of kids.

_____   _____

_____   _____

_____   _____

_____   _____

_____   _____

Step 2. During our daily obligations as employees, students, homemakers, etc., we use a variety of personal resources. Do an audit of the personal resources you use the most during your daily obligations. These can be physical resources such as strength, endurance, and energy, or psychological resources such as concentration, self-control, patience, self-esteem, creativity, optimism, empathy, or assertiveness. List the three personal resources you use the most during your daily obligations in the spaces below.

1. _____   3. _____

2. _____

Step 3. Circle all of the activities in Step 1 that use any of the resources listed in Step 2. For example, playing chess requires concentration. If you wrote "playing chess" as a leisure activity in Step 1 and "concentration" as a personal resource in Step 2, circle "playing chess" in Step 1. Any activities you draw circles around reveal leisure time activities you are participating in that require the same resources you use during your daily obligations. These circles indicate that you are not giving these resources a break during your leisure time. Consider replacing the circled leisure activities with others you enjoy that don't draw on resources you need to use during your daily obligations. In the spaces below, indicate any leisure time activities you might want to change and the activities you might replace them with.

I will change these activities: **I will replace them with these activities:**

_____   _____

_____   _____

_____   _____

_____   _____

Step 4. Return to the list of activities in Step 1 and identify which ones allow you to achieve the following:

    a. Experience the freedom of having chosen the activity for yourself
    b. Achieve a feeling of competence, growth or mastery
    c. Enjoy quality time with friends or family

These three things represent basic psychological needs that should be met to produce a boost. Activities that satisfy all three needs give you the biggest boost, but as long as you satisfy all the needs through different activities you will still be boosting. Consider dropping activities from your leisure time that don't satisfy any of these needs and replace them with some that do. What new activities can you think of that would help you satisfy any of the needs you are missing or satisfy all three needs even more? Write them in the spaces below and make a point of fitting them into your uptime.

_____   _____

_____   _____

Step 5. In order to get a boost, you need to relax and mentally "turn off" from your obligations. During your next period of leisure, write down each of the activities you engage in and indicate how relaxed each one makes you feel on a scale from 1 (not at all relaxed) to 5 (completely relaxed). You may be surprised at which activities you find most relaxing once you start paying attention. Do more of the activities that relax you. Also, think of the activities in which you get completely absorbed. Maybe it's building model airplanes, or gardening. Absorbing activities will help you to mentally disengage and "turn off" from your obligations. Schedule some time tomorrow evening or this weekend to engage in at least one of these activities.

Step 6. Take each of the activities you listed in Step 1 and use the spaces below to indicate how happy each one makes you feel. Happiness, or psychological well-being, is a key part of boosting. Ideally you would like to have a number of activities listed in the "Enormously Happy" column below. If you don't, you are missing out on opportunities to boost. Think of the activities that make you the happiest. Now identify what stands in the way of you engaging in these activities more often. Develop a plan to overcome or reduce these barriers so you can enjoy more activities that bring you tremendous joy during your leisure time. This may involve bringing the kids to their grandparents' house for an afternoon, making a point of inviting some friends over, or just scheduling some "me time" to take a bite out of a good book. Whatever it takes, make it happen.

Enormously Happy	Moderately Happy	Not Particularly Happy
_____	_____	_____
_____	_____	_____
_____	_____	_____

Now that you have been able to zone in on what uptime activities will help you rejuvenate and reenergize, read on to optimize the way you do these activities to get the biggest boost!

REFERENCES

Binniwies, C., Sonnentag S., & Mojza, E. J. (2009). Daily performance at work: feeling recovered in the morning as a predictor of day-level job performance. *Journal of Organizational Behavior, 30*, 67–93.

Binnewies, C., Sonnentag, S., & Mojza, E. J. (2010). Recovery during the weekend and fluctuations in weekly job performance: A week-level study examining intra-individual relationships. *Journal of Occupational and Organizational Psychology, 83*, 419–441.

Coulson, J. C., McKenna, J., & Field, M., (2008). Exercising at work and self-reported work performance. *International Journal of Workplace Health Management, 1*, 176–197.

Cropley, M., Derk-Jan, D., & Stanley, N. (2006). Job strain, work rumination and sleep in school teachers. *European Journal of Work and Organizational Psychology, 15*, 181–196.

Deci, E. L., & Ryan, R. M. (2000). The "what" and "why" of goal pursuits: Human needs and the self-determination of behavior. *Psychological Inquiry, 11*, 227–268.

Fritz, C., & Sonnentag, S. (2005). Recovery, health, and job performance: Effects of weekend experiences. *Journal of Occupational Health Psychology, 10*, 187–199.

Guerts, S. A. E., & Sonnentag, S. (2006). Recovery as an explanatory mechanism in the relation between acute stress reactions and chronic health impairment. *Scandinavian Journal of Work, Environment & Health, 32*, 482–492.

Hagger, M. S., Wood, C., Stiff, C., & Chatzisarantis, N. L. D. (2010). Ego depletion and the strength model of self-control: A meta-analysis. *Psychological Bulletin, 136*, 495–525.

Hamilton, N. A., Nelson, C. A., Stevens, N., & Kitzman, H. (2007). Sleep and psychological well-being. *Social Indicators Research, 82*, 147–163.

Holder, M. D., Coleman, B., Sehn, Z., L. (2009). The contribution of active and passive leisure to children's well-being. *Journal of Health Psychology, 14*, 378–386.

Hunter, E. M., & Wu, C. (2016). Give me a better break: Choosing workday break activities to maximize resource recovery. *Journal of Applied Psychology, 101*, 302–311.

Kivimäki, M., Leino-Arjas, P., Luukkonen, R., Riihimäki, H., Vahtera, J., & Kirjonen, J. (2002). Work stress and risk of cardiovascular mortality: Prospective cohort study of industrial employees. *British Medical Journal, 325*, 857–861.

Mausbach, B. T., Patterson, T. L. Von Kanel, R., Mills, P. J., Dimsdale, J. E., Ancoli-Israel, S., & Grant, I. (2007). The attenuating effect of personal mastery on the relations between stress and Alzheimer caregiver health: A five-year longitudinal analysis. *Aging & Mental Health, 11*, 637–644.

McEwen, B. S. (1998). Stress, adaptation, and disease: Allostatis and allostatic load. *Annals of the New York Academy of Sciences, 840*, 33–44.

Meijman, T. F., & Mulder, G. (1998). Psychological aspects of workload. In P. J. D. Drenth, H. Thierry, & C. J. de Wolff (Eds.), *Handbook of Work and Organizational Psychology* (2nd ed., pp 5–33). East Sussex, UK: Psychology Press.

Pereira, D., & Elfering, A. (2014). Social stressors at work and sleep during weekends: The mediating role of psychological detachment. *Journal of Occupational Health Psychology, 19*, 85–95.

Robertson, J., Hatton, C., Wells, E., Collins, M., Langer, S., Welch, V., & Emerson, E. (2011). The impacts of short break provision on families with a disabled child: An international literature review. *Health and Social Care in the Community, 19*, 337–371.

Ryan, R. M., & Deci, E. L. (2000). Self-determination theory and the facilitation of intrinsic motivation, social development, and well-being. *American Psychologist, 55*, 68–78.

Sluiter, J. K., van der Beek, A. J., & Frings-Dresen, M. H. W. (1999). The influence of work characteristics on the need for recovery and experienced health: a study on coach drivers. *Ergonomics, 42*, 573–583.

Sonnentag, S. (2001). Work, recovery activities, and individual well-being: A diary study. *Journal of Occupational Health Psychology, 6*, 196–210.

Sonnentag, S. (2012). Psychological detachment from work during leisure time: The benfits of mentally disengaging from work. *Current Directions in Psychological Science, 21*, 114–118.

Sonnentag, S., Binnewies, C., & Mojza, E. J. (2008). "Did you have a nice evening?" A day-level study on recovery experiences, sleep, and affect. *Journal of Applied Psychology, 93*, 674–684.

Sonnentag, S., & Fritz, C. (2007). The recovery experiences questionnaire: Development and validation of a measure for assessing recuperation and unwinding from work. *Journal of Occupational Health Psychology, 12*, 204–221.

Sonnentag, S., & Natter, E. (2004). Flight attendants' daily recovery from work: Is there no place like home? *International Journal of Stress Management, 11*, 366–391.

Stansfeld, S., & Candy, B. (2006). Psychosocial work environment and mental health—a meta-analytic review. *Scandinavian Journal of Work, Environment & Health, 32*, 443–462.

Strauss-Blasche, G., Reithofer, B., Schobersberger, W., Ekmekcioglu, C., & Marktl, W. (2005). Effect of vacation on health: Moderating factors of vacation outcome. *Journal of Travel Medicine, 12*, 94–101.

Trougakos, J. P., Hideg, I., Cheng, B., & Beal, D. J. (2014). Lunch breaks unpacked: The role of autonomy as a moderator of recovery during lunch. *Academy of Management Journal, 57*, 405–421.

CHAPTER 2

HOW TO REAP THE BOOSTING BENEFITS OF NATURE

With gleaming stars punching through the black sky above him and the hard, frozen lake beneath him, Andrew fell asleep in his down-filled sleeping bag surrounded by silence except for the occasional howling of a wolf. He was alone on a winter wilderness trek in northern Ontario and he had never felt more at peace.

"It's really beautiful," says the 50-year-old. "You are able to experience the world as it is when it is, where it is. It's just like when you were a kid and you wanted to explore in the river until your mom called you in for dinner. Only as an adult you can do it for days or weeks on end."

Andrew has hiked hundreds of kilometers through some of the most remote areas in Canada with just his backpack. Let's just say this civil engineer and father of four is all about staying off the beaten path. For Andrew, being surrounded by untouched landscapes is the greatest escape, whether it's the thick forest of northern Ontario or the desert-like tundra of the arctic.

Unlike at his job where he is designing sophisticated bridges, cutting through red tape and making big decisions on multi-million-dollar projects, when Andrew is deep in the wilderness all he has to worry about is finding a place to camp and deciding what to cook for dinner.

"The responsibilities are totally different from my work. In fact, I don't think about work at all. I daydream. That's one of the good things about it."

Boost: The Science of Recharging Yourself in an Age of Unrelenting Demands, pp. 17–31

When Andrew returns home from a trek, he is often sunburned, covered in bug bites and scratches and badly in need of a shower. But this dose of wilderness therapy always leaves him feeling recharged.

NATURE AND ANCIENT WISDOM

The idea that nature can recharge our batteries and offer psychological and physical health benefits is as old as time. People have always had an intuitive sense that there is something special, perhaps even sacred, about humankind's relationship with nature. It is a sense that we are not apart from nature, but rather we are *a part of* nature and that living to our full potential necessarily involves a connection with the natural environments which give us physical and psychological nourishment. It is no coincidence that in the Jewish, Christian, and Islamic religious traditions paradise is symbolized by a garden, and in Buddhist folklore Buddha is said to have been born, achieved enlightenment, and died under trees (Cooper Marcus & Barnes, 1999). Such descriptions reveal that our traditions regard nature as fundamental to well-being and suggest that exposure to nature is a need that must be satisfied (Ward Thompson, 2011).

History reveals a strong and persistent current of thought attesting to the importance of our connection with nature. For example, the idea that being exposed to nature can help us deal with stress dates all the way back to ancient Persia, China, and Greece (Ulrich, 1999). Records of early Roman thinkers, such as Cornelius Celsus, show that strolling in gardens, being exposed to light and water, as well as other activities involving nature were advocated to improve mental health and sleep (Selhub & Logan, 2012). In the Middle Ages hospitals and monasteries incorporated the use of healing gardens when caring for the sick (Cooper Marcus & Barnes, 1999). Monastic cloister gardens were also thought to preserve health and foster the recovery of religious devotees fatigued by their spiritual studies and physical work (Ward Thomas, 2011).

In more recent times, as noted by Eva Selhub and Alan Logan, authors of *Your Brain on Nature* (2012), when North American cities started growing at an unprecedented rate, doctors began prescribing nature exposure to help patients reduce their stress level and improve their mental outlook. They sent their patients to sanitariums deep within natural settings with names that evoked nature retreats such as The Pines, Lake View, and Blue Hills. However, none of these prescriptions for getaways into the countryside were based on scientific evidence. They were based on the same ancient intuition that had guided physicians in ancient Egypt to recommend walks in palace gardens to kings and queens who were psychologically disturbed (Davis, 1998). Only recently has there been actual research in this area, but the research has provided an overwhelming amount of empirical evidence to confirm the intuitive idea that nature has profound boosting effects.

WHY DOES NATURE GIVE US A BOOST?

Much of the research conducted on the boosting effect of nature reflects the notion that our desire for contact with trees, rivers, and flowers, and their ability to replenish us, is rooted in our biology. This idea is called the biophilia hypothesis and reflects what some people consider to be our natural predisposition to be drawn to life and lifelike processes (Wilson, 1984). The biophilia hypothesis is based on the idea that in facing the numerous rewards and threats present in the natural landscapes in which our distant ancestors evolved, some of our prehistoric relatives developed an inclination to prefer certain natural environments which enhanced their likelihood of survival. For example, being attracted to certain natural features, such as water, made it more likely that our early kin could find nourishment, which often grows close to streams and lakes. Close proximity to water also provided them with protection from predators, who couldn't pounce on them quickly from across a river. As a result, those ancestors with biophilic tendencies outlived their counterparts who didn't have this inclination, and were able to pass on their genes, and the associated attraction to nature, to future generations (Ulrich, 1993). Importantly, the biophilia hypothesis suggests that non-threatening natural environments promote positive emotions, recovery, and improve mental functioning, all of which supports getting a boost (Ulrich, 1993).

The biophilia hypothesis is not without its critics (e.g., Joye & De Block 2011), but the criticisms tend to focus on the mechanisms and processes through which our apparently innate enchantment with nature developed and operates. Although some people have suggested that theory and research on the biophilia hypothesis has been sloppy (Joye & De Block, 2011), the work nonetheless generally supports the idea that human beings have a natural affinity for nature (Gullone, 2000), something even the critics acknowledge.

There are two main approaches to understanding the dynamics underlying how nature gives us a boost. The first approach is called stress reduction theory (SRT). As you can imagine, life for our evolutionary ancestors was no picnic. They had to constantly contend with the threat of being wounded or killed by animals, the struggle to find shelter from the elements when searching for food, and the risk of confrontations with unfriendly neighbors (Ulrich, 1993). Being able to quickly recover from such stressors would have been valuable for these folks. In line with the biophilia hypothesis, SRT suggests that our ancient relatives who developed a tendency to find unthreatening natural environments restorative had advantages over others, such as quickly recovering from stressful episodes and recharging physical energy. SRT suggests that as a result of eons of evolution, unthreatening natural environments quickly elicit in us unconscious, automatic restorative emotional responses and reductions in physiological arousal (Ulrich et al., 1991). Essentially, such settings give us "a breather" (Ulrich et al., 1991), just as they did for some of our ancestors. Evidence for the deep-seated biological basis of SRT includes research showing that the physiological reactions people have in response to nature are invariant across cultures (Chang, 2004).

The second approach to understanding how nature gives us a boost is called attention restoration theory (ART). Whereas SRT focuses on the emotional and physiological benefits of exposure to nature, ART focuses on the cognitive benefits (Hansmann, Hug, & Seeland, 2007). According to ART, natural environments are boosting because they grab our attention without requiring any mental effort. Within ART this is called fascination (Kaplan, 1995). Fascination promotes recovery because it releases us from needing to engage in effortful attention. Effortful attention is required any time we need to actively concentrate on something, like work, or school, or making sure we arrive at the bus stop on time. Fascination involves *in*voluntary attention, which means we don't need to direct our attention because our attention is instinctively and effortlessly drawn to the interesting features of the natural environment (Kaplan & Talbot, 1983). Since fascination is automatic and effortless, during periods of involuntary attention attentional resources that we have used up have a chance to rest and replenish themselves. It's easy, undemanding and therefore, rejuvenating. When Andrew is spending his days hiking through the wilderness, he doesn't have to exert effort on concentrating. His focus is spontaneously drawn to the moose he sees trampling through the forest, the orange glow of the sunset, and the branches blowing in the wind. Some evidence for ART comes from research that shows that when people are fatigued, they are less inclined to spend time in human-made, city environments and instead are attracted to spending time in natural environments which they believe will better help them recover (Hartig & Staats, 2006).

All of this suggests that contact with nature represents a basic human requirement. When we have contact with nature we promote our own well-being and replenishment, and when we don't we deprive ourselves of this opportunity (Joye & De Block, 2011). As suggested by Catharine Ward Thompson (2011), a professor of landscape architecture at the Edinburgh College of Art, "Throughout history and across cultures, people have considered access to some form of "nature" as a fundamental human need" (p. 194).

It is therefore concerning that the current trend is for people to spend less time in nature during their leisure time. People are doing less camping, less fishing, and spending less time interacting with nature in general than they used to. Researchers in the U.S. have found that although there was a steady increase in visits to national parks from 1939 to 1987, since then there has been a consistent decrease (Pergams & Zaradic, 2008). Around the globe nature recreation is declining at a rate of approximately 1.2% per year, with a total reduction of between 18% and 25% since the peak that occurred between 1981 and 1991.

Although SRT and ART differ in what they propose as underlying mechanisms, they both agree that natural environments are restorative. Experiences with nature give us a boost because they fill all of the ReNU buckets. Restoring attention through fascination fills the rebuild bucket. Contact with nature satisfies our evolutionarily derived need for such exposure and fills the nourish bucket. Also, just as SRT predicts, there is research showing that when people spend time interacting with nature they feel more relaxed (Korpela & Kinnunen, 2011). So, contact with nature fills the unhook bucket too.

THE BOOSTING BENEFITS OF NATURE

If exposure to natural environments fills all of the ReNU buckets, we should expect that hiking through a forest, lounging at a cottage by a lake, or taking short strolls though a local garden on our lunchbreaks should give us a boost. Indeed, they all do. Research on the boosting power of nature has revealed that exposure to natural environments fosters psychological well-being, physical health, and enhancement (Velarde, Fry, & Tveit, 2007).

Psychological Well-Being

Numerous studies have shown that nature promotes psychological well-being. In one such study, researchers had people who suffer from depression take a 2.8 mile walk through either a tree-lined, secluded arboretum or a busy downtown street, and measured their positive emotions before and after the walks. Exercise can have beneficial effects on people's moods, as we will discuss in the chapter on exercise, so we would expect both walks to improve the mood of participants. However, the walk through the arboretum increased the participants' positive emotions much more than the walk on the street, demonstrating the additional boosting power of nature (Berman et al., 2012).

In a similar study, researchers had people take a 50-minute walk through either a vegetation and wildlife preserve or through city streets lined with office-buildings and retail stores. As in the study just described, they measured positive emotions before and after the walks, but also measured participants' levels of anger and aggressiveness. The results showed that the walks through the nature preserve increased people's positive emotions and decreased their levels of anger and aggressiveness. Walks through the city had the opposite effect—they decreased people's positive emotions and increased their feelings of anger and aggressiveness (Hartig, Evans, Jammer, Davis, & Gärling, 2003).

These sorts of effects are common. Nature has predictable effects on people's emotions. A 2015 study by U.S. researchers summarized all of the experiments that have looked at the relationship between contact with natural environments and both positive and negative emotions. Their statistical summary of 32 experiments showed that exposure to nature consistently increases people's positive emotions and, to a somewhat lesser extent, consistently decreases their negative emotions (McMahan & Estes, 2015).

Other studies have found that nature affects other aspects of psychological well-being. Compared to walks through human-made environments, walking through natural environments increases people's level of vitality, which involves having energy as well as a sense of enthusiasm and aliveness (Ryan et al., 2010). Walking through nature also has a stronger effect on decreasing anxiety and rumination than walking through city streets (Bratman, Daily, Levy, & Gross, 2015). The decrease in rumination has been shown to correspond to less neural activity in the subgenual prefrontal cortex, an area of the brain associated with sadness (Bratman, Hamilton, Hahn, Daily, & Gross, 2015).

As these studies suggest, nature has a significant and consistent positive effect on psychological well-being. Unfortunately, people underestimate the benefits of being in nature (Nisbet & Zelenski, 2011). This may partly explain the trend toward less nature recreation we noted earlier. Buck this trend. Get outside!

Physical Health

Exposure to nature also has beneficial consequences for our physical health. A German study found that people who regularly walked along a highly vegetated trail beside a local canal had lower levels of the stress hormone cortisol (Honold, Lakes, Beyer, & van der Meer, 2016). An elevated level of cortisol has traditionally been considered one of the main mechanisms through which chronic stressors produce disease (Miller,

Chen, & Zhou, 2007). Nature exposure short-circuits this mechanism and keeps us healthy.

Compared to walking through urban areas, walking through natural environments such as forests lowers our pulse rate, and both our systolic and diastolic blood pressure. More generally, forest exposure increases activity in our parasympathetic nervous system and decreases activity in our sympathetic nervous system, which helps bring the body back to its normal resting state (Park, Tsunetsugu, Kasetani, Kagawa, & Miyazaki, 2010). Remember the concept of allostatic load? Essentially, being in nature promotes physical health by reducing allostatic load.

Research has also shown that spending time in nature enhances our immune system. Our bodies have natural killer cells, or NK cells, which are a type of white blood cell that make up part of the immune system. Leisurely walks through a forest increase NK activity and the number of NK cells in the blood, and these effects last a minimum of 7 days (Li, 2010). So, if you think you are coming down with a cold, take a walk in the woods.

These fine-grained physiological studies are consistent with studies conducted at a more macro-level. A study of the greenspace in Toronto, Canada, found that people who live in city blocks that have more trees consider their health to be better than those who live in areas with fewer trees. The benefit of this enriched health perception is equivalent to the effect of earning a pay raise of $10,000 or being 7 years younger (Kardan et al., 2015). A similar study by researchers in The Netherlands found that people who live within a one-kilometer (.62 mile) radius of an area that has 10% more greenspace than average have lower rates of certain disease clusters. For example, they have reduced rates of heart disease, infectious intestinal diseases, back pain, upper respiratory tract infections, asthma, headaches, and diabetes (Maas et al., 2009). Not only does nature make us feel good, it keeps us healthy.

Enhancement

Numerous studies have documented that exposure to nature also enhances our abilities and improves our performance on a variety of tasks. In the study discussed earlier involving people who suffer from depression walking through either an arboretum or a city street, the researchers found that people's performance on a memory test improved after the stroll through the arboretum (Berman et al., 2012). A different study using the same memory test and non-depressed people found identical results which the authors interpreted as demonstrating that nature improves our ability to pay attention (Berman, Jonides, & Kaplan, 2008). Children experience the same benefits from nature. One study found that children who suffer from attention deficits perform better on a concentration task after walking through a park compared to when they spend time in less natural settings (Faber Taylor & Kuo, 2009).

A group of U.S. researchers found that after spending time in nature people are better at memorizing a list of ordered letters while simultaneously solving math problems (Bratman et al., 2015). Another study found that exposure to a wooded area with a view of a creek reduced the number of errors people made on a test of their ability to pay attention (Mayer, McPherson Frantz, Bruehlman-Senecal, & Dolliver, 2009). This study also found that people exposed to nature reported an enhanced ability to "tie up loose ends" with respect to problems they were facing. This enhanced ability to deal with problems may be due to the fact that our creativity and problem-solving skills improve when we are exposed to nature. A study of backpackers on a wilderness trip found that the backpackers' level of creativity was 50% higher while on the trip (Atchley, Strayer, & Atchley, 2012). Based on this, it's likely that Andrew, who we met in the opening of this chapter, returns to work after his stints in nature with solutions to business problems that may have plagued him before he left.

Some parts of the world have already caught on to the fact that taking in some nature gives you a boost. In 1982 the Japanese government Forest Agency introduced "Shinrin-yoku" which translates as "forest bathing" and involves spending time in a forest to reap psychological and physical health benefits (Tsunetsugu, Park, & Miyazaki, 2010). Shinrin-yoku has become increasingly popular because of its boosting abilities. So much so that it has migrated beyond the Far East, and spawned associations and numerous articles in the popular media attesting to its healing properties. So, during your leisure time jump into a kayak and race down a river. Go for a walk in the woods. Or just sit quietly in a local garden. Spending time in nature is an effective way to get a boost.

STAYING INDOORS

That being said, you don't need to get outside to reap the boosting benefits of nature. In fact, some of the most influential research on nature exposure looks at its effects while people are indoors. Even when we're not outside, exposure to nature promotes psychological well-being, physical health, and enhancement (Velarde, Fry, & Tveit, 2007). There are many ways to transform your downtime into uptime while still indoors. We have already discussed the various boosting effects of nature in some depth, so we will now quickly consider some of the ways you can get a boost from nature while enjoying uptime indoors.

Decorate With Plants and Flowers

Spending leisure time in an area that has plants will help you get a boost. Research shows that indoor plants reduce our stress, improve our mood and performance, and promote our health (McSweeney, Rainham, Johnson, Sherry, & Singleton, 2015). For example, patients in a waiting room experience less stress when plants are present and visible (Beukeboom, Langeveld, & Tanja-Dikstra, 2012). To enhance boosting it is a good idea to decompress in an area that is different from where you perform your obligations. Decorate that area with plants and flowers to help yourself recover and feel good. And if you don't have the luxury of moving to a different spot during your breaks, decorate the area where you spend most of your time with lots of things that grow. How many plants can you fit in your bedroom?

Gaze at Nature Through a Window

There's a considerable amount of research showing that having a window view of outdoor nature gives us a boost (Velarde, Fry, & Tveit, 2007). For example, being able to view nature from a window is associated with feeling positive, focused, and relaxed (Kaplan, 2001). If you can't get outside during your leisure time, get close to a window with a view of a park, garden, or wooded area. Even better, open the window so you can hear the birds and feel the fresh air on your face. And you don't need to do this for long. Viewing nature for as little as five minutes can induce positive changes in your heart rate, blood pressure, and muscle tension (Ulrich, 2002, as cited in Velarde et al., 2007).

Watch a Video, Look at Photos, or Put Up a Poster of Nature

If you have absolutely no way of getting close to any plants, hills, trees, or other elements of nature, you can still get a boost by looking at images of them. In one of the first studies of the indoor effects of nature exposure, researchers found that after people were intentionally stressed by showing them a video of gruesome work accidents, simply watching videos of natural outdoor scenes increased their positive emotions, and decreased their anger and fear (Ulrich et al., 1991). In fact, after watching the nature videos people felt even better than they did before being exposed to the stressful video. Watching videos of nature also reduce our stress and increases our happiness (van den Berg, Koole, & van der Wulp, 2003).

Photographs and posters are effective too. Viewing photos of nature increases our vitality (Ryan et al., 2010) and improves decision quality by making people less impulsive (Berry, Sweeney, Morath, Odum, & Jordan, 2014). In the study discussed above in which plants reduced the stress of patients in a waiting room, posters of plants in the waiting room had an equally beneficial effect (Beukeboom et al., 2012).

When it comes to selecting videos, photos, or posters of nature, try to choose ones with blue space. A consistent research finding is that people love water and find it boosting. In one study that investigated the features depicted in wall murals that provided the biggest boost to university students taking a study break, the researcher found that murals depicting natural scenes with water were the most restorative (Felsten, 2009). But don't overdo it. People tend to feel happier when viewing natural scenes with some water more than when viewing scenes completely flooded with water, such as a panoramic view of an ocean (White et al., 2010). A little blue space is better than a ton.

Essentially, putting up posters and photographs of nature, or downloading a screen saver that loops through videos of beaches, forests, and savannas can help you recover, particularly if the scenes have some water elements.

We should note that although being exposed to nature while indoors can give you a boost, that boost isn't likely to be as big as if you actually get out into the wilderness. Plants in your break room don't have the same fascinating configuration as trees in the woods. Paintings of forests do not release chemicals of the trees they depict, and they do not let you hear the sounds of birds chirping, or feel a breeze on your face. Research has shown that although watching videos of nature can give you a boost, people who actually spend time in nature have a higher level of positive emotions and enjoy cognitive benefits, such as an enhanced ability to solve problems (Mayer et al., 2009). Exposing yourself to nature while indoors has an unquestionable boosting impact, but if you can venture into the great outdoors, that is even better.

SUMMARY

Nature fills all three of the ReNU buckets and helps us feel rejuvenated. The restorative properties of nature allow our attentional resources to replenish and thus fill the rebuild bucket. Spending time in nature satisfies our need for such exposure and fills the nourish bucket. People also find interacting with nature relaxing which fills the unhook bucket. Natural environments are also conducive to psychologically detaching from our obligations, which again helps to fill the unhook bucket. You will recall that Andrew, the civil engineer, mentioned that he doesn't think about work at all when he is on his hiking trips. One effective way to turn your downtime into uptime and get a boost is to spend more time interacting with nature. Like Andrew, try to find opportunities to give yourself some wilderness therapy.

Boosting Bites

Practice Shinrin-yoku. Find a local woodland or big park and do some forest bathing.

Put plants in the area in which you spend a lot of leisure time.

Change the screen saver on your computer to depict a lake, mountain, or some other natural element.

Take up a hobby such as hiking, mountain climbing, or kayaking, which requires being outdoors.

Put up pictures or posters of nature.

Incorporate blue space: Ensure that images of nature you select include water elements.

Take a break in a room that allows you to have a view of outdoor nature.

UPTIME ACTION PLAN

Step 1. Do a nature audit. Identify all of the spaces close to you that will allow you to get out into nature. Is there a garden or park close by where you can take a break? Go online and find all of the wooded areas, bike paths, parks, botanical gardens, conservation areas, national parks, lakes, beaches, and other natural spaces within a reasonable distance from you. In the spaces below list six places you can go to get a dose of nature.

_____ _____ _____

_____ _____ _____

Step 2. Incorporate visits to these areas into your uptime. Plan to eat lunch in a park. Visit a garden when you take a break. Schedule a hike through a forest on the weekend. To build nature exposure into your routine, participate in regularly scheduled activities that take place in nature. For example, join a walking group or get some binoculars and join a group of bird watchers. In the space below jot down the times you think you can incorporate nature exposure into your busy routine.

_____

_____

_____

_____

Step 3. Organize your break area and other spots where you enjoy time away from your obligations. If you can, take breaks near windows that give you views of nature. If you do not have such views and tend to take breaks in a particular spot, how can you incorporate nature into it? What about at home? Indicate three ways you'd like to bring real (e.g., plants) or simulated (e.g., posters) nature into the areas in which you enjoy leisure time.

_____

_____

_____

REFERENCES

Atchley, R., Strayer, D. L., & Atchley, P. (2012). Creativity in the wild: Improving creative reasoning through immersion in natural settings. *PLOS ONE, 7,* e51474.

Berman, M. G., Jonides, J., & Kaplan, S. (2008). The cognitive benefits of interacting with nature. *Psychological Science, 19,* 1207–1212.

Berman, M. G., Kross, E., Krpan, K. M., Askren, M. K., Burson, A., Deldin, P. J., Kaplan, S., Sherdell, L., Gotlib, I. H., & Jonides, J. (2012). *Journal of Affective Disorders, 140,* 300–305.

Berry, M. S., Sweeney, M. M., Morath, J., Odum, A. L., & Jordan, K. E. (2014). The nature of impulsivity: Visual exposure to natural environments decreases impulsive decision-making in a delay discounting task. *PLOS ONE, 9,* 1–7.

Beukeboom, C. J., Langwveid, D., & Tanja-Dikstra, K. (2012). Stress-reducing effects of real and artificial nature in a hospital waiting room. *The Journal of Alternative and Complementary Medicine, 18,* 329–333.

Bratman, G. N., Daily, G. C., Levy, B. J., & Gross, J. J. (2015). The benefits of nature experience: improved affect and cognition. *Landscape and Urban Planning, 138,* 41–50.

Bratman, G. N., Hamilton, J. P., Hahn, K. S., Daily, G. C., & Gross, J. J. (2015). Nature experience reduces rumination and subgenual prefrontal cortex activation. *Proceedings of the National Academy of Sciences, 112,* 8567–8572.

Chang, C. Y. (2004). Psychophysiological responses to different landscape settings and a comparison of cultural differences. *Acta Horticulturae, 639,* 57–65.

Cooper Marcus, C., & Barnes, M. (1999). Introduction: Historical and cultural perspectives on healing gardens. In C. Cooper Marcus & M. Barnes (Eds.), *Healing gardens: Therapeutic benefits and design recommendations* (pp. 1–26). New York, NY: John Wiley & Sons.

Davis, S. (1998). Development of the profession of horticultural therapy. In S. Pastor Simson & M. C. Straus (Eds.), *Horticulture as therapy: Principles and practice* (pp. 3–18). New York, NY: The Food Products Press.

Faber Taylor, A., & Kuo, F. E. (2009). Children with attention deficits concentrate better after a walk in the park. *Journal of Attention Disorders, 12,* 402–409.

Felsten, G. (2009). Where to take a study break on the college campus: An attention restoration theory perspective. *Journal of Environmental Psychology, 29,* 160–167.

Gullone, E. (2000). The biophilia hypothesis and life in the 21st century: increasing mental health or increasing pathology? *Journal of Happiness Studies, 1,* 293–321.

Hansmann, R., Hug, S., & Seeland, K. (2007). Restoration and stress relief through physical activities in forests and parks. *Urban Forestry & Urban Greening, 6,* 213–225.

Hartig, T., Evans, G. W., Jammer, L. D., Davis, D. S., & Gärling, T. (2003). Tracking restoration in natural and urban field settings. *Journal of Environmental Psychology, 23,* 109–123.

Hartig, T., & Staats, H. (2006). The need for psychological restoration as a determinant of environmental preferences. *Journal of Environmental Psychology, 26,* 215–226.

Honold, J., Lakes, T., Beyer, R., & van der Meer, E. (2016). Restoration in urban spaces: Nature views from home, greenways and public parks. *Environment and Behavior, 48,* 796–825

Joye, Y., & De Block, A. (2011). "Nature and I are two" A critical examination of the biophilia hypothesis. *Environmental Values, 20,* 189–215.

Kaplan, S. (1995). The restorative benefits of nature: Toward an integrative framework. *Journal of Environmental Psychology, 15,* 169–182.

Kaplan, R. (2001). The nature of the view from home: Psychological benefits. *Environment and Behavior, 33,* 507–542.

Kaplan, S., & Talbot, J. F. (1983). Psychological benefits of a wilderness experience. In I. Altman, & J. F. Wohlwill (Eds.), *Behavior and the natural environment* (pp. 163–203). New York, NY: Plenum Press.

Kardan, O., Gozdyra, P., Misic, B., Moola, F., Palmer, L. J., Paus, T., & Berman, M. G. (2015). Neighborhood greenspace and health in a large urban center. *Scientific Reports, 5,* 1–14.

Korpela, K., & Kinnunen, U. (2011). How is leisure time interacting with nature related to the need for recovery from work demands? Testing multiple mediators. *Leisure Sciences, 33,* 1–14.

Li, Q. (2010). Effect of forest bathing trips on human immune function. *Environmental Health and Preventative Medicine, 15,* 9–17.

Maas, J., Verheji, R. A., Spreeuwenberg, P., Schellevis, F. G., & Groenewegen, P. P. (2009). Morbidity is related to a green living environment. *Journal of Epidemiology and Community Health, 63,* 967–973.

Mayer, F. S., McPherson Frantz, C., Bruehlman-Senecal, E., & Dolliver, K., (2009). Why is nature beneficial? The role of connectedness to nature. *Environment and Behavior, 41,* 607–643.

McMahan, E. A., & Estes, D. (2015). The effect of contact with natural environments on positive and negative affect: A meta-analysis. *The Journal of Positive Psychology, 10,* 507–519.

McSweeney, J., Rainham, D., Johnson, S. A., Sherry, S. B., & Singleton, J. (2015). Indoor nature exposure (INE): A health-promotion framework. *Health Promotion International, 30,* 126–139.

Miller, G. E., Chen, E., & Zhou, E. S. (2007). If it goes up, must it come down? Chronic stress and the hypothalamic-pituitary-adrenocortical axis in humans. *Psychological Bulletin, 133,* 25–45.

Nisbet, E., & Zelenski, J. M. (2011). Underestimating nearby nature: Affective forecasting errors obscure the happy path to sustainability. *Psychological Science, 22,* 1101–1106.

Park, B. J., Tsunetsugu, Y., Kasetani, T., Kagawa, T., & Miyazaki, Y. (2010). The physiological effects of Shinrin-yoku (taking in the forest atmosphere or forest bathing): Evidence from field experiments in 24 forests across Japan. *Environmental Health and Preventative Medicine, 15,* 18–26.

Pergams, O. R. W., & Zaradic, P. A. (2008). Evidence for a fundamental and pervasive shift away from nature-based recreation. *Proceedings of the National Academy of Sciences, 105*, 2295–2300.

Ryan, R. M., Weinstein, N., Bernstein, J., Brown, K. W., Mistretta, L., & Gagné, M. (2010). Vitalizing effects of being outdoors and in nature. *Journal of Environmental Psychology, 30*, 159–168.

Selhub, E. M., & Logan, A. C. (2012). *Your brain on nature: The science of nature's influence on your health, happiness, and vitality.* Mississauga, ON: John Wiley & Sons.

Tsunetsugu, Y., Park, B., & Miyazaki, Y. (2010). Trends in research related to "Shinrin-Yoku" (taking in the forest atmosphere or forest bathing) in Japan. *Environmental Health and Preventative Medicine, 15*, 27–37.

Ulrich, R. S. (1993). Biophilia, biophobia, and natural landscapes. In S. R. Kellert & E. O. Wilson (Eds.), *The biophilia hypothesis* (pp. 73–137). Washington, DC: Island Press.

Ulrich, R. S. (1999). Effects of gardens on health outcomes: theory and research. In C. Cooper Marcus & M. Barnes (Eds.), *Healing gardens: Therapeutic benefits and design recommendations* (pp. 27–86). New York, NY: John Wiley & Sons.

Ulrich, R. S., Simons, R. F., Losito, B. D., Fiorito, E., Miles, M. A., Zelson, M. (1991). Stress recovery during exposure to natural and urban environments. *Journal of Environmental Psychology, 11*, 201–230.

van den Berg, A. E., Koole, S. L., & van der Wulp, N. Y. (2003). Environmental preference and restoration: (How) are they related? *Journal of Environmental Psychology, 23*, 135–146.

Velarde, M. D., Fry, G., & Tveit, M. (2007). Health effects of viewing landscapes— landscape types in environmental psychology. *Urban Forestry & Urban Greening, 6*, 199–212.

Ward Thompson, C. (2011). Linking landscape and health: A recurring theme. *Landscape and Urban Planning, 99*, 187–195.

White, M., Smith, A., Humphryes, K., Pahl, S., Snelling, D., & Depledge, M. (2010). Blue space: The importance of water for preference, affect, and restorativeness ratings of natural and build scenes. *Journal of Environmental Psychology, 30*, 482–493.

Wilson, E. O. (1984). *The biophilia hypothesis.* Boston, MA: Harvard University Press.

CHAPTER 3

CUTTING THE VIRTUAL CORD

When Bailey started Proactive Movement, her own corporate wellness business, it wasn't uncommon for her to start her day in her home office at 9 A.M. and stay there until 11 P.M.

"The line between work and home was very blurred," says the 31-year-old. "I'm not married and I don't have kids so there was no one telling me to stop. When you run your own business you can continuously work around the clock."

After a couple of years of this constant connection to work, Bailey began to notice the intense passion she once had for her career had faded and been replaced with resentment. That's when she knew things had to change.

"I realized I needed to create a separation."

So Bailey laid down some hard rules for herself such as no work after 6 P.M. during the week. To ensure this happens, she sets a timer, books time off in her calendar and makes plans in the evenings that require her to get out of the house—anything from meeting friends for dinner to running errands.

"After 6 P.M. there is no more work and no more work conversation."

On weekends she takes it a step further by avoiding her home office and completely ignoring her e-mail until Monday. And when she goes on vacations, she leaves her phone at home.

"When I take a vacation I set things up so that there won't be anything urgent I need to respond to. I want to make sure that I can disconnect from the rest of the world."

Boost: The Science of Recharging Yourself in an Age of Unrelenting Demands, pp. 33–50

Completely disconnecting from work is difficult for some, but Bailey has found it clears her mind. This change in lifestyle has spurred Bailey to appreciate the time she has away from work.

"I value time so much. The time I have to be able to be with loved ones, to meditate, to go for a run or to travel is priceless to me."

By committing to a few simple rules Bailey set for herself, she was able to draw a healthy line between work and home life.

TECHNOLOGY AND THE MODERN WORLD

Information and communication technologies such as computers, the internet, and smartphones, have transformed and enriched our lives, and made it much easier and convenient to do so many things. Unlike in our grandparents' day, today we can get instantaneous news updates from around the globe, see with our own eyes if our babies are sleeping at home in their cribs while we enjoy dinner at a restaurant, map a detailed, cross-country road trip in seconds, and listen to virtually any song that has ever been recorded. One of the most significant changes brought about by modern technologies is that today we can obtain, send and receive information anytime and almost anywhere. This allows us to be much more flexible and efficient because we can, for example, handle work tasks at home, and access needed information, or people, any time of the day or night.

Nobody would deny that there are significant benefits brought about by modern technologies. But there are potential disadvantages too. Communication technologies can become "a leash" that keep us connected to our obligations (Middleton & Cukier, 2006). For example, a 2016 study found that 84% of employees report having to be available after hours at least some of the time (Dettmers, Bamberg, & Seffzek, 2016). This state of affairs is enabled by the technologies that make us easily accessible and blur the boundary between obligation time and leisure time. To get a boost we need to strengthen and protect that boundary.

Bailey, the entrepreneur who opened this chapter, learned that she could rekindle her passion for her work by creating boundaries between obligation time and leisure time. Andrew, the engineer we met in the last chapter, explained that being out in the wilderness helps him avoid thinking about his work obligations. In the language of the ReNU model, he experiences psychological detachment and fills the unhook bucket. However, he would be unlikely to enjoy detachment if he was constantly checking his phone. All of us can benefit from cutting the virtual cord that keeps us connected to our obligations. This is a key part of transforming our downtime into uptime.

Why is it that so many of us stay connected to our obligations in our leisure time? One reason of course is simply because we can. We can take handheld computers with us wherever we go. Ninety-five percent of Americans now own a cellphone and 77% have a smartphone, an increase of 120% since 2011 (Pew Research Center, 2017). Although any electronic device can interfere with boosting, smartphones pose the biggest problem because they couple connectivity with mobility (Chesley, 2005). Modern technology makes it easy for us to be constantly connected and available no matter where we are, regardless of whether our weekly obligations are employment-related or not.

However, this availability can prevent boosting. Being constantly connected creates unpredictability because you never know when you will be propelled from leisure mode into obligation mode. This unpredictability causes stress, insecurity, and a constant state of activation that prevents recovery (Dettmers et al., 2016). But we are generally unaware of these negative consequences. Research has suggested that one reason people stay connected to their obligations is because they don't appreciate that staying connected takes a significant toll on their lives (Boswell & Olson-Buchanan, 2007). With that in mind, let's consider the consequences of staying electronically connected to our obligations during our leisure time.

MODERN TECHNOLOGY AND THE RₑNU BUCKETS

Over the last few years there has been a burgeoning research interest in how information and communication technologies affect us when we are away from our obligations. Much of this research focuses on what is called interrole conflict, which is when activities and interests in one domain of life interfere with activities and interests in a different domain (Schwind Wilson & Baumann, 2015). Most research on interrole conflict focuses on how work interferes with home life, or vice versa, and numerous studies have shown that staying electronically connected to work during our leisure time interferes with our ability to attend to things we like to do at home, such as playing with our kids (e.g., Schieman & Young, 2013). However, the domains that are relevant to interrole conflict are broader than just work and home (Schwind Wilson & Baumann, 2015). Just because you are at home doesn't mean you are free to attend to matters that can help you boost, so we'll adopt a broader understanding of how activities in one domain can interfere with activities in other domains. For example, we can consider how taking care of elderly parents interferes with our ability to relax, or how meeting childcare obligations prevents us from taking a long, uninterrupted walk. These are examples of how home obligations conflict with personal activities and interests. Communication technologies that keep us connected to our obligations intensify interrole conflict because they keep us tied to those obligations when we could use a boost. This is not to suggest that you should abandon your obligations and choose to not be available when others may need you. Far from it. But it does highlight the value of allowing yourself the luxury of making yourself unavailable when circumstances allow it.

The first reason cutting the virtual cord will give you a boost is because it allows you to fill the rebuild bucket by giving your resources a break. It goes without saying that if you participate in obligation-related activities during your leisure time, you need to draw on obligation-related resources. However, doing so compromises your ability to replenish those resources and prevents you from boosting. For example, if you manage to get out for a pleasant stroll alone only to have your partner phone you 10 minutes into it to ask how to calm the crying baby, you need to get into "parent" mode and draw on resources that may already be depleted. Cutting the cord erects a boundary between your obligation time and your uptime which gives your limited resources a chance to replenish themselves and helps you recover. This is one of the main reasons why people who cut the virtual cord when they are on vacation, like Bailey does, end up feeling more recovered when they return (Kirillova & Wang, 2016).

Cutting the cord also help us satisfy our needs and fill the nourish bucket. Staying electronically connected to our obligations in our leisure time, and the interrole conflict it produces, increases how tired we feel but, paradoxically, also compromises the quality of our sleep (Van Hooff, Guerts, Kompier, & Taris, 2006). This happens because interrole conflict interferes with our ability to rest and unwind, which is necessary to promote good sleep (Nylén, Melin, & Laflamme, 2007). Ultimately, staying connected impedes our ability to satisfy our physical needs.

It also interferes with our ability to satisfy our psychological needs. Research shows that when facing a high level of interrole conflict, people who do not electronically detach from their obligations are less likely to satisfy their psychological needs for competence and autonomy (Derks, ten Brummelhuis, Zecic, & Bakker, 2014). This happens because when we stay electronically connected we have trouble carving out time to engage in leisure activities, such as hobbies, that allow us to master challenges, and we lose control over who contacts us, how often, and when (Derks, ten Brummelhuis, et al., 2014).

Cutting the cord also helps satisfy our psychological need for relatedness. For example, when employees are on call, which means they have no choice but to remain tethered to work, they spend less time participating in social activities (Bamberg, Dettmers, Funck, Krähe & Vahle-Hinz, 2012). As a result, staying connected hinders our engagement with friends and family. This helps to explain why our significant others find our use of communication technologies even more disruptive to leisure time than we do (Boswell & Olson-Buchanan, 2007). When we stay connected to our obligations during our leisure time it can generate resentment in our partners (Ferguson et al., 2016). Known as "technoference," the frequent use of communication technology at home can interfere with the interactions we have with our partners and hurt our relationships (McDaniel & Coyne, 2016). In fact, research shows that when two people are having a face-to-face conversation, the *mere presence* of a cell phone undermines their relationship. In one study, when researchers left a cell phone sitting on a desk beside two people having a casual discussion, the conversation partners felt less close and connected to each other, compared to people who interacted with no phone present (Przybylski & Weinstein, 2013). A more specific form of technoference is "phubbing." This involves snubbing someone to spend time on a smartphone, which also compromises relationships. Essentially, staying electronically connected hinders our ability to satisfy our need for relatedness.

A number of studies have demonstrated that cutting the virtual cord also fills the unhook bucket. For example, one study found that people experiencing high interrole conflict are more likely to psychologically detach and experience relaxation when they do not use smartphones in their leisure time (Derks, ten Brummelhuis, et al., 2014). A similar study found that people who use information and communication technologies less frequently at home during non-work hours are more successful at psychologically detaching (Park, Fritz, & Jex, 2011). Given this, it's not surprising that a study out of the Netherlands revealed that employees are less likely to psychologically detach on the days they use their smartphones more intensely during their leisure time (Derks, van Mierlo, & Schmitz, 2014). Importantly, this study took people's workload into account, so the researchers were able to determine that people weren't failing to detach simply because they were busy and needed to stay connected. Instead, the technology itself was the culprit.

WILL CUTTING THE CORD GIVE YOU A BOOST?

Because staying electronically connected to our obligations during our leisure time prevents us from filling the buckets of the ReNU model, it also prevents us from getting a boost. Most of the research in this area has focused on the psychological well-being component of boosting, but it presents a consistent picture of the value of cutting the cord.

People who allow their electronic devices to compromise the boundary between their obligation time and leisure time experience stress (Voydanoff, 2005), and an associated increase in the stress hormone cortisol (Dettmers,

Vahle-Hinz, Bamberg, Friedrich, & Keller, 2016). They also experience anxiety and depression (Schieman & Young, 2013), are more irritated and suffer from worse moods (Bamberg et al., 2012), fewer positive emotions (Ohly & Latour, 2014), and exhaustion (Derks, van Mierlo, et al., 2014), which increases over time (Dettmers, 2017). These effects take a toll on our health. Research shows that compared to employees who are never contacted outside of normal working hours for work-related matters, those who are contacted *even occasionally* suffer numerous health impairments, such as musculoskeletal issues, gastrointestinal disorders, and cardiovascular problems (Arlinghaus & Nachreiner, 2013).

The research is pretty clear. Constant electronic connection to our obligations and extended availability interferes with our ability to get a boost. Despite this, many people today are almost always electronically connected and never cut the cord. They are perpetually available. We might say they suffer from availableism.

AVAILABLEISM

Availableism is the condition in which people experience a need to be available continuously through technology and therefore are constantly electronically connected and available to others (Gruman, 2017). There are a number of reasons people suffer from availableism. First, communication technologies have become so common and familiar that some people feel anxious if they are not connected through their wireless devices (Cheever, Rosen, Carrier, & Chavez, 2014). This has colloquially been referred to as FOMO, fear of missing out; FOBO, fear of being offline; and nomophobia, fear of being out of cell phone contact (Rosen, 2015). Another reason is that people sometimes strongly identify with a particular role they occupy in their lives, such as the role of employee or caregiver, and find it enjoyable and rewarding to stay connected in order to fulfil that role (Ashforth, Kreiner, & Fugate, 2000). A third reason is that, as we suggested, some people feel that their employers and colleagues expect them to be always available (Derks, ten Brummelhuis, et al., 2014). However, as we have seen, constant connection has serious drawbacks and prevents people from boosting.

Progressive organizations understand this and are implementing policies that allow their employees to cut the virtual cord. For example, the *New York Times* reported that at the Toronto office of the global public relations firm, Edelman, there is a "7-to-7" rule whereby employees are not only discouraged from, but reprimanded if they are caught, e-mailing colleagues before 7:00 A.M. or after 7:00 P.M. (Thompson, 2014). This helps to discourage availableism. In the absence of rules like these however, each of us needs to work on addressing availableism for ourselves. The first step in this process is to determine if you suffer from this affliction.

Complete the following test to get a sense of whether or not you suffer from availableism. Respond to each of the eight items below by indicating a score from one to five using the scale provided. Then add up your scores for each question to get a total score. Total scores of 16 or less suggest that you do not suffer from availableism. Scores between 17 and 28 suggest that you like to be electronically connected but that it doesn't consume you, and you are likely able to cut the virtual cord in order to get a boost. Scores above 29 suggest that you suffer from availableism, and would benefit from finding new ways to disconnect.

Availableism Test

1	2	3	4	5
Disagree Strongly	Disagree	Neutral	Agree	Agree Strongly

1. I get anxious if I don't have my phone with me. _____

2. I can always be contacted. _____

3. I feel that I should always be available if people want to contact me. _____

4. I always have my phone with me. _____

5. It is important to me that I always be accessible to people by phone or other electronic device. _____

6. It makes me uncomfortable to think that someone might not be able to contact me when they want to. _____

7. I make a point of always being accessible. _____

8. I'm concerned that bad things might happen if people can't contact me anytime they want. _____

If you scored 16 or less on this scale, you should feel free to skip the rest of this chapter; You don't need any advice on how to cut the virtual cord. However, if you scored 17 or higher, read on to learn about boundary management tactics that can help you cut the cord and transform your downtime into uptime.

TURN DOWNTIME INTO UPTIME WITH BOUNDARY MANAGEMENT TACTICS

Boundary management tactics are strategies people use to separate the different domains of their lives (Kossek, Lautsch, & Eaton, 2006). Most of the research on boundary management tactics focuses on how people separate the work and home domains. However, in the same way that inter-role conflict can occur in domains other than work and home, boundary management tactics can be applied in other domains too. For example, they can also be used to separate non-employment-related obligations, like schoolwork, from the personal activities and interests we prefer to pursue during our uptime (Van Steenbergen, Ybema, & Lapierre, 2017).

People differ in the extent to which they build walls between their obligations and their leisure time (Kreiner, Hollensbe, & Sheep, 2009). This is called a segmentation preference. People with a high segmentation preference (segmenters) like to keep different domains such as work and home completely separate, whereas people with a low segmentation preference (integrators) do not mind blurring the boundaries between domains, and are more likely to use communication technologies to, for instance, attend to work matters while at home. However, research shows that people with a high segmentation preference are better at boosting because, for example, they are more successful at psychologically detaching in their leisure time (Park et al., 2011), and experience less interrole conflict (Kossek et al., 2006). It is important to note that segmentation and integration are not all-or-none deals. We can vary in the extent to which we prefer segmentation versus integration, and the ways in which we manage the associated boundaries (Kreiner et al., 2009).

With these points in mind, let's consider some of the ways boundary management tactics can help you cut the virtual cord and get a boost. We will consider boundary management tactics that reduce availableism and help to segment obligation time and uptime more generally. There are four categories of boundary management tactics—physical, temporal, behavioral, and communicative (Kreiner et al., 2009).

Physical Boundary Management Tactics

Physical boundary management tactics involve using physical space or items to create a separation between obligations and uptime (Kreiner et al., 2009). For example, closing or locking the door to a home office in the evening creates a physical and psychological barrier and keeps you away from your computer, which will help you boost. Using separate calendars for obligation-related and leisure-related matters, and different key rings for each domain, will also support a mental boundary between obligations and uptime (Nippert-Eng, 1996). If you can, use different electronic devices for your obligations and personal matters (Kossek, 2016). This way when you are enjoying uptime you can ignore your work phone and not have it with you while you focus on activities that help you recharge.

Putting physical distance between obligation-related items and uptime is also valuable. Keeping papers, agendas, and other obligation-related materials away from spaces regularly used during leisure time will help you detach and devote your full attention to non-obligation-related matters (Basile & Beauregard, 2016). Similarly, someone who is a homemaker and attends to housework all day should physically get away from it all by leaving their house when they want to enjoy some uptime. Putting physical distance between obligation-related "things" and uptime helps to promote psychological distance. And of course, when they leave the house they might also want to put some physical space between themselves and their devices by leaving their phone at home.

Temporal Boundary Management Tactics

Temporal boundary management tactics involve setting boundaries around when you will address, and how much time you will devote to, your obligations. Perhaps the most common temporal boundary tactic is to schedule blocks of time during which you will not be available and being resolute about protecting that time (Kreiner et al., 2009). For example, an employee can be firm about not checking work-related messages in the evenings, weekends, or on vacations, just like Bailey does. Or a mother can be adamant about not being phoned while she enjoys a weekly girls' night out with her friends. Setting temporal boundaries opens up time for boosting and positions recovery as a priority in your life. In the same way that you might schedule blocks of time to workout at the gym, temporal boundaries delineate the blocks of time during which you don't attend to obligation-related matters.

To delineate the temporal boundary between obligation time and uptime it is helpful to practice transition rituals, which are routines that signify the move from one role to another (Ashforth, Kulik, & Tomiuk, 2008). A pair of researchers in the U.K. interviewed teleworkers about the boundary management tactics they used to separate work from home. One of their interviewees explained a transition ritual that supports one of her temporal boundary management tactics: "I have dogs to walk. So there is always at least a natural break around five o'clock where I meet up with friends and we walk the dogs. So that signals that it is the end of the working day for me" (Basile & Beauregard, 2016, p. 108). For her, walking her dogs was a daily ritual that demarcated the separation of obligation time from uptime and it was reinforced by involving other people. Being accountable to others helps to create stronger boundaries (Basile & Beauregard, 2016).

The rituals you implement to establish boundaries aren't just symbolic. Research has shown that when people enact rituals they feel more in control

(Norton & Gino, 2014), and become more effective at their tasks (Wood Brooks et al., 2016). Rituals also result in us enjoying and savoring our experiences more intensely (Vohs, Wang, Gino, & Norton, 2013). So, not only can transition rituals make you more effective at cutting the virtual cord, they can increase the degree to which you derive pleasure from your uptime.

There are countless transition rituals you can employ to support the creation of boundaries: Change your clothes. Pour a glass of wine or herbal tea. Go for a bike ride. Put on some music. Light a candle. Feed your bird. Take a shower. Do 15 minutes of people-watching in a park. The point is to do something that signifies that you are now moving into uptime, and are no longer tied to your obligations.

Behavioral Boundary Management Tactics

Behavioral boundary management tactics involve behaving in a way that allows you to cut the virtual cord. One of the interviewees in the U.K. study we just discussed explained what is probably the most effective behavioral boundary management tactic available: "I wouldn't answer the phone after close of business time because the danger with that is then that people think you are available 24/7 and those calls become later and later and later. I actually switch the phone off so that I am not even tempted to hear it" (Basile & Beauregard, 2016, p. 107). Essentially, by answering phone calls, e-mails, and texts related to your obligations after work hours, you are perpetuating the expectation that you will be available during these hours of the day. However, if a boundary is established and maintained, the expectation won't develop in the first place. Other tactics identified by the researchers included turning off laptops, logging off of computer systems, and turning off the ringer on phones used for work.

Another behavioral boundary management tactic involves social media. Although most of our discussion focuses on phones, social media can also prevent us from separating from our obligations by keeping us connected to the people with whom we interact while handling them. One effective tactic is to use different social media platforms with different groups of people and limit obligation-related contacts to a particular platform. You can then avoid that platform in your uptime.

Additional behavioral boundary management tactics include involving other people, and exploiting technology (Kreiner et al., 2009). Involving other people allows you to offload some of your responsibilities or have others serve as gatekeepers. For example, you can create a buddy system with co-workers who perform similar functions as you so that only one of you is on call at any given time after hours. As another example, all the partners in a consulting firm do not need to be available to all clients and at all times. Availability can rotate among the partners to allow each of them to have regular, uninterrupted uptime. Another option is to have colleagues or partners screen your calls and messages. In a study of the boundary management tactics of Episcopal parish priests, one of the priests explained that he had his wife answer phone calls on his day off and she only involved him if it was an emergency (Kreiner et al., 2009).

Exploiting technology involves leveraging features and applications that allow you to control your boundaries. For example, you can put your phone into airplane mode or "do not disturb" mode to protect periods of uptime. Alternatively, you can set up your devices to send automatic replies to people who try contacting you advising them that you are not available and noting when you will be. You can also use applications, like Sanity, that filter your phone calls and allow you to control which ones you will receive (Henry, 2013).

Communicative Boundary Management Tactics

Communicative boundary management tactics involve establishing expectations and addressing people who violate those expectations (Kreiner et al., 2009). The first step, establishing expectations, is about communicating to others when you will and will not be available. This step prevents other people from being surprised, disappointed, or upset when they can't reach you. It is important to note that setting expectations may require some negotiation (Kreiner et al., 2009). People with whom you interact when it comes to handling your obligations may have their own needs or preferences with respect to when and how much you will be available in your leisure time. Negotiating expectations allows you to work through any differences and satisfy the needs and preferences of all parties.

The second step is addressing violators, which involves taking corrective action when others ignore the boundaries you have established. In some instances, violations will be due to ignorance and simply informing people of the expectations you have established will suffice. Other times violations will be intentional. When that happens, the way you respond must take into account your relationship with the violator. You likely would not rebuke a senior work colleague the same way you might admonish a child. However, you should be firm in explaining that your leisure time is to be respected. Remember, whatever behavior you are willing to tolerate is precisely the behavior you will have to endure. When you demonstrate respect for yourself, others respect you more. Protect your uptime.

Another issue regarding communication is to make sure that any exchanges you have with other people during your obligation time are crystal clear so that nobody is confused about things and feels compelled to clarify details with you when you are trying to disengage (Boswell, Olson-Buchanan, Butts, & Becker, 2016). Also, consider advising people that you would prefer text-based communication as opposed to phone calls during your leisure time. This allows people to contact you whenever the urge strikes them, but gives you control over when you respond, which should be once you are back in obligation mode (Boswell et al., 2016).

Boundary management tactics are an effective way to cut the virtual cord. They can be applied to help us disconnect from our obligations and to prevent or reduce availableism. These are important factors in helping us get a boost.

THE WHOLE STORY

The main theme of this chapter is that to get a boost in our uptime we need to put away our tablets, phones and computers so we can psychologically disconnect from our obligations. Overall, the available research supports this conclusion. However, sometimes completely segmenting obligation time and leisure time simply is not possible. Particularly when deadlines loom, crises occur, or pressing issues arise, getting work done during leisure time and being available may be necessary. Even in less urgent situations, occasional availability may sometimes be required. In these circumstances, boundary management remains valuable. Research shows that even when we can't escape our obligations completely in our uptime, implementing boundary management tactics allows us to mitigate the anti-boosting effects of constant connection (Barber & Jenkins, 2014). Also, erecting partial boundaries can be helpful (Kreiner et al., 2009). Erecting partial boundaries involves prioritizing tasks and only attending to those that require attention. To foster boosting, your goal in these circumstances is to address any burning issues so you can move past them and put them out of your mind. If you must address obligations during your leisure time, and have the option, schedule your availability for when you are most alert so you can address issues efficiently and effectively and then move on (Kossek, 2016).

On occasion, letting obligations creep into our uptime may actually help us fill the ReNU buckets. There is a natural human tendency for people to continue thinking about tasks they have not completed. This is called the Zeigarnik effect (Zeigarnik, 1938). Not only does ruminating about unfinished business prevent us from psychologically detaching from our obligations, research shows that it has other anti-boosting effects such as interfering with our ability to get a good night's sleep (Syrek, Weigelt,

Peifer, & Antoni, 2017). If a small amount of work, or checking your phone, helps you tie up loose ends, clear your mind, and attend to other matters, it can be beneficial for boosting (Ohly & Latour, 2014). This helps to explain why people who prefer not to segment their work and home lives have less work-home conflict when they use their smartphones at home (Derks, Bakker, Peters, & van Wingerden, 2016). The flexibility afforded by technology lets them attend to their obligations and then frees them up to attend to other leisurely matters. However, we urge you to be cautious with this tactic. Blurring the line between obligation time and leisure time can easily degenerate into the reduction or elimination of uptime.

Another point to consider is that although psychologically detaching by not thinking about our obligations gives us a boost, thinking *positively* about our obligations can promote the same end. Research shows that if during your leisure time you think about good things that happened while you were engaged in your obligations, it can promote psychological detachment (Bono, Glomb, Shen, Kim, & Koch, 2013). The fly in the ointment is that research also shows people who tend to engage in this sort of positive reflection during their leisure time also tend to engage in negative reflection, which undermines boosting (Binnewies, Sonnentag, & Mojza, 2009).

To reconcile all of this remember that getting a boost is less about the activities we engage in than it is about filling the ReNU buckets. Whether you should completely cut the virtual cord and not think at all about your obligations, or allow yourself to stay connected somewhat by checking your phone or thinking positively about your responsibilities, depends on which of your buckets happens to need filling. If you had a tough week and need to mentally step away in your uptime to fill the unhook bucket, do it. If you had a great week and want to savour the delights of a job well done for a little bit, which will satisfy your need for competence and fill the nourish bucket, go for it. But then, turn your brain to something else and unhook.

SUMMARY

Modern technology makes our lives more convenient, but it also makes it much easier to stay connected to our obligations in our leisure time. Although we tend to be unaware of it, research shows that remaining attached to our obligations when we're trying to unwind has lots of undesirable consequences that compromise our ability to fill the ReNU buckets and get a boost. Implementing boundary management tactics is an effective way to put some space between you and your obligations, and transform your downtime into uptime. As Bailey learned, cutting the virtual cord is an important part of recovery.

Boosting Bites

Turn off your obligation-related electronic devices in your uptime.

Schedule "unavailable" time in your agenda.

Use an application that precludes the use of obligation-related functions during uptime.

Have two phones and put away the work phone after hours.

Keep obligation-related materials away from you during uptime.

Advise other people of when you will and won't be available.

Schedule after hours obligations for a specific time so you can then put them out of your mind.

UPTIME ACTION PLAN

Step 1. Think about the ways in which your electronic devices keep you connected to your obligations in your uptime. Do your devices allow you to escape your obligations as much as you would like? If not, indicate what prevents you from cutting the virtual cord.

_____

_____

_____

_____

_____

Step 2. Based on your response in Step 1, design and implement boundary management tactics to segment your obligation time from your uptime. In the space below, indicate what physical, temporal, behavioral, and communicative boundary management tactics will you find most helpful.

Physical _____

_____

_____

Temporal _____

_____

_____

Behavioral _____

_____

_____

Communicative _____

_____

_____

Step 3. Develop a transition ritual. Think about an activity that you can use to demarcate the separation between obligation time and uptime. Select something that will be easy to implement on an ongoing basis.

_____

_____

_____

_____

_____

REFERENCES

Arlinghaus, A., & Nachreiner, F., (2013). When work calls—associations between being contacted outside of regular working hours for work-related matters and health. *Chronobiology International, 30*, 1197–1202.

Ashforth, B., E., Kulik, C. T., & Tomiuk, M. A. (2008). How service agents manage the person-role interface. *Group & Organization Management, 33*, 5–45.

Ashforth, B., Kreiner, G. E., & Fugate, M. (2000). All in a day's work: Boundaries and micro role transitions. *Academy of Management Review, 25*, 472–491.

Bamberg, E., Dettmers, J., Funck, H., Krähe, B., & Vahle-Hinz, T. (2012). Effects of on-call work on well-being: Results of a diary study. *Applied Psychology: Health and Well-Being, 4*, 299–320.

Barber, L. K., & Jenkins, J. S. (2014). Creating technological boundaries to protect bedtime: Examining work-home boundary management, psychological detachment and sleep. *Stress & Health, 30*, 259–264.

Basile, K. A., & Beauregard, A. (2016). Strategies for successful telework: How effective employees manage work/home boundaries. *Strategic HR Review, 15*, 106–111.

Binnewies, C., Sonnentag, S., & Mojza, E. J. (2009). Feeling good and thinking about the good sides of one's work. *Journal of Occupational Health Psychology, 14*, 243–256.

Bono, J. E., Glomb, T. A., Shen, W., Kim, E., & Koch, A. J. (2013). Building positive resources: Effects of positive events and positive reflection on work stress and health. *Academy of Management Journal, 56*, 1601–1627.

Boswell, W. R., & Olson-Buchanan, J. B. (2007). The use of communication technologies after hours: the role of work attitudes and work-life conflict. *Journal of Management, 33*, 592–610.

Boswell, W. R., Olson-Buchanan, J. B., Butts, M. M., & Becker, W. J. (2016). Managing "after hours" electronic work communication. *Organizational Dynamics, 45*, 291–297.

Cheever, N. A., Rosen, L. D., Carrier, L. M., & Chavez, A. (2014). Out of sight is not out of mind: The impact of restricting wireless mobile device use on anxiety levels among low, moderate, and high users. *Computers in Human Behavior, 37*, 290–297.

Chesley, N. (2005). Blurring boundaries? Linking technology use, spillover, individual distress, and family satisfaction. *Journal of Marriage and Family, 67*, 1237–1248

Derks, D., Bakker, A. B., Peters, P., & van Wingerden, P. (2016). Work-related smartphone use, work-family conflict and family role performance: The role of segmentation preference. *Human Relations, 69*, 1045–1068.

Derks, D., ten Brummelhuis, L. L., Zecic, D., & Bakker, A. B. (2014). Switching on and of...: Does smartphone use obstruct the possibility to engage in recovery activities? *European Journal of Work and Organizational Psychology, 23*, 80–90.

Derks, D., van Mierlo, H., & Schmitz, E. B. (2014). A diary study on work-related smartphone use, psychological detachment and exhaustion: Examining the role of the perceived segmentation norm. *Journal of Occupational Health Psychology, 19*, 74–84.

Dettmers, J. (2017). How extended work availability affects well-being: The mediating roles of psychological detachment and work-family-conflict. *Work & Stress, 31*, 24–41.

Dettmers, J., Bamberg, E., & Seffzek, K. (2016). Characteristics of extended availability for work: The role of demands and resources. *International Journal of Stress Management, 23*, 276–297.

Dettmers, J., Vahle-Hinz, T., Bamberg, E., Friedrich, N., & Keller, M. (2016). Extended work availability and its relation with start-of-day mood and cortisol. *Journal of Occupational Health Psychology, 21*, 105–118.

Ferguson, M., Carlson, D., Boswell, W., Whitten, D., Butts, M. M., & Kacmar, K. M. (2016). Tethered to work: A family systems approach to linking mobile device use to turnover intentions. *Journal of Applied Psychology, 101*, 520–534.

Gruman, J. (2017, Spring). Put away your devices and chill. *Your Workplace, 19*, 14–15.

Henry, A. (2013, February 13). How to work an on call job and keep your sanity. *Life Hacker*. Retrieved from http://lifehacker.com/5983847/how-to-work-an-on-call-job-and-keep-your-sanity

Kirillova, K., & Wang, D. (2016). Smartphone (dis)connectedness and vacation recovery. *Annals of Tourism Research, 61*, 157–169.

Kossek, E., E. (2016). Managing work-life boundaries in the digital age. *Organizational Dynamics, 45*, 258–270.

Kossek, E. E., Lautsch, B. A., & Eaton, S. C. (2006). Telecommuting, control, and boundary management: Correlates of policy use and practice, job control, and work-family effectiveness. *Journal of Vocational Behavior, 68*, 347–367.

Kreiner, G. E., Hollensbe, E. C., & Sheep, M. L. (2009). Balancing borders and bridges: Negotiating the work-home interface via boundary work tactics. *Academy of Management Journal, 52*, 704–730.

McDaniel, B. T., & Coyne, S. (2016). "Technoference": The interference of technology in couple relationships and implications for women's personal and relational well-being. *Psychology of Popular Media Culture, 5*, 85–98

Middleton, C. A., & Cukier, W. (2006). Is mobile email functional or dysfunctional? Two perspective on mobile email usage. *European Journal of Information Systems, 15*, 252–260.

Nippert-Eng, C. E. (1996). *Home and work: Negotiating boundaries through everyday life*. Chicago, IL: University of Chicago Press.

Norton, M., & Gino, F. (2014). Rituals alleviate grieving for loved ones, lovers, and lotteries. *Journal of Experimental Psychology: General, 143*, 266–272.

Nylén, L., Melin, B., & Laflamme, L. (2007). Interference between work and outside-work demands relative to health: Unwinding possibilities among full-time and part-time employees. *International Journal of Behavioral Medicine, 14*, 229–236.

Ohly, S., & Latour, A. (2014). Work-related smartphone use and well-being in the evening: The role of autonomous and controlled motivation. *Journal of Personnel Psychology, 13*, 174–183.

Park, Y., Fritz, C., & Jex, S. M. (2011). Relationships between work-home segmentation and psychological detachment from work: The role of communication use at home. *Journal of Occupational Health Psychology, 16*, 457–467.

Pew Research Center. (2017, January 12). *Mobile fact sheet*. Retrieved from http://www.pewinternet.org/fact-sheet/mobile/

Przybylski, A. K., & Weinstein, N. (2013). Can you connect with me now? How the presence of a mobile communication technology influences face-to-face conversation quality. *Journal of Social and Personal Relationships, 30*, 237–246.

Rosen, L. D. (2015, January 18). Iphone separation anxiety: It's real and it's not good for you. *Psychology Today*. Retrieved from https://www.psychologytoday.com/blog/rewired-the-psychology-technology/201501/iphone-separation-anxiety

Schieman, S., & Young, M. C. (2013). Are communications about work outside of regular working hours associated with work-to-family conflict, psychological distress and sleep problems? *Work & Stress, 27*, 244–261.

Schwind Wilson, K., & Baumann, H. (2015). Capturing a more complete view of employees' lives outside of work: The introduction and development of new interrole conflict constructs. *Personnel Psychology, 68*, 235–282.

Syrek, C. J., Weigelt, O., Peifer, C., & Antoni, C. H. (2017). Zeigarnik's sleepless nights: How unfinished tasks at the end of the week impair employee sleep on the weekend through rumination. *Journal of Occupational Health Psychology, 22*, 225–238.

Thompson, C. (2014, August 28). End the tyranny of 24/7 email. *The New York Times*. Retrieved from https://www.nytimes.com/2014/08/29/opinion/end-the-tyranny-of-24-7-email.html?_r=0

Van Hooff, M. L. M., Geurts, S. A. E., Kompier, M. A. J., & Taris, T. W. (2006). Work-home interference: How does it manifest itself from day to day? *Work & Stress, 20*, 145–162.

Van Steenbergen, E. F., Ybema, J. F., & Lapierre, L. M. (2017). Boundary management in action: A diary study of students' school-home conflict. *International Journal of Stress Management*. Advance online publication. http://dx.doi.org/10.1037/str0000064

Vohs, K. D., Wang, Y., Gino, F., & Norton, M. I. (2013). Rituals enhance consumption. *Psychological Science, 24*, 1714–1721.

Voydanoff, P. (2005). Consequences of boundary-spanning demands and resources for work-to-family conflict and perceived stress. *Journal of Occupational Health Psychology, 10*, 491–503.

Wood Brooks, A., Schroeder, J., Risen, J. L., Gino, F., Galinsky, A. D., Norton, M. I., & Schweitzer, M. E. (2016). Don't stop believing: Rituals improve performance by decreasing anxiety. *Organizational Behavior and Human Decision processes, 137*, 71–85.

Zeigarnik, B. (1938). On finished and unfinished tasks. In W. D. Ellis (Ed.), *A source book of Gestalt psychology* (pp. 300–314). London, England: Kegan Paul, Trench & Company.

CHAPTER 4

QUALITY TIME WITH
THE SANDMAN

Boost With Smart Sleeping Practices

After more than a decade of sacrificing sleep for her career, Laurel finally hit a wall. At the time she was working 70 hours a week as the director of sales for a professional sports league and spending another 35 hours a week studying for her masters of business.

"I was chronically sleep-deprived," says the 39-year-old. "I felt like I could cry at the drop of a dime because I was so exhausted. I couldn't go to the gym. Some mornings I didn't even have the energy to lift my head off the pillow."

To fit everything in, Laurel allowed herself just four hours of sleep a night.

"I had so much on my plate that I would wake up in the middle of the night thinking about all the things I had to do."

She was trying to be as productive as possible, but in the end found the lack of shut-eye was only slowing her down.

"If you are not getting sleep, your mental agility is not the same. Your clarity and your ability to make decisions are impacted. It takes more effort to think about things."

On the advice of her doctor, Laurel decided to finally make sleep a priority. She began turning off her alarm in the morning and sleeping until 7 a.m. or climbing into bed at night before 10 P.M.—anything to ensure she was getting at least 7 or 8 hours of sleep a night. She arranged her travel schedule for work around her new healthy sleep habits, and even put sleep ahead of her once strict exercise regime. Instead of hitting the gym every day like she used to, Laurel would skip her workout to make room for a little bit of extra sleep on the days she felt she needed it.

"Within a week or two I was feeling unbelievable. My overall performance improved. I felt healthier, more energetic and my presence was warmer with people. I was more positive and happier."

Now a year later, Laurel continues to dedicate enough time to the sandman and even throws in regular 15-minute power naps on weekends for good measure.

DO YOU GET ENOUGH SLEEP?

Sleep is a fundamental human need. The benefits of sleep are so significant that almost all species on the planet sleep or demonstrate some state similar to sleep (Miyazaki, Liu, & Hayashi, 2017). Although scientists are still unsure about the ultimate function of sleep (Miyazaki et al., 2017), one thing we do know for sure is that sleep gives us a boost. In fact, some researchers have suggested that sleep is among the most important recovery mechanisms that exist (Cropley, Dijk, & Stanley, 2006). In a summary of the relationship between sleep and recovery, Swedish sleep researchers have noted that "[s]leep will not only reset alertness, mood, and performance capacity to normal levels after a night of sleep. It will also regenerate the CNS [central nervous system], the metabolic system, the endocrine system, and the immune system" (Åkerstedt, Nilsson, & Kecklund, 2009, p. 234). Laurel learned firsthand about the regenerative power of sleep. When she started exploiting sleep's recuperative value it gave her a big boost and improved several aspects of her life.

Given the importance of sleep for boosting, it is alarming that so many people report not sleeping enough. The American Academy of Sleep Medicine recommends that in order to avoid physical and psychological health consequences, healthy adults should get between seven and nine hours of sleep a night (Watson et al., 2015). However, a study by the U.S. Centers for Disease Control and Prevention (CDC) found that 35.3% of the population gets less than seven hours of nightly sleep (Centers for Disease Control and Prevention, 2015). Between 1985 and 2012 the average amount of time people sleep has declined, and the percentage of adults who sleep less than 6 hours a night has increased by 31% (Ford, 2015). Compared to 60 years ago, people today tend to get 1 to 2 hours less sleep every night (National Health Interview Survey, as cited in Van Cauter, Spiegel, Tasali, & Leproult, 2008). The ensuing fatigue causes almost 40% of these sleep-deprived people to fall asleep unintentionally during the day, and 5% do so while driving (Centers for Disease Control and Prevention, 2015).

Fatigue is a global problem affecting between 11% and 30% of employees in Europe and approximately 14% of men and 20% of women in the U.S. and Canada (Querstret & Cropley, 2012). And it's not restricted to the working population. For example, fatigue affects 17% of the general adult population of Japan (Aritake et al, 2015), and 22% in Norway (Loge, Ekeberg, & Kaasa, 1998). In a survey involving 10 countries around the globe, 24% of the population reported sleeping poorly, with the lowest rates in Austria at 10%, and the highest rates in Belgium with 32% (Soldatos, Allaert, Ohta, & Dikeos, 2005). Numbers like these have led the CDC to consider inadequate sleep a public health problem.

WHAT EXACTLY IS SLEEP?

There is no agreed upon definition of sleep among experts, but scientific definitions tend to be similar to our commonsense thoughts of sleep as a state of reduced responsiveness and immobility that is quickly reversible (Siegel, 2005). The reduced responsiveness part of the definition distinguishes sleep from calm wakefulness, and the reversibility part distinguishes it from states that are not quickly or easily changed, such as being in a coma (Cirelli & Tononi, 2008).

People cycle through five different stages of nightly sleep. Each cycle lasts between 90 and 110 minutes and most people will go through three to six cycles each night (Paterson, 2012).

The first stage, stage one sleep, is the lightest stage and is characterized by slow drifting eye movements. Stage one sleep represents a transition phase between being awake and being asleep and lasts only 3 to 5 minutes (Siegel, 2002). This stage of sleep doesn't really have any recuperative value (Åkerstedt et al., 2009).

Stage two sleep represents actual sleep (Paterson, 2012). In stage two sleep the slow drifting eye movements disappear (Siegel, 2002), our muscle tone is reduced, our heart rate and breathing slow down, and our brain wave pattern demonstrates reduced frequency and increased amplitude. This pattern reveals slower, more synchronized brain activity (Paterson, 2012). Stage two sleep, which typically lasts up to half an hour (Siegel, 2002), allows simple recovery to occur and represents 50% of a typical sleep episode (Åkerstedt et al., 2009).

The next stages of sleep, stages three and four, are often considered together and are referred to as slow wave sleep (SWS). During SWS muscle tone is reduced even more, and breathing and heart rate slow down even further (Åkerstedt et al., 2009; Paterson, 2012). Brain patterns in SWS demonstrate synchronous slow waves with very large amplitude (Paterson, 2012) which are thought to be a significant part of the brain mechanism that produces recovery (Vyazovskiy & Delogu, 2014). The deepest level of sleep, stage four, typically starts slightly less than an hour after falling asleep and lasts 20 to 30 minutes. People then rapidly cycle back into stage three and then stage two. After that, there is a quick shift into the final stage of sleep, REM (or rapid eye movement) sleep, which typically occurs 90 to 100 minutes after falling asleep (Siegel, 2002).

REM sleep is when we dream. During REM sleep our brain patterns demonstrate activity that resembles wakefulness but we experience a complete loss of muscle tone (Paterson, 2012). This paralysis likely evolved to prevent us from flailing about and hurting ourselves or others by acting out our dreams. After REM sleep, the first episode of which will last only 5 to 10 minutes, we cycle through stages two, three, and four again before returning to the REM stage, a process that takes roughly 90 minutes (Siegel, 2002). Over the course of the night, successive cycles display less SWS and longer periods of REM, with the final REM episode lasting up to 50 minutes (Siegel, 2002). This overall nightly pattern is typically understood to suggest that the most significant recovery occurs in the early part of sleep (Åkerstedt et al., 2009). However, that doesn't mean that REM sleep is not important for boosting. Although the ultimate function of REM sleep is even less well understood than that of SWS sleep, REM sleep seems to play a role in brain development, memory formation, and the processing of emotional information (Vyazovskiy & Delogu, 2014).

It is important to note that the brain is very active when we are not awake. While brain activity slows down when we are sleeping, blood flow to the brain drops by only 20%. Sleep is not merely a time for the brain and body to passively decompress from the stressors of the day. It is an active and regulated process that is vital for neural reorganization and effective functioning (Hobson, 2005)

SLEEP QUALITY

As we have seen, a lot of people don't sleep for long enough each night. However, getting a boost requires that we not only get a sufficient *quantity* of sleep but that we also achieve an adequate *quality* of sleep. For instance, if you are in bed for 8 hours each night but wake up every hour and a half, the quality of your sleep, and your ability to boost, is compromised. There are a number of different dimensions we can use to assess sleep quality (Krystal & Edinger, 2008). For example, sleep duration is the total amount of time you sleep, which is different from the total amount of time you are in bed each night. Sleep onset latency refers to how long it takes you to fall asleep after going to bed. Sleep efficiency is the percentage of time you spend asleep between sleep onset and final awakening in the morning. Sleep fragmentation is the number of times you wake up at night. Subjective sleep quality is your own personal assessment of how well you sleep. All or a subset of these measures can be used to calculate an overall sleep quality score.

Research has investigated all of these forms of sleep disruption and the results of the studies are consistent. Regardless of whether researchers measure the quantity of sleep or the quality of sleep, any form of sleep disruption has negative neurophysiological consequences and prevents boosting (Krizan & Hisler, 2016). Any kind of sleep disruption acts as a stressor representing a form of allostatic load that inhibits the body from recovering (McEwen, 2006). With these sleep details in mind, let's take a brief look at how sleep fits within the ReNU model and its relationship with boosting.

SLEEP AND THE ReNU MODEL

Sleep is essential for us to function effectively (Cirelli & Tononi, 2008). In terms of the ReNU model, sleep is a physical need that must be satisfied in order to get a boost. Sleep therefore helps to fill the nourish bucket. But remember, the ReNU buckets are connected. Filling up the nourish bucket by getting enough sleep of sufficient quality will also help to fill other buckets too, notably the rebuild bucket.

Recall that the rebuild bucket involves replenishing resources. Sleep is essential for topping up resources, particularly the resource of self-regulation. Have you ever seen what toddlers act like when they miss their naps? They are like tiny psychopaths. They completely lose the ability to regulate themselves. Adults are not much different. Without adequate sleep adults can start acting like tired 2-year-old children unable to control their behavior (Krizan & Hisler, 2016). Research in numerous areas has shown that disturbed sleep compromises self-regulation. Compromised sleep impairs our capacity to pay attention to things, modulate our behavior, and control our emotions (Krizan & Hisler, 2016). When we don't sleep well we lose the ability to invest effort and persist on tasks, set goals and monitor how well we are achieving them, and restrain ourselves when needed (Krizan & Hisler, 2016). Sleep restores our self-regulation resources and puts us back in control of ourselves.

Adequate sleep can also reinforce filling the nourish bucket because sleep affects other aspects of that bucket. For example, when we don't sleep well we are less effective at recognizing the emotions of our romantic partners and are more prone to experience conflict in our relationships

(Gordon & Chen, 2014). This undermines our ability to satisfy our need for relatedness. Also, when we have trouble regulating our behavior our performance on various tasks is compromised which will hinder our ability to satisfy our need for competence. So, sleeping well not only directly satisfies our physical needs, it also indirectly helps to satisfy our psychological needs.

Finally, sleep can help fill the unhook bucket. In order to cut the virtual cord and achieve psychological detachment we must have a certain amount of self-control. Sleep helps us unhook by rebuilding the resources we need to restrain the inclination to stay connected, monitor the relaxation and detachment goals we set for ourselves, and persist in our efforts to achieve them. Sleep helps us put our rudder in the water and sail in the direction we desire.

SLEEP GIVES US A BOOST

As you might expect, sleep gives us a huge boost. And compromised sleep produces a plethora of nasty anti-boosting consequences we want to avoid. There is a lot of research on the outcomes associated with sleep. Let's consider a sampling of this research as it relates specifically to the three aspects of boosting.

Psychological Well-Being

In general, there is a consistent and strong relationship between sleep and various aspects of well-being (Barber, Rupprecht, & Munz, 2014). Just take Laurel's experience as a perfect example. Once she began to get enough sleep, she felt happier, more energetic and was a nicer person to be around. Research has shown that sleep quality is associated with subjective well-being and leads us to be satisfied with various domains of our lives such as in our relationships and our connection to the community (Weinberg, Noble, & Hammond, 2016). Also, people who get an optimal number of hours of sleep each night report less anxiety and depression, and higher levels of well-being that includes a sense of personal growth, purpose in life, and self-acceptance (Hamilton, Nelson, Stevens, & Kitzman, 2007).

In addition to experiencing less anxiety, adequate sleep leads people to feel less stress and anger when exposed to mild stress (Minkel et al., 2012). Getting more sleep is also associated with lower levels of general mental distress (Strine & Chapman, 2005). A number of studies have shown that good sleep results in a better mood and poor sleep leads to a worse mood. For example, in a study that followed employees at a large insurance company, the researchers found that on days employees slept poorly they reported feeling more hostile and less jovial (Scott & Judge, 2006). Researchers in Australia recently reviewed studies that have been done on the relationship between sleep and emotions and noted that "sleep deprivation decreas[es] vigor, happiness, cheerfulness, activation, pride, and delight, and increase[es] fatigue, confusion, depression, anxiety, and dissociation" (Watling, Pawlik, Scott, Booth, & Short, 2017, p. 398). Even a modest amount of sleep deprivation negatively and substantially affects our moods (Pilcher & Huffcutt, 1996). The overall picture is pretty clear. Sleep promotes psychological well-being.

Physical Health

The picture is even clearer when it comes to physical health. If you want to be physically healthy, you need adequate sleep. And if your sleep is compromised your health will be too. Sleep, particularly SWS, plays a vital role in allowing the body to modulate hormones, including inhibiting the release of stress hormones that contribute to allostatic load (Van Cauter et al., 2008). One of the hormones we release when sleeping is growth hormone, which is required for mending tissue and needed to promote physical health (Åkerstedt et al., 2009). Sleep is also involved in controlling blood glucose levels and appetite regulation, which sheds light on why sleep problems are associated with obesity and diabetes (Van Cauter et al., 2008) Compared to people who sleep poorly, those who sleep well have fewer gastrointenstinal problems (33% vs 9%), breathing problems (25% vs 6%), urinary problems (20% vs 10%), neurologic disease (7% vs 1%), and have lower incidence of high blood pressure (43% vs 19%) (Taylor et al., 2007). They also have stronger immune systems (Irwin, 2015). If that's not enough, the restorative value of sleep has been found to reduce the experience of pain (Davies et al., 2008). On the flip side, people who sleep poorly have a 45% greater likelihood of cardiovascular disease (Sofi et al., 2014). Perhaps the most serious health outcome of inadequate sleep is a shortened lifespan (Grandner, Hale, Moore, & Patel, 2010). It's safe to say that quality sleep is a key component of good health.

Enhancement

The harmful cocktail of fatigue and compromised self-regulation caused by poor sleep affects how well we execute our obligations and can lead to lots of undesirable outcomes (Barnes, 2012). For Laurel, sleep deprivation made her less productive at work. Concentrating on tasks and making decisions took more effort. One reason unfavorable consequences can occur is that our judgment and decision making is hampered when we don't sleep well. When we are sleep deprived we are more easily distracted, inflexible and less likely to adjust or re-think tactics when needed. We are also less creative and innovative, give up more easily on tasks, have trouble receiving and sending messages, and are less able to handle unexpected events (Harrison & Horne, 2000). Sleep deprivation degrades our most basic cognitive skills. It negatively impacts how well our memory systems work, how quickly we can process information, and our ability to pay attention (Lim & Dinges, 2010). As you might expect, these deficits severely impact how effective we are at our obligations. When we don't get enough quality sleep our performance suffers on both cognitive tasks, such as those involving logical reasoning, and motor tasks, such as those involving manual dexterity (Pilcher & Huffcutt, 1996). Even a small amount of sleep deprivation compromises our performance (Pilcher & Huffcutt, 1996), and our performance gets worse over time as the number of days of sleep deprivation continues (Barnes, 2012). Not only that, but after multiple days of poor sleep our inferior performance stabilizes at a lower level resulting in consistently degraded output (Belenky et al., 2003). To perform at our best, we need proper sleep.

HOW OBLIGATIONS AFFECT SLEEP

The stress of our obligations can have a detrimental effect on the quantity and quality of our sleep. People who find their obligations hectic and strenuous tend not to sleep as well as those whose obligations are less taxing (Åkerstedt, Fredlund, Gillberg, & Jansson, 2002). For example, stress has been shown to compromise the sleep quality of college students dealing with school obligations (Lund, Reider, Whiting, & Prichard, 2010), and mothers dealing with the obligations of caring for children with developmental disabilities (Lee, 2013). And the sleep-restricting effect of stress is not limited to the day the stress occurs. For instance, when people experience stress at work during the week it affects their sleep on the weekend. Research shows that when employees experience stress between Monday and Friday, on Sunday they have longer sleep onset latency (they take longer to fall asleep), show more sleep fragmentation (they wake up more times during the night), have lower sleep efficiency (they have a lower percentage of time spent asleep), and have lower sleep duration (they sleep for less time) (Pereira & Elfering, 2014). This poor quality sleep prevents boosting.

The primary reason our obligations compromise our sleep is that during our leisure time we ruminate about the hassles, demands, and tensions produced by those obligations. This rumination and associated stress and worry interferes with sleep (Åkerstedt et al., 2012). The stress associated with rumination causes psychological and physiological activation which is incompatible with the deactivation required for a good night's rest (Åkerstedt, 2006). The activation can arise from continuing to think about obligation-related matters once they have ended, or from anticipating stressful obligation-related issues before they begin (Åkerstedt, 2006). The latter is probably what accounts for the results noted above in which stressed employees slept poorly on Sunday but not Saturday.

In terms of the ReNU model, obligation-related stress hinders psychological detachment, which then compromises sleep. Studies have shown that rumination and a lack of psychological detachment is the causal mechanism linking obligation-related stress and sleep impairment (Berset, Elfering, Lüthy, Lüthi, & Semmer, 2011). This is another example of how the ReNU buckets are connected. If you can psychologically detach and fill the unhook bucket in your uptime you will sleep better and fill the nourish bucket, which together will give you a bigger boost.

THE BOOSTING POWER OF NAPS

Because sleep is so important for recovery, and because so many people don't get adequate sleep, one highly effective boosting strategy is to take naps during the day. A lot of prominent historical figures, such as Albert Einstein, Salvador Dali, and Napoleon Bonaparte were proponents of naps. Another avid napper, Winston Churchill, said that "You must sleep sometime between lunch and dinner…. That's what I always do. Don't think that you will be doing less work because you sleep during the day. That's a foolish notion held by people who have no imaginations. You will be able to accomplish more. You get two days in one—well at least one and a half" (Dhand & Sohal, 2006, p. 380).

Numerous studies have demonstrated the boosting power of naps. For example, one study found that people who took a short nap after lunch were more alert and performed better on a transcription task than those who didn't nap (Takahashi, Fukuda, & Arito, 1998). Among its benefits, napping restores our vigilance, logical reasoning, reaction time, and accuracy, and, of course, reduces how sleepy we feel (Milner & Cote, 2009). Naps reinstate our alertness and bring our slumping performance levels back up to baseline after fatigue has kicked in (Gillberg, Kecklund, Axelsson, & Åkerstedt, 1996). Naps also positively affect our moods by, for example, making us feel more joyful and relaxed (Luo & Inoué, 2000). They also have beneficial physiological effects. For instance, compared to people who haven't had a daytime nap, the cardiovascular systems of people who have had a nap recover faster after exposure to a stressor (Brindle & Conklin, 2012). For people who haven't slept well at night, naps can be particularly valuable. Research has shown that if a nap allows us to make up the sleep we fail to get at nighttime, we fully recover and maintain our performance at normal levels (Mollicone, Van Dongen, Rogers, & Dinges, 2008). Overall, the evidence is overwhelming that napping gives us a boost.

How long a nap do we need to get a boost? The answer to that question depends partly on how poorly we sleep at night and how tired we are during the day. However, research has consistently shown that naps as short as 10 minutes can restore alertness and improve performance. In fact, short naps can be more effective than long naps because shorter naps help us avoid sleep inertia (Brooks & Lack, 2006). Sleep inertia is the grogginess we sometimes feel after waking up (Tassi & Muzet, 2000). It is caused by SWS and results in a decline in performance, which we generally want to avoid. Shorter naps (i.e., 10 to 30 minutes) are long enough to allow us to reach the restorative stage two sleep stage and short enough that we don't enter the deeper sleep stages that produce sleep inertia. And we don't need much stage two sleep to get a boost. Research has shown naps that allow us to get a mere three minutes of stage two sleep restore alertness and performance (Hayashi, Motoyoshi, & Hori, 2005). Shorter naps are also ideal because longer naps can interfere with our ability to sleep at night (Mastin, Bryson, & Corwyn, 2006). In a journal article that reviewed the benefits of napping, researchers at the Sleep Research Laboratory at Brock University in Canada, recommend that healthy adults should ideally nap for about 10 to 20 minutes (Milner & Cote, 2009). In short, we don't need to nap for very long to derive benefits that can last all day.

In addition to length, the timing of your nap matters too. The body goes through daily cycles during which it is more or less alert. As you are likely aware, we tend to get sleepy in the mid-to-late afternoon. Some researchers have suggested that the ideal time to nap is therefore around 3 p.m., which coincides with the typical afternoon dip in alertness (Dhand & Sohal, 2006). However, the best time to nap depends on your individual needs. If you had sufficient sleep last night and are just feeling tired from the day's activities, a mid-to-late afternoon nap is likely best. If, however, you slept poorly and are exhausted, an earlier afternoon nap is advisable (Milner & Cote, 2009). Listen to your body.

Progressive organizations allow their employees to nap on the job. Uber has nap rooms. Google provides nap pods for employees. Zappos, Capital One Labs, Ben & Jerry's, and PricewaterhouseCoopers all allow their employees to nap at work (Henry, 2015). But these companies are still in the minority. There remains a pervasive taboo against workplace napping. However, the taboo is outdated. It doesn't acknowledge the existing scientific evidence demonstrating the boosting benefits of naps and therefore prevents us from exploiting naps' positive effects on performance. If you work or handle other obligations at home, feel free to enjoy short, guilt-free naps. They make you better at what you do.

HOW TO SLEEP WELL AT NIGHT

Now that we're clear about the boosting benefits of sleep, let's consider how to get a good night's rest. The recommendations below are based on empirical research related to sleep hygiene (Irish, Kline, Gunn, Buysse, & Hall, 2015), which refers to the practices associated with high quality sleep, the literature on treating insomnia (Morin, 2004), and the advice offered by professional associations, such as the National Sleep Foundation (2017a, 2017b) and the American Academy of Sleep Medicine (2017). You can feel confident that applying these recommendations will improve the quality and quantity of your sleep. Research shows that effective sleep hygiene differentiates good sleepers from poor sleepers (Gellis & Lichstein, 2009). Also, when people start implementing better sleep practices their sleep improves. For example, they fall asleep almost 20 minutes faster (Trauer, Qian, Doyle, Rajaratnam, & Cunnington, 2015). However, don't feel obliged to implement all of these recommendations. Select the ones you believe are most relevant to you, and will best help you get a good night's sleep.

1. ***Do a bedroom audit.*** Ensure the room you sleep in is conducive to getting high quality sleep. Research shows that nighttime tempera-ture and environmental noise distinguish good and bad sleepers (Gellis & Lichstein, 2009). Your room should be cool with the tem-perature about 65 F, or 18.5 C (National Sleep Foundation, 2017b) and it should be quiet because noise at night results in lighter sleep (Irish et al., 2015). There should also be no light. Use whatever is required to control light and sound such as eye shades, ear plugs or fans that can produce white noise. If your partner snores and it dis-turbs you, sleep in another room. Your pillow and mattress should also be comfortable.
2. ***Psychologically detach.*** Get obligation-related thoughts out of your head. Schedule a small amount of "worry time" in the late after-noon or early evening so you can document your thoughts and then put them out of your mind (Hauri, 1993). Take a few minutes to write down your worries and the things that are causing you stress and indicate one action you will take tomorrow to address each con-cern. Then forget about them. Research shows that creating plans that address where, when, and how we can tackle obligation-related

goals helps people who are heavily invested in their roles to psychologically detach (Smit, 2016). In the same document, write down any important thoughts, creative ideas, or other tidbits that you want to remember the next day. Again, the purpose is to note them so you can forget about them. Keep a pad of paper beside your bed so you can record and then ignore any important thoughts that spontaneously come to mind when you are trying to sleep. Laurel, the NHL director who opened this chapter, complained that she tended to wake up in the middle of the night thinking about all the things she had to do at work. Don't let this happen to you. Writing things down and making brief notes on how to address them the following day will clear your head and help you sleep through the night.

3. ***Don't push.*** If you have trouble getting thoughts about your obligations out of your mind while you are trying to fall asleep, it is not helpful to try to suppress them. Research shows that active attempts to push thoughts out of your head backfire and are related to lower quality sleep. It is better to write them down, or distract yourself with different, non-stressful thoughts (Ree, Harvey, Blake, Tang, & Shawe-Taylor, 2005). Think about other, happy things. Recall enjoyable experiences, or try to just let negative thoughts dissolve away. The chapter on meditation and mindfulness presents more detail on how to calm your mind.

4. ***Maintain a regular sleep schedule***. Go to bed and wake up at roughly the same time every day, including on your days off. You know how traveling to another time zone produces jetlag? Well, when we vary the time of day we go to sleep and wake up it creates what is called social jetlag, which produces comparable effects (Wittmann, Dinich, Merrow, & Roenneberg, 2006). We tend to think that sleeping in on our days off will refresh us and make us feel great, and a slight amount of extra time in bed may do so. However, research shows that when adults sleep for much longer than usual—roughly an hour more—it actually puts them in a *worse* mood. And this effect grows stronger as we get older (Wrzus, Wagner, & Riediger, 2014). So, go to bed and get out of bed at the same time each day. If you find that you are not sleepy at your normal bedtime, stay up just a bit longer but then always wake up at the same time. Wake-time seems to be a more important factor in producing high quality sleep than bedtime (Irish et al., 2015). When establishing your schedule, make sure you set a bedtime that is early enough to give you at least 7 hours of sleep. Also try to time your sleep so you wake up at the end of a sleep cycle, not in the

middle of it when you are in SWS. The online sleep calculator at sleepyti.me can help with this.

5. ***Don't get excited.*** With the exception of having sex, don't do anything arousing before bedtime. Research shows that poor sleepers are more likely to do things that excite or upset them close to bedtime, such as engage in a difficult phone conversation; or do things that demand a lot of concentration, like finishing up obligation-related tasks; or worry, plan and ponder important matters, such as whether or not to move into a new apartment (Gellis & Lichstein, 2009). Don't do that. Engage in arousing and cognitively demanding activities earlier in the evening so they do not stimulate you when you are trying to wind down.

6. ***Develop a relaxing routine.*** Implement a bedtime ritual that relaxes you. Read, meditate, engage in progressive muscle relaxation, or practice deep breathing techniques. Intentionally relaxing before bedtime helps us sleep better. For example, research has shown that when people who have sleep complaints start listening to music in order to help them relax before bedtime, the quality of their sleep improves (de Niet, Lendemeijer, & Hutschemaekers, 2009). Ideally, you want to focus on relaxing both your body and your mind (Morin, 2004).

7. ***Restrict your sleep.*** You may have trouble sleeping at night because you stay in bed for too long. In the same way that long naps can interfere with nighttime sleep because they provide you with too much rest in a 24-hour period, an excessive amount of time in bed one night can interfere with sleep the next night (Morin, 2004). If you think this affects you, try cutting back on the number of hours you are in bed each night by going to bed later, but don't drop below the 7-hour minimum without consulting a healthcare professional.

8. ***Exercise regularly.*** Research has shown that exercise helps people sleep well, although the effects are not particularly strong (Young-stedt, 2005). Some sleep hygiene guidelines suggest that exercising close to bedtime will compromise sleep quality, and indeed, people who exercise in the morning report better sleep quality than those who exercise later in the day (Buman, Phillips, Youngstedt, & Kline, 2014). However, research has demonstrated that exercise done in the evening doesn't diminish the quality of our sleep (Buman et al., 2014). You might want to avoid very strenuous exercise within an hour of bedtime in order to avoid the sleep disturbing effects of having a raised heart rate and body temperature, but generally exercise will help you sleep well. Go ahead. Break a sweat.

9. ***Keep electronic devices at bay.*** Our daily biological rhythm is heavily influenced by light. Light in the morning tells our bodies that it is time to wake up, and diminished light in the evening signals that it is time to sleep. The light emitted from electronic devices can wreak havoc with our natural daily rhythms when they are used close to bedtime. For example, researchers have found that people who use e-readers before going to sleep stay more alert at bedtime, take longer to fall asleep, have less REM sleep, and are less alert the next morning (Chang, Aeschbach, Duffy, & Czeisler, 2015). Stay away from light-emitting electronic devices close to bedtime, and expose yourself to bright light in the morning to help set your daily biological clock.

10. ***Avoid stimulants.*** In general, it is a good idea to not drink caffeinated drinks or smoke close to bedtime. Research shows that high doses of caffeine close to bedtime severely disrupt sleep in many ways. However, people differ in how sensitive they are and how much tolerance they have developed to caffeine, so its effects on sleep vary (Irish et al., 2015). The same isn't true of nicotine. Even after years of smoking, smokers display worse sleep than non-smokers (Irish et al., 2015). At high levels in particular, caffeine and nicotine compromise sleep. It's best to reduce your consumption in the evening in order to promote high quality sleep.

11. ***Control your alcohol intake.*** Consuming alcohol near bedtime can make you fall asleep faster and put you into a deep sleep in the first part of the night, but after that, light, non-restorative stage one and REM sleep increase and you wake up more often (Irish et al., 2015). This prevents boosting. The disruptive effect of alcohol is related to the amount consumed; Light doses aren't as disruptive as high doses. However, even the occasional drink shortly before bedtime can negatively affect sleep (Irish et al., 2015). If you want to sleep well, limit how much booze you drink.

12. ***Don't drink anything close to bedtime.*** Jamie's grandmother tells him that she doesn't drink anything in the late evening so that she doesn't have to get up in the middle of the night. This piece of advice doesn't often appear on sleep hygiene lists, but grandma is a smart lady. We recommend that you heed her counsel.

13. ***Restrict use of the bedroom.*** Use your bedroom only for sleep and sex. Do not watch TV, read, exercise, study, eat, play games, do puzzles, or any other activity in your bedroom. Train yourself to associate your bedroom with falling asleep.

14. ***Take naps with caution.*** Although naps are great for recharging our batteries during the day, it is possible for them to interfere with nighttime sleep. Naps are great for producing boosting effects in

people suffering from sleep deprivation or those who are sleepy, but can exacerbate sleep problems in people who suffer from insomnia. If you have trouble with nighttime sleep, it may be best to avoid napping (Morin, 2004).

15. ***Get up.*** If after 20 minutes of lying in bed you are still not asleep, get up. Do something relaxing under dim light for a short while and return to bed when you feel sleepy. Do the same thing if you wake up during the night and cannot get back to sleep (Morin, 2004). Your bed is a place to sleep, not a place to feel anxious about not sleeping.

SUMMARY

Sleep is a vital ingredient in transforming downtime into uptime. It is a basic human need and is among the most important factors in giving us a boost. When we sleep well, we feel good, are healthier, and perform well. And without high quality sleep virtually every aspect of our functioning is compromised. In this harried world where there always seems like there is so much to do and so little time to do it, it is easy to cut into sleep time in order to get more done. But that is a mistake. As Laurel learned, sleep refreshes us, recharges us, and improves virtually all aspects of our lives. The better we sleep, the better we live. Happy slumber.

Boosting Bites

Sleep between 7 and 9 hours a night.

Ensure that you get not only enough quantity, but also quality, of sleep.

Nap during the day to get a boost, but only if it doesn't interfere with your nighttime sleep.

Take extra steps to ensure adequate sleep if, and when, you find your obligations stressful.

Implement effective sleep hygiene practices.

UPTIME ACTION PLAN

Step 1. Using the scale below, indicate the quality of your sleep in a typical week.

1	2	3	4	5	6	7
very poor	poor	somewhat poor	average	fairly good	good	excellent

Step 2. Do a sleep practices audit. If you think your sleep could stand some improvement, assess the extent to which you implement the 15 sleep practices presented at the end of this chapter. In the space below, indicate which of your typical sleep practices might require some attention in order to help you sleep better.

_____

_____

_____

_____

_____

Step 3. For each of the practices you listed above, develop a plan to improve it. The plans should be specific enough so that you know whether or not you are being successful in implementing them. For example, noting that you won't drink coffee *within 4 hours* of bedtime is better than noting that you simply won't drink coffee *before* bedtime.

_____

_____

_____

_____

_____

Step 4. Implement the new and improved sleep practices for 2 weeks.

Step 5. After 2 weeks of implementing the new and improved sleep practices, reassess how well you are sleeping by responding to this item: Indicate the quality of your sleep in the last 3 days.

1	2	3	4	5	6	7
very poor	poor	somewhat poor	average	fairly good	good	excellent

REFERENCES

Åkerstedt, T. (2006). Psychosocial stress and impaired sleep. *Scandinavian Journal of Work, Environment & Health, 32*, 493–501.

Åkerstedt, T., Fredlund, P., Gillberg, M., & Jansson, B. (2002). Work load and work hours in relation to disturbed sleep and fatigue in a large representative sample. *Journal of Psychosomatic Research, 53*, 585–588.

Åkerstedt, T., Nilsson, P. M., & Kecklund, G. (2009). Sleep and recovery. In S. Sonnentag, P. L. Perrewé, & D. C. Ganster (Eds.), *Current perspectives on job-stress recovery* (pp. 205–247). Bingley, United Kingdom: Emerald.

Åkerstedt, T., Orsini, N., Petersen, H., Axelsson, J., Lekander, M., & Kecklund, G. (2012). Predicting sleep quality from stress and prior sleep – A study of day-to-day covariation across six weeks. *Sleep Medicine, 13*, 674–679.

American Academy of Sleep Medicine. (2017). *Healthy sleep habits*. Retrieved from http://www.sleepeducation.org/essentials-in-sleep/healthy-sleep-habits

Aritake, S., Kaneita, Y., Ohtsu, T., Uchiyama, M., Mishima, K., Akashiba, T., ... Ohida, T. (2015). Prevalance of fatigue symptons and correlations in the general adult population. *Sleep and Biological Rhythms, 13*, 146–154.

Barber, L. K., Rupprecht, E. A., & Munz, D. C. (2014). Sleep habits may undermine well-being through the stressor appraisal process. *Journal of Happiness Studies, 15*, 285–299.

Barnes, C. M. (2012). Working in our sleep: Sleep and self-regulation in organizations. *Organizational Psychology Review, 2*, 234–257.

Belenky, G., Wesensten, N. J., Thorne, D. R., Thomas, M. L., Sing, H. C., Redmond, D. P., ... Balkin, T. J. (2003). Patterns of performance degradation and restoration during sleep restriction and subsequent recovery: A sleep dose-response study. *Journal of Sleep Research, 12*, 1–12.

Berset, M., Elfering, A., Lüthy, S., Lüthi, S., & Semmer, N. K. (2011). Work stressors and impaired sleep: Rumination as a mediator. *Stress & Health, 27*, e71–e82.

Brindle, R. C., & Conklin, S. M. (2012). Daytime sleep accelerates cardiovascular recovery after psychological stress. *International Journal of Behavioral Medicine, 19*, 111–114.

Brooks, A., & Lack, L. (2006). A brief afternoon nap following nocturnal sleep restriction: Which nap duration is most recuperative? *Sleep, 29*, 831–840.

Buman, M. P., Phillips, B. A., Youngstedt, S. D., & Kline, C. E. (2014). Does night-time exercise really disturb sleep? Results from the 2013 National Sleep Foundation Sleep in America Poll. *Sleep Medicine, 15*, 755–761.

Centers for Disease Control and Prevention, CDC Features, Data & Statistics. (2015, September 3). *Insufficient sleep is a public health concern*. Retrieved from https://www.cdc.gov/features/dssleep/

Chang, A.-M., Aeschbach, D., Duffy, J. F., & Czeisler, C. A. (2015). Evening use of light-emitting eReaders negatively affects sleep, circadian timing, and next-morning alertness. *Proceedings of the National Academy of Sciences, 112*, 1232–1237

Cirelli, C., & Tononi, G. (2008). Is sleep essential? *PLOS Biology, 6*, e216. doi:10.1371/journal.pbio.0060216

Cropley, M., Dijk, D.-J., & Stanley, N. (2006). Job strain, work rumination, and sleep in school teachers. *European Journal of Work and Organizational Psychology, 15*, 181–196.

Davies, K. A., Macfarlane, G. J., Nicholl, B. I., Dickens, C., Moriss, R., Ray, D., & McBeth, J. (2008). Restorative sleep predicts the resolution of chronic widespread pain: Results from the EPIFUND study. *Rheumatology, 47*, 1809–1813.

de Niet, G., Lendemeijer, T. B., & Hutschemaekers, G. (2009). Music-assisted relaxation to improve sleep quality: Meta-analysis. *Journal of Advanced Nursing, 65*, 1356–1364.

Dhand, R., & Sohal, H. (2006). Good sleep, bad sleep! The role of daytime naps in healthy adults. *Current Opinion in Pulmonary Medicine, 12*, 379–382.

Ford, E. S. (2015). Trends in self-reported sleep duration among US adults from 1985 to 2012. *Sleep, 38*, 829–833.

Gellis, L. A., & Lichstein, K. L. (2009). Sleep hygiene practices of good and poor sleepers in the United States: An internet-based study. *Behavior Therapy, 40*, 1–9.

Gillberg, M., Kecklund, G., Axelsson, J., & Åkerstedt, T. (1996). The effects of a short daytime nap after restricted night sleep. *Sleep, 19*, 570–575.

Gordon, A. M., & Chen, S. (2014). The role of sleep in interpersonal conflict: Do sleepless nights mean worse fights? *Social Psychological and Personality Science, 4*, 168–175.

Grandner, M. A., Hale, L., Moore, M., & Patel, N. P. (2010). Mortality associated with short sleep duration: The evidence, the possible mechanisms, and the future. *Sleep Medicine Reviews, 14*, 191–203.

Hamilton, N. A., Nelson, C. A., Stevens, N., & Kitzman, H. (2007). Sleep and psychological well-being. *Social Indicators Research, 82*, 147–163.

Harrison, Y., & Horne, J. A. (2000). The impact of sleep deprivation on decision making: A review. *Journal of Experimental Psychology: Applied, 6*, 236–249.

Hayashi, M., Motoyoshi, N., & Hori, T. (2005). Recuperative power of a short daytime nap with or without stage 2 sleep. *Sleep, 28*, 829–836.

Hauri, P. J. (1993). Consulting about insomnia: A method and some preliminary data. *Sleep, 16*, 344–350.

Henry, Z. (2015, September 4). 6 companies (including Uber) where it's ok to nap. Retrieved from https://www.inc.com/zoe-henry/google-uber-and-other-companies-where-you-can-nap-at-the-office.html

Hobson, J. A. (2005). Sleep is of the brain, by the brain, and for the brain. *Nature, 437*, 1254–1256.

Irish, L. A., Kline, C. E., Gunn, H. E., Buysse, D. J., & Hall, M. H. (2015). The role of sleep hygiene in promoting public health: A review of empirical evidence. *Sleep Medicine Reviews, 22*, 23–36.

Irwin, M. R. (2015). Why sleep is important for health: A psychoneuroimmunology perspective. *Annual Review of Psychology, 66*, 143–172

Krizan, Z., & Hisler, G. (2016). The essential role of sleep in self-regulation. In K. D. Vohs & R. F. Baumeister (Eds.), *Handbook of self-regulation: Research, theory, and applications* (3rd ed., pp. 182–202). New York, NY: The Guilford Press.

Krystal, A. D., & Edinger, J. D. (2008). Measuring sleep quality. *Sleep Medicine, 9*, S10–S17.

Lee, J. (2013). Maternal stress, well-being, and impaired sleep in mothers of children with developmental disabilities: A literature review. *Research in Developmental Disabilities, 34*, 4255–4273.

Lim, J., & Dinges, D. F. (2010). A meta-analysis of the impact of short-term sleep deprivation on cognitive variables. *Psychological Bulletin, 136*, 375–389.

Loge, J. H., Ekeberg, Ø., & Kaasa, S. (1998). Fatigue in the general Norwegian population: Normative data and associations. *Journal of Psychosomatic Research, 45*, 53–65.

Lund, H. G., Reider, B. D., Whiting, A. B., & Prichard, J. R. (2010). Sleep patterns and predictors of disturbed sleep in a large population of college students. *Journal of Adolescent Health, 46*, 124–132.

Luo, Z., & Inoué, S. (2000). A short daytime nap modulates levels if emotions objectively evaluated by the emotion spectrum analysis method. *Psychiatry and Clinical Neurosciences, 54*, 207–212.

Mastin, D. F., Bryson, J., & Corwyn, R. (2006). Assessment of sleep hygiene using the sleep hygiene index. *Journal of Behavioral Medicine, 29*, 223–227.

McEwen, B. S. (2006). Sleep deprivation as a neurobiologic and physiologic stressor: Allostasis and allostatic load. *Metabolism Clinical and Experimental, 55*, S20–S23.

Milner, C. E., & Cote, K. A. (2009). Benefits of napping in healthy adults. Impact of nap length, time of day, age, and experience with napping. *Journal of Sleep Research, 18*, 272–281.

Minkel, J. D., Banks, S., Htaik, O., Moreta, C., Jones, C. W., McGlinchey, E. L., ... Dinges, D. F. (2012). Sleep deprivation and stressors: Evidence for elevated negative affect in response to mild stressors when sleep deprived. *Emotion, 12*, 1015–1020.

Miyazaki, S., Liu, C.-Y., & Hayashi, Y (2017). Sleep in vertebrate and invertebrate animals, and insights into the function and evolution of sleep. *Neuroscience Research, 118*, 3–12.

Mollicone, D. J., Van Dongen, H. P. A., Rogers, N. L., & Dinges, D. F. (2008). Response surface mapping of neurobehavioral performance: Testing the feasibility of split sleep schedules for space operations. *Acta Astronautica, 63*, 833–840.

Morin, C. M. (2004). Cognitive-behavioral approaches to the treatment of insomnia. *Journal of Clinical Psychiatry, 65*, 33–40.

National Sleep Foundation. (2017a). *Healthy sleep tips.* Retrieved from https://sleepfoundation.org/sleep-tools-tips/healthy-sleep-tips

National Sleep Foundation. (2017b). *Inside your bedroom: Use your senses!* Retrieved from https://sleepfoundation.org/bedroom/index.php

Paterson, L. M. (2012). The science of sleep: What it is, what makes it happen and why do we do it? In A Green & A. Westcombe (Eds.), *Sleep: Multi-professional perspectives* (pp. 18–40). London, UK: Jessica Kingsley.

Pereira, D., & Elfering, A. (2014). Social stressors at work and sleep during the weekends: The mediating role of psychological detachment. *Journal of Occupational Health Psychology, 19*, 85–95.

Pilcher, J. J., & Huffcutt, A. I. (1996). Effects of sleep deprivation on performance: A meta-analysis. *Sleep, 19*, 318–326.

Querstret, D., & Cropley, M. (2012). Exploring the relationship between work-related rumination, sleep quality, and work-related fatigue. *Journal of Occupational Health Psychology, 17*, 341–353.

Ree, M. J., Harvey, A. G., Blake, R., Tang, N. K. Y., & Shawe-Taylor, M. (2005). Attempts to control unwanted thoughts in the night: Development of the thought control questionnaire-insomnia revised (TCQI-R). *Behaviour Research and Therapy, 43*, 985–998.

Siegel, J. (2002). *The neural control of sleep and waking*. New York, NY: Springer.

Siegel, J. M. (2005). Clues about the function of mammalian sleep. *Nature, 437*, 1264–1271.

Scott, B. A., & Judge, T. A. (2006). Insomnia, emotions, and job satisfaction: A multilevel study. *Journal of Management, 32*, 622–645.

Smit, B. W. (2016). Successfully leaving work at work: The self-regulatory underpinnings of psychological detachment. *Journal of Occupational and Organizational Psychology, 89*, 493–514.

Sofi., F., Cesari, F., Casini, A., Macchi, C., Abbate, R., & Gensinin, G. (2014). *European Journal of Preventative Cardiology, 21*, 57–64.

Soldatos, C. R., Allaert, F. A., Ohta, T., & Dikeos, D. G. (2005). How do individuals sleep around the world? Results from a single-day survey in ten countries. *Sleep Medicine, 6*, 5–13.

Strine, T. W., & Chapman, D. P. (2005). Associations of frequent sleep insufficiency with health-related quality of life and health behaviors. *Sleep Medicine, 6*, 23–27.

Takahashi, M., Fukuda, H., & Arito, H. (1998). Brief naps during post-lunch rest: effects on alertness, performance, and autonomic balance. *European Journal of Applied Physiology, 78*, 93–98.

Tassi, P., & Muzet, A. (2000). Sleep inertia. *Sleep Medicine Reviews, 4*, 341–353.

Taylor, D. J., Mallory, L. J., Lichstein, K. L., Durrence, H. H., Riedel, B. W., & Bush, A. J. (2007). Comorbidity of chronic insomnia with medical problems. *Sleep, 30*, 213–218.

Trauer, J., Qian, M. Y., Doyle, J. S., Rajaratnam, S. M. W., & Cunnington, D. (2015). Cognitive behavioral therapy for chronic insomnia: A systematic review and meta-analysis. *Annals of Internal Medicine, 163*, 191–205

Van Cauter, E. Spiegel, K., Tasali, E., & Leproult, R. (2008). Metabolic consequences of sleep and sleep loss. *Sleep Medicine, 9*(Suppl 1), S23–S28.

Vyazovskiy, V. A., & Delogu, A. (2014). NREM & REM sleep: complementary roles in recovery after wakefulness. *The Neuroscientist, 20*, 203–219.

Watling, J., Pawlik, B., Scott, K., Booth, S., & Short, M. A. (2017). Sleep loss and affective functioning: More than just mood. *Behavioral Sleep Medicine, 15*, 394–409.

Watson, N. F., Badr, M.S., Belenky, G., Bliwise, D. L., Buxton, O. M. Buysse, S. F., … Tasali, E. (2015). Joint consensus statement of the American Academy of Sleep Medicine and sleep research society on the recommended amount of sleep for a healthy adult: Methodology and discussion. *Journal of Clinical Sleep Medicine, 11*, 931–958.

Weinberg, M. K., Noble, J. M., & Hammond, T. G. (2016). Sleep well feel well: An investigation into the protective value of sleep quality on subjective well-being. *Australian Journal of Psychology, 68*, 91–97.

Wittmann, M., Dinich, J., Merrow, M., & Roenneberg, T. (2006). Social jetlag: misalignment of biological and social time. *Chronobiology International, 23*, 497-509.

Wrzus, C., Wagner, G. G., & Riediger, M. (2014). Feeling good when sleeping in? Day-to-day associations between sleep duration and affective well-being differ from youth to old age. *Emotion, 14*, 624-628.

Youngstedt, S. D. (2005). Effects of exercise on sleep. *Clinical Sports Medicine, 24*, 355-365.

CHAPTER 5

VOLUNTEERING

How Unpaid Work Pays Off

It's Tuesday night. The one night a week Kevin takes time away from his family to do his own thing. After reading stories to his 5-year-old daughter before bed, he says a quick goodbye to his wife and heads out into the dark winter night towards the emergency homeless shelter down the street. He can tell the temperature has dropped by the long line of people trying to keep warm as they wait for the doors to open. It's a sight that would seem daunting to some, but to Kevin it's a welcomed challenge, a change of pace and scenery from his desk job as a senior executive in sales.

"No matter how bad a day I have had, no matter how tired I am, I am always happy to go," says the 39-year-old.

Instead of making sales pitches or listening in on conference calls, his weekly shifts at the shelter are spent spreading mats on the church basement floor, making sandwiches for hundreds of people, managing unruly crowds and striking up conversations.

He has been volunteering at the shelter for more than 2 years and has come to know the regulars. The elderly woman who despite her tiny frame, has a huge appetite and wears size 10 men's shoes because she finds them more comfortable. The sports fanatic who admits he can't afford a place to live because he keeps gambling away his pension. The man from India who was driven from the hospital to the shelter by ambulance one night and dropped off with just the suitcase he was carrying. The encounters Kevin

Boost: The Science of Recharging Yourself in an Age of Unrelenting Demands, pp. 73–88

has with the people he meets at the shelter are brief, but their stories stick with him.

"There are all kinds of things I could be doing with my time, but they wouldn't be as rewarding," he says.

At the end of his shift, Kevin's feet are a little sore and his back aches temporarily yet he feels completely re-energized. He is filled with a sense of satisfaction and an eagerness to take on the rest of the week.

THE BOOSTING BENEFITS OF VOLUNTEERING

It sounds contradictory that adding more work to your days would give you a boost, but science has found that voluntarily participating in certain industrious activities in your uptime promotes recovery. Even though passive, relaxing activities like watching TV or reading a book can certainly help you recover, you can also give yourself a boost with more active pursuits (Rook & Zijlstra, 2006). Volunteering is one of them. Numerous studies have shown that spending some of your leisure time coaching a little-league baseball team, serving as a volunteer firefighter, or working at a homeless shelter like Kevin does, is an effective way to recharge your batteries.

Volunteering is a popular activity. Across the globe roughly a billion people offer their time as volunteers (Scheller, 2014). In the U.S. about 25% of the population volunteers, which translates into almost 63 million people (United States Department of Labor, 2015). In Australia, about 6 million people, or 31% of the population participate in voluntary work (Australian Bureau of Statistics, 2014). And in Canada, over 13 million people, about half of the population, volunteer their time for others. This translates into over 2 billion hours of volunteer work a year, most of which is devoted to fundraising and organizing events (Vézina & Crompton, 2012).

As we'll discuss, research has shown that we can fill all of the ReNU buckets by volunteering our time, and we get a boost as a result. Volunteering is a selfless act of kindness. Obviously, such selfless, altruistic acts benefit the recipients of our kindness. But recent research reveals the surprising fact that when we help other people by engaging in altruistic acts, those acts benefit not only the recipients of our benevolence, but us too. When we give, we receive.

HELPING OTHERS IS GOOD FOR YOU

Over the last few years researchers have become very interested in studying how acts of kindness, altruism, and benevolence benefit the "giver." The results of these studies support ancient religious teachings that proclaim if we want to live the good life, it's smart to help others.

In one recent study researchers asked people to either perform a kind act for someone else, such as watching their neighbor's children for a while, or to perform a kind act for themselves, such as going for a massage. Over the 6 weeks of the study the researchers found that the people who acted kindly towards others had higher levels of psychological well-being compared to those who acted kindly towards themselves. In fact, the people who acted kindly towards themselves had a slight dip in their well-being. Performing acts of kindness for others also led people to enjoy higher levels of positive emotions (Nelson, Layous, Cole, & Lyubomirsky, 2016). In short, the study showed that demonstrating kindness to other people makes us feel better ourselves.

Similar results were found in another study where researchers measured people's level of happiness in the morning and then gave them up to $20 to spend either on themselves or others before 5 P.M. that day. At the end of the day the researchers phoned the participants to re-assess how happy they felt. The results revealed that participants who had spent the money on other people by buying a little gift for someone or making a donation to charity, were happier than those who used the money to pay a bill or buy themselves a gift (Dunn, Aknin, & Norton, 2008). This positive relationship between happiness and spending money on other people is a pervasive phenomenon that exists worldwide (Nelson et al., 2016).

Generosity can even lighten our physical burdens. For example, as part of a Chinese study, researchers told participants to wait in the lobby of a building on campus because they had yet to determine which room they'd be using (This wasn't true. Researchers are sneaky). When each participant arrived in the lobby, a female assistant greeted them standing beside two cartons at the bottom of a flight of stairs. In one condition, the assistant pretended to have trouble carrying the cartons up the stairs, accidentally dropped one, and asked the participant if they'd be willing to help her. In the other condition, the assistant simply said that the first part of the study involved having participants carry a carton up the stairs. Afterwards, participants in both conditions were asked to estimate the weight of the carton. Amazingly, the participants who acted altruistically by helping the assistant carry the carton up the stairs estimated the weight of the carton as lighter than those who simply carried the carton because they thought it was part of the study (Li & Xie, 2017). Helping others literally lightens our load and make life feel easier.

Over and over, the research on altruism shows that when we help others we derive tremendous benefits ourselves. Kindness and benevolence not only benefit us psychologically, they benefit us physically. Researchers from The Ohio State University and the University of North Carolina recently published a paper summarizing the benefits of self-focused versus other-focused behavior. They concluded that "in daily life, giving is often beneficial for givers. It is associated with positive psychological health, good physical health, and decreased mortality, and improved relationships" (Crocker, Canevello, & Brown, 2017, p. 302). Volunteering is an altruistic, other-focused act. The many beneficial effects of altruism, kindness, and benevolence are an important part of the story that explains why volunteering gives us a boost.

FILL THE ReNU BUCKETS WITH VOLUNTEERING

Volunteering allows us to fill up the ReNU buckets. Whether we deliver magazines to patients recovering from surgery at a hospital, run a self-help group meeting for people with unruly dogs, or organize a church picnic, our volunteer activities satisfy the requirements we need for boosting.

We can replenish resources through volunteering and fill the rebuild bucket. When we volunteer to play music at a nursing home or supervise lunches at an elementary school, we are often performing tasks that are different from those we engage in as part of our obligations. As a result, we draw on different resources. Engaging in volunteer activities that use different skills and abilities helps to replenish resources we've depleted during our obligation time (Mojza, Sonnentag, & Bornemann, 2011). During Kevin's weekly stints at the emergency shelter, he is able to develop and make use of his more physical skills, such as preparing meals, making beds, or breaking up squabbles between patrons. Since the environment where he volunteers is so different from where he works, he is able to give the skills he uses daily for his job in sales a break so they can recharge. As a result, after a night of volunteering, Kevin feels more energized and enthusiastic for work the following morning.

This raises an important point about which volunteer activities you should pursue. As a result of the experiences you have during your obligations, you develop skills and competence in certain areas. Because of this you're likely to be inclined to pursue volunteer opportunities that leverage those skills, experiences, and competencies. In fact, our volunteer work often imitates our obligations precisely because we like to leverage the experiences and skills our obligations have allowed us to develop (Wilson, 2000). However, doing this will prevent you from giving your resources a break. You want to choose volunteer roles that allow you to get away from your obligations, not replicate your obligations in another setting. So, if you're a chef, don't volunteer to cook at a soup kitchen in your leisure time. Instead, serve the food. If you spend your weeks as a caregiver for an elderly parent, don't volunteer to read stories to people in a nursing home in your leisure time. Instead, clean up a roadway. If you're a taxi driver, don't volunteer to drive people to their medical appointments. Instead, help organize a political campaign. If your specific expertise or skills are requested for volunteer activities on occasion, great, it's nice to be needed, but as a general rule try to select volunteer roles that draw on resources that are different from those you use in your obligation time.

We should also note that volunteering not only rebuilds depleted resources, but it can also help us build new resources (Ruderman, Ohlott, Panzer, & King, 2002). For example, research has shown that volunteering is associated with self-esteem, confidence (Brown, Hoye, & Nicholson, 2012), and optimism (Mellor et al., 2008). Volunteering can also help us extend our network of relationships which can serve as a valuable resource (Wilson & Musick, 2003). If you think your resources could do with a little enhancement, it's a good idea to devote some time to helping others in your uptime.

Volunteering can also fill the nourish bucket. For example, the challenges people master in their volunteer roles can satisfy their need for competence. The latitude they are given in executing their volunteer duties can satisfy their need for autonomy. And the relationships they form and nurture while engaged in volunteer activities can satisfy their need for relatedness. In a study designed to examine the benefits of volunteer work, researchers in Germany asked 105 employed people to fill in a survey every evening for 2 weeks indicating how much time they spent doing volunteer activities each day and how well their psychological needs for competence, autonomy and relatedness were satisfied each day. The results demonstrated that the amount of time people spent volunteering each day was significantly related to how successfully they felt their psychological needs had been satisfied (Mojza et al., 2011). Satisfying their psychological needs also helped people boost by reducing the amount of negative emotions they felt the next day.

We can also fill the unhook bucket by volunteering. Volunteering is especially effective at helping us to psychologically detach. By providing us with the opportunity to become absorbed in different activities, volunteering encourages us to mentally escape from our daily obligations (Mojza, Lorenz, Sonnentag, & Binnewies, 2010). In the study just mentioned, the researchers also discovered that the amount of time people spent engaged in volunteer activities each day was related to how much psychological detachment they experienced at bedtime (Mojza et al., 2011). The more they volunteered the more they detached.

In summary, volunteering allows us to fill all of the ReNU buckets. It fills the rebuild bucket by allowing us to replenish and build new resources. It fills the nourish bucket by satisfying our psychological needs. And it fills the unhook bucket by helping us psychologically detach.

VOLUNTEERING GIVES US A BOOST

Given that all of the ReNU buckets are filled by volunteering, we should expect that participating in volunteer activities will recharge our batteries and give us a boost. Sure enough, research on the topic shows this to be true.

Psychological Well-Being

We noted earlier that the more time people spend volunteering each day the less negative emotions they feel the following day (Mojza et al., 2011). This is just one example of many which show that volunteering promotes well-being.

One of the most common well-being outcomes researchers look at when it comes to volunteering is depression. And research has consistently shown that people suffer from less depression when they volunteer. This relationship has been observed across the lifespan in different age groups such as young college students (Lederer, Autry, Day, & Oswalt, 2015), middle-aged people (Musick & Wilson, 2003), and seniors (Li & Ferraro, 2005). Volunteering keeps the negative experience of depression at bay.

On the more positive side of things, research shows that when we volunteer we feel more satisfied with our lives (Mellor et al., 2009), experience more positive emotions (Windsor, Anstey, & Rodgers, 2008), and enjoy higher levels of social well-being, which reflects our overall assessment of how well we are functioning in the community (Son & Wilson, 2012). Volunteering also makes us happier (Thoits & Hewitt, 2001), and makes us feel as though we are self-actualizing, or realizing our true nature (Son & Wilson, 2012). In short, when we volunteer our psychological well-being improves.

Physical Health

About 70% of volunteers say that volunteering makes them feel healthier (Post, 2017), and research shows that, in fact, people who volunteer their time for others enjoy better health. A U.S. study of adults found that people who volunteer for more organizations have better physical health than those who volunteer for fewer organizations (Yeung, 2017). Another study found that even after controlling for initial levels of health, people who spend more time volunteering end up being healthier than people who spend less time volunteering (Thoits & Hewitt, 2001). Using data on 139 countries from the World Gallup Poll, an international team of researchers found that the positive relationship between volunteering and health is an almost universal phenomenon that transcends geographical, cultural, and economic boundaries (Kumar, Calvo, Avendano, Sivaramakrishnan, & Berkman, 2012).

Much of the research on the relationship between volunteering and physical health has been conducted with older people. Just like the research done with younger people, these studies consistently show that volunteering in old age is associated with better physical health. For example, it has been shown that people 70-years-old or older who volunteer at least 100 hours a year have better health and live longer than those who volunteer less than 100 hours annually (Lum & Lightfoot, 2005). You might reasonably think that the relationship between volunteering and longevity is explained by the fact that healthier people are simply able to do more volunteering, and not by the reverse—that volunteering makes people healthier and they therefore live longer. It is certainly true that healthier people do volunteer more (Wilson, 2000), but research has shown that even when we take people's level of health into account, and can therefore ignore the impact of health on their ability to volunteer their time, volunteers live longer than people who don't volunteer (Oman, Thoresen, & McMahon, 1999). Overall, there is strong scientific evidence showing that volunteering results in better health (Piliavin & Siegl, 2015).

Enhancement

Volunteering can also improve how we handle our obligations. Jamie, the lead author of the book you are reading, has experienced this first hand. Writing this book was a huge, exhausting undertaking that ate up a lot of time. One of the things that helped Jamie boost while working on the book was his volunteer work. During one particularly draining week, Jamie was struggling to complete this very chapter. Not only was he feeling depleted, he was also stressed because he was scheduled to facilitate a day-long strategic planning session for a non-profit organization he's been volunteering with for many years. Although Jamie enjoys facilitating these sessions, he worried that a full day away from working on the book would compromise his ability to make the chapter deadline. However, his concern was misplaced. The opportunity to immerse himself in an activity that was very different from writing ended up allowing him to psychologically detach from working on the book, rebuild resources, and sit down at his computer the following day feeling refreshed and recharged. Volunteering to facilitate the session gave him a boost! The day after his volunteer work he spent twice as long working on this chapter than he'd originally planned because the work felt easier and words flowed effortlessly from his fingertips onto the computer screen. He made up the lost writing time easily and even developed some ideas for the chapter that he hadn't previously considered, including this anecdote.

Research supports Jamie's experience. A number of studies have shown that volunteering enhances our ability to perform well at our obligations. For example, the psychological detachment and need satisfaction produced by volunteering has been shown to increase people's ability to engage in active listening the day after they volunteer (Mojza et al., 2011). Spending time helping others can also lead to enhancement because when we volunteer we learn a variety of things that improve our performance. In a survey of over 37,000 Canadians, a substantial percentage of volunteers reported that their volunteer work had allowed them to improve their interpersonal skills (64%), communication skills (44%), organization or managerial skills (39%), technical or office skills (27%), and had increased their knowledge (34%) (Vézina & Crompton, 2012). These gains in skill and knowledge partly explain why volunteering earlier in one's career is associated with higher occupational status later in one's career (Wilson & Musick, 2003).

WON'T VOLUNTEERING OVERWHELM ME?

Each of us occupies a number of roles in our lives. We are fathers, mothers, sons, daughters, brothers, sisters, in-laws, employees, caregivers, students, and so on. When we start donating our time to others we add the role of volunteer. It is reasonable to wonder what effect adding more roles to our lives will have on us? Traditionally, people who contemplated these sorts of questions thought that adding extra roles to our already hectic schedules would pose problems for us. The idea behind this line of thinking is that each of us has a limited amount of energy to spend on the various activities that make up our lives, and depleting some of that energy on volunteer activities leaves less energy for other activities, notably those that are required of us and demand quality performance. This line of thinking can be represented by a metaphorical pie; When we cut a slice of the pie and use up energy by fulfilling one role in our lives, there is less pie and less energy left for other roles (Ruderman et al., 2002). Social scientists refer to this as role scarcity. Based on this view, volunteering is like moonlighting and should hurt how well we perform our obligations because it pulls from the energy we need to succeed at our daily tasks (Rodell, 2013). The strain and burdens caused by additional roles should also cut into our well-being and health (Thoits, 2012).

An alternative line of thinking argues that adding more roles to our lives should actually be beneficial for us. The idea behind this perspective is that the more roles we occupy the more opportunity we have to make friends, build a power base, and feel satisfied (Chrouser Ahrens & Ryff, 2006).

Multiple roles can help us deal with stress because stress in one role can be buffered by accomplishment and enjoyment in another role. Multiple roles can provide more opportunities for social support, which promotes well-being. They can also provide more opportunities to experience success and build resources such as self-confidence. Additionally, occupying multiple roles can expand our frame of reference and help us keep problems and stressors in perspective (Barnett & Hyde, 2001). Social scientists refer to this as role enhancement. In this view, because of all the benefits that come from having multiple roles, volunteering shouldn't compromise our performance or well-being at all. In fact, the suggestion in this view is that multiple roles should lead to improvement in these areas.

So, which is it? Would you guess that research supports the role scarcity view or the role enhancement view? It turns out that when scientists conduct research to test these competing views, they find very little evidence supporting the former, and lots of evidence supporting the latter. Having multiple roles proves beneficial for us. As noted by Peggy Thoits, a professor of sociology at Indiana University and one of the leading authorities on this topic, "[a] large body of research shows that holding multiple roles reduces psychological distress and enhances physical health. The more roles individuals occupy, the better their mental and physical well-being" (Thoits, 2012, p. 360). In fact, American researchers found that as the number of roles people occupy increases, so does their well-being, including the extent to which they enjoy positive emotions, the sense that they are effectively managing their everyday affairs, and the amount of meaning they have in their lives. Not only that, but the quality of their relationships also improves (Chrouser Ahrens & Ryff, 2006).

Roles can be obligatory or voluntary. Obligatory roles, such as being a parent, are emotionally intense, relatively demanding, and difficult to leave. Voluntary roles, such as being a volunteer, tend to be less emotionally intense, less demanding and easier to enter and exit (Thoits, 2003). The beneficial effects of multiple roles come primarily from voluntary roles, which are freely and willingly chosen. For example, the number of obligatory roles people occupy, such as being a parent or employee, has relatively little effect on well-being. However, when people take on more voluntary roles by, for example, becoming a group member or volunteer, they experience higher self-esteem, a higher sense of mastery, better physical health, and less distress (Thoits, 2003). Obligatory roles promote well-being only when the demands they place on us are not excessive, but voluntary roles promote well-being fairly consistently (Thoits, 1992). In general, voluntarily taking on extra roles doesn't hurt you, it gives you a boost.

WHAT KIND OF VOLUNTEERING IS BEST?

Earlier we noted that the volunteer work we select should draw on resources that are different from those we use during our obligations. There are a few other ideas to consider when deciding what volunteer role will give you the biggest boost.

First, volunteer for the right reasons. People have a number of different motivations for volunteering. Some people volunteer to relieve loneliness, some want to get ahead in their careers, while others want to spend time with people who share similar interests (Clary et al., 1998). However, people tend to only be satisfied with their volunteer experiences when they engage in them for the right reasons. Being satisfied with our volunteer roles is important because satisfaction often includes feeling challenged and rewarded which can nourish the need for competence (Dwyer, Bono, Snyder, Nov, & Berson, 2013). But research shows that people tend to only find satisfaction in their volunteer experiences when they engage in them to express important values like helping others, or to make themselves feel useful and important (Dwyer et al., 2013). Because of this, it is important to think of boosting as a byproduct, and not the main purpose, of volunteering.

When it comes to the type of volunteer activities that are best for boosting, you want to select opportunities that allow you to make a difference, help others, and feel good about yourself. You do this by volunteering for groups or causes that you deem to be important. Volunteering for roles that are meaningful to us enhances our psychological well-being and physical health (Thoits, 2012). So, get involved in an activity that allows you to feel like you're making a difference at something of great significance. This will make you feel as though your involvement matters. This is a crucial point because research has shown that feeling as though our participation matters is a vital link in the connection between volunteering and well-being (Piliavin & Siegel, 2007). Put another way, part of the reason volunteering promotes well-being is because it makes people feel as though they matter. And when you volunteer for a cause that is important to you, you will enjoy a heightened sense of purpose and meaning in your life (Thoits, 2012).

As for how much time to commit to your volunteer role, you don't want to overdo it. Relative to none or lots, a modest amount of volunteering is most effective at giving you a boost. What is considered modest depends partly on your age, life circumstances, and stage of life. For example, researchers in Australia compared the number of hours older people volunteered annually to their level of well-being and found that the highest levels of well-being occurred among those who volunteered between 100 and 800 hours a year (Windsor, Anstey, & Rodgers, 2008). That translates into roughly between 2 to 15 hours a week. For older, retired people, volunteering 15 hours a week may be doable, but for younger people with heavy weekly obligations that degree of involvement is likely excessive. Most younger people should invest considerably less time volunteering. Overdoing it isn't beneficial for boosting. For example, we know that volunteering can produce psychological detachment, but on days that adults spend more than 3½ hours of their leisure time volunteering, they fail to detach (Mojza et al., 2010). One reason this can happen is because volunteering starts to feel like work. Similarly, undergraduate students who volunteer more than 10 hours a week end up feeling less rested (Lederer et al., 2015).

For Kevin, who has a young child and a full-time job, spending a few hours one night a week is enough to fill his ReNU buckets without taking up too much time away from his family. And according to the current research, it seems Kevin is right on track as far as how much time he should be devoting to his volunteering.

Researchers have suggested that to produce boosting benefits it is optimal to spend two to three hours per week volunteering (Anderson et al., 2014). This general guideline was originally suggested for seniors, but has recently been promoted more broadly in the medical community by Dr. Stephen Post, Director of the Center for Medical Humanities, Compassionate Care, and Bioethics at Stony Brook University (Post, 2017). Investing just a few hours volunteering one weekday evening, Saturday morning or Sunday afternoon will help you effectively recover from your daily obligations and make you feel great about yourself without overwhelming you. It is admirable to devote lots of time to making a difference in other people's lives, but relentless devotion to such tasks is reserved for saintly souls with time to spare. For busy people with daily obligations, a modest amount of volunteering is a more attainable goal that can provide a needed boost.

THE WHOLE STORY

Because volunteering tends to place fewer demands on us than our obligations, and because it allows us to fill the ReNU buckets, we generally profit from volunteering by getting a boost. However, when the demands of our volunteer experiences exceed the benefits, volunteering can be harmful to us. For example, research has shown that people who volunteer to help in disaster settings, such as helping out with hurricane relief efforts, sometimes find the experience stressful and suffer lower well-being as a result (Thormar et al., 2010). Unlike professional emergency workers, volunteers in disaster settings often have little training and are therefore unprepared for the difficulty of the role. They also often don't have the opportunity to receive social support from a network of people with similar experiences (Thormar et al., 2010). As a result, the demands of the volunteer experience can exceed the benefits people derive and they suffer negative outcomes.

In the broader literature on helpfulness it has been shown that although altruism and kindness can benefit the "giver," the stress associated with helping others on an ongoing basis can be detrimental to our well-being. For example, taking care of an ill or disabled family member can take a toll on our physical and mental health (Crocker et al., 2017). The last thing stressed caregivers need is volunteer work that places additional burdens on them. Such burdens further deplete the ReNU buckets; they don't fill them. We would not want to suggest that you shouldn't volunteer for potentially stressful roles like helping out in a disaster. Providing assistance in such circumstances is noble and commendable. But those volunteer roles may not be the best choices if you're hoping to indirectly get a boost as a result. To recover from your daily obligations, it is better to select volunteer roles that don't tax you and can be enjoyed and sustained over a long period.

SUMMARY

Recovering from our weekly obligations does not require inactivity, or that we spend our leisure time participating only in passive, relaxing endeavors. Volunteering is an active leisure time pursuit that can help to recharge our batteries and rejuvenate us. If we select volunteer roles that are sufficiently different from our weekly obligations and don't overtax us, we can replenish our resources, satisfy our psychological needs, and psychologically detach. This fills all of the ReNU buckets and gives us a boost. As Kevin, the sales executive and father who opened this chapter knows, unpaid work can really pay off. Including a small amount of volunteer work in your schedule is an immensely satisfying and effective part of transforming your downtime into uptime.

Boosting Bites

Perform random acts of kindness.

Choose volunteer roles that are different from your weekly obligations.

Volunteer for causes that are important to you.

Spend two to three hours a week volunteering.

Select volunteer opportunities that aren't overly stressful or taxing.

UPTIME ACTION PLAN

Step 1. Consider what issues/causes/groups of people are most important to you. To help determine this, think about what significant events have shaped you as a person? Which media stories tend to grab your attention? What topics do you tend to search on the internet? Write down your priority issues/causes/groups in the spaces below.

1. _____ 2. _____

3. _____ 4._____

Step 2. Evaluate your typical schedule and decide what part of the week is most convenient for you to spend a few hours helping others or supporting an important cause.

Step 3. Search the Internet for organizations in your area that serve the people or support the issues or causes you noted in Step 1. Research the organization online or contact the organizations to determine which ones offer volunteer opportunities. Ask about any training or support that may be needed to assist you in your volunteer duties, and select the opportunity that best fits your interests.

Step 4. Speak with fellow volunteers or other knowledgeable folks, and read about the issue/cause/group for which you are volunteering so you can learn how to make a substantial difference and have as big an impact as possible.

REFERENCES

Anderson, N. D., Damianakis, T., Kröger, E., Wagner, L. M., Dawson, D. R., Binns, M. A., ... Cook, S. L. (2014). The benefits associated with volunteering among seniors: A critical review and recommendations for future research. *Psychological Bulletin, 140*, 1505–1533.

Australian Bureau of Statistics. (2014). *General social survey: Summary results, Australia, 2014.* (Report No. 4159.0). Canberra, Australia. Retrieved from http://www.abs.gov.au/ausstats/abs@.nsf/Latestproducts/4159.0Main%20Features152014

Barnett, R., & Hyde, J. (2001). Women, men, work, and family: An expansionist theory. *American Psychologist, 56*, 781–796

Brown, K. M., Hoye, R., & Nicholson, M. (2012). Self-esteem, self-efficacy, and social connectedness as mediators of the relationship between volunteering and well-being. *Journal of Social Service Research, 38*, 468–483.

Chrouser Ahrens, C., & Ryff, C. D. (2006). Multiple roles and well-being: Sociodemographic and psychological moderators. *Sex Roles, 55*, 801–815.

Clary, E. G., Snyder, M., Ridge, R. D., Copeland, J., Stukas, A. A., Haugen, J., & Miene, P. (1998). Understanding and assessing the motivations of volunteers: A functional approach. *Journal of Personality and Social Psychology, 74*, 1516–1530.

Crocker, J., Canevello, A., & Brown, A. A. (2017). Social motivation: Costs and benefits of selfishness and otherishness. *Annual Review of Psychology, 68*, 299–325.

Dunn, E. W., Aknin, L. B., & Norton, M. I. (2008). Spending money on others promotes happiness. *Science, 319*, 1687–1688.

Dwyer, P. C., Bono, J. E., Snyder, M., Nov, O., & Berson, Y. (2013). Sources of volunteer motivation: Transformational Leadership and personal motives influence volunteer outcomes. *Nonprofit Management & Leadership, 24*, 181–205

Kumar, S., Calvo, R., Avendano, M., Sivaramakrishnan, K., & Berkman, L. F. (2012). Social support, volunteering and health around the world: Cross-national evidence from 139 countries. *Social Science & Medicine, 74*, 696–706.

Lederer, A., Autry, D. M., Day, C. R. T., & Oswalt, S. B. (2015). The impact of work and volunteer hours on the health of undergraduate students. *Journal of American College Health, 63*, 403–408.

Li, Y., & Ferraro, K. F. (2005). Volunteering and depression in later life: Social benefit or selection processes? *Journal of Health and Social Behavior, 46*, 68–84.

Li, X., & Xie, X. (2017). The helping behavior helps lighten physical burden. *Basic and Applied Social Psychology, 39*, 183–192.

Lum, T. Y., & Lightfoot, E. (2005). The effects of volunteering on the physical and mental health of older people. *Research on Aging, 27*, 31–55.

Mellor, D., Hayashi, Y., Firth, L., Stokes, M., Chambers, S., & Cummins, R. (2009). Volunteering and well-being: Do self-esteem, optimism, and perceived control, mediate the relationship? *Journal of Social Service Research, 34*, 61–70.

Mellor, D., Hayashi, Y., Stokes, M., Firth, L., Lake, L., Staples, M., ... Cummins, R. (2009). Volunteering and its relationship with persona and neighborhood well-being. *Nonprofit and Voluntary Sector Quarterly, 38*, 144–159.

Mojza, E. J., Lorenz, C., Sonnentag, S., & Binnewies, C. (2010). Daily recovery experiences: The role of volunteer work during leisure time. *Journal of Occupational Health Psychology, 15*, 60–74

Mojza, E. J., Sonnentag, S., & Bornemann, C. (2011). Volunteer work as a valuable leisure-time activity: A day-level study on volunteer work, non-work experiences, and well-being at work. *Journal of Occupational and Organizational Psychology, 84*, 123–152.

Musick, M. A., & Wilson, J. (2003). Volunteering and depression: The role of psychological and social resources in different age groups. *Social Science & Medicine, 56*, 259–269.

Nelson, S. K., Layous, K., Cole, S. W., & Lyubomirsky, S. (2016). Do unto others or treat yourself? The effects of prosocial and self-focused behavior on psychological flourishing. *Emotion, 16*, 850–861.

Oman, D., Thoresen, C. C., & McMahon, K. (1999). Volunteerism and mortality among the community-dwelling elderly. *Journal of Health Psychology, 4*, 301–316.

Piliavin, J. A., & Siegel, E. (2007). Health benefits of volunteering in the Wisconsin Longitudinal Study. *Journal of Health and Social behavior, 48*, 450–464.

Piliavin, J. A., & Siegl, E. (2015). Health and well-being consequences of formal volunteering. In D. A. Schroeder & W. G. Graziano (Eds.), *The Oxford Handbook of Prosocial Behavior* (pp. 494–523). New York, NY: Oxford University Press.

Post, S. G. (2017). Rx it's good to be good (G2BG) 2017 commentary: Prescribing volunteerism for health, happiness, resilience, and longevity. *American Journal of Health Promotion, 3*, 163–172.

Rodell, J. B. (2013). Finding meaning through volunteering: Why do employees volunteer and what does it mean for their jobs? *Academy of Management Journal, 56*, 1274–1294.

Rook, J. W., & Zijlstra, F. R. H. (2006). The contribution of various types of activities to recovery. *European Journal of Work and Organizational Psychology, 15*, 218–240.

Ruderman, M. N., Ohlott, P. J., Panzer, K., & King, S. N. (2002). Benefits of multiple roles for managerial women. *Academy of Management Journal, 45*, 369–386.

Scheller, A. (2014, December 2). The countries where you'll find the most volunteers. *The Huffington Post*. Retrieved from http://www.huffingtonpost.ca/entry/volunteering-by-country_n_6221046

Son, J., & Wilson, J. (2012). Volunteer work and hedonic, eudaimonic and social well-being. *Sociological Forum, 27*, 658–681.

Thoits, P. A (1992). Identity structures and psychological well-being: Gender and marital status comparisons. *Social Psychology Quarterly, 55*, 236–256.

Thoits, P. A., & Hewitt, L. N. (2001). Volunteer work and well-being. *Journal of Health and Social Behavior, 42*, 115–131.

Thoits, P. A. (2003). Personal agency in the accumulation of multiple role-identities. In P. J. Burke, T. J. Owens, R. T. Serpe, & P. A. Thoits (Eds.), *Advances in identity theory and research* (pp. 179–194). New York, NY: Academic/Plenum.

Thoits. P. A. (2012). Role-identity salience, purpose and meaning in life, and well-being among volunteers. *Social Psychology Quarterly, 75*, 360–384

Thormar, S. B., Gersons, B. P. R., Juen, B., Marschang, A., Djakababa, M. N., & Olff, M. (2010). The mental health impact of volunteering in a disaster setting: A review. *Journal of Nervous and Mental Disease, 198*, 529–538.

United States Department of Labor, Bureau of Labor Statistics. (2015). *Volunteering in the United States–2015.* (Report No. USDL-16-0363). Retrieved from https://data.bls.gov/search/query/results?cx=01373803619591 9377644%3A6ih0hfrgl50&q=volunteering

Vézina, M., & Crompton, S. (2012, April 16). *Volunteering in Canada* (Report No. 11-008-X). Canada: Statistics Canada. Retrieved from http://www.statcan.gc.ca/pub/11-008-x/2012001/article/11638-eng.htm

Wilson, J. (2000). Volunteering. *Annual Review of Sociology, 26*, 215–240.

Wilson, J., & Musick, M. (2003). Doing well by doing good: Volunteering and occupational achievement among American women. *The Sociological Quarterly, 44*, 433–450.

Windsor, T. D., Anstey, K. J., & Rodgers, B. (2008). Volunteering and psychological well-being among young-old adults: How much is too much? *The Gerontologist, 48*, 59–70.

Yeung, J. W. K. (2017). Religion, volunteerism, and health: Are religious people really doing well by doing good? *Social Indicators Research.* Advance online publication. doi:10.1007/s11205-017-1671-8

CHAPTER 6

MEDITATION, MINDFULNESS, AND MORE

Five Minutes to a Better Life

Erica had been looking after her 81-year-old widowed mother for almost a decade yet had never had a real conversation with her. She would drop in at her house at least two or three times a week, but her visits were always rushed and consisted of filling the fridge with groceries and making sure the house was in order before darting out the door. Between caring for her mother and her teenaged son, Erica felt consumed by her daily 'to do' list and was in a constant rush to get to the next task.

"My mother had become another person that I was responsible for," says the 49-year-old. "It was physically and emotionally draining. Suddenly it felt like all my free time had been sucked up."

That is until she discovered meditation. Taking a few minutes each day to stop and focus her mind helps Erica to concentrate on the present rather than being preoccupied with what she has to do next. Instead of viewing the visits to her mother's house as another chore, she looks at them as an opportunity to strengthen their once strained relationship. Now after Erica stocks her mother's fridge and tidies up, she makes a pot of tea and the two of them sit down and talk.

"I take the time to sit down with her. It's quality time and the visits now feel different because I am actually spending time with her."

Meditation has also helped Erica manage the anger she sometimes feels towards her mother.

Boost: The Science of Recharging Yourself in an Age of Unrelenting Demands, pp. 89–106
Copyright © 2018 by Information Age Publishing

"I am better at examining my emotions and I don't let them dictate what I do. In the past my mother would make comments that would infuriate me, but now I take a breath, pause and don't let myself get carried away."

Erica finally has the relationship with her mother that she has craved since she was a teenager.

"We have the best relationship we have ever had. It's not an ideal relationship but there is less tension and less anger. We are definitely moving in the right direction."

WHAT IS MEDITATION?

As we will discuss in this chapter, meditation has numerous and significant boosting effects. But before delving into how meditation can help us recover from, and handle, our obligations, let's get a better handle on what exactly meditation means.

Meditation refers to "a family of self-regulation practices that focus on training attention and awareness in order to bring mental processes under greater voluntary control and thereby foster general mental well-being and development and/or specific capacities such as calm, clarity, and concentration" (Walsh & Shapiro, 2006, pp. 228–229). As this definition implies, when Erica started meditating she was better able to self-regulate her anger, stay calm, and enjoy a better relationship with her mother, thus fostering greater well-being. Although on the surface it can seem like an esoteric, mystical topic, the mechanisms that underlie the numerous beneficial effects of meditation have long-standing scientific roots. For example, one of the things people learn to do when they meditate is control and direct their attention, and the exact same attentional processes that are emphasized in meditation have been the focus of extensive scientific study in fields like psychology and neuroscience (Lutz, Slagter, Dunne, & Davidson, 2008).

Meditation has a long history dating back to ancient Indian scriptures from about 3500 B.C.E (Sedlmeier et al., 2012). Spiritual instruction on the methods and purpose of meditation often prescribe a series of stages that take meditators from being novices learning the basics of breathing exercises and thought control to, ultimately, a state of liberation and enlightenment. However, the scientific study of meditation focuses almost exclusively on the early stages of this process and the effect of meditation on non-spiritual phenomena such as enhancing our concentration and minimizing our stress (Sedlmeier et al., 2012). In this chapter, we will focus on these less esoteric, non-religious benefits.

Research has generally focused on two specific forms of meditation (Lutz et al., 2008). The first form is called focused attention meditation and involves maintaining focus on a particular object, such as one's breathing, and bringing attention back to that object anytime the mind wanders. The main purpose of this form of meditation is to cultivate the ability to sustain focused attention, and to do so with diminishing effort over time, resulting in what is referred to as effortless concentration (Lutz et al., 2008). An example of this form is loving-kindness meditation in which the meditator focuses on herself or others while generating kind intentions (Zeng, Chiu, Oei, & Leung, 2015). As we practice focused attention meditation we develop three interrelated skills. First, we develop the ability to be aware of distractions without losing our focus. Second, we learn to divorce ourselves from distractions. Third, we cultivate the ability to refocus our attention when needed (Lutz et al., 2008).

The second form is called open monitoring meditation. Whereas focused attention meditation involves concentrating on an object, open monitoring meditation involves concentrating on attention itself in an open, non-evaluative, non-reactive way. We simply watch our inner and outer experiences without directing or judging them. Thus, while focused attention meditation leads us to generate a narrower span of attention, open monitoring meditation produces a broader span of attention (Lippelt, Hommel, & Colzato, 2014). The main purpose of this form of meditation is to become more aware of our patterns of cognitive and emotional activity (Lutz et al., 2008). An example of this form is mindfulness meditation during which meditators focus on observing their own experiences, paying close attention to conscious awareness with "an attitude of curiosity, openness, and acceptance" (Eberth & Sedlmeier, 2012, p. 174). Typically, novice meditators start with focused attention meditation and develop skill in regulating attention before advancing to open monitoring meditation (Lutz et al., 2008).

WHAT HAPPENS WHEN WE MEDITATE?

As suggested above, one of the things that happens when we mediate is that we build skills related to directing and sustaining our attention. The cultivation of these skills quiets what is often referred to as our "monkey mind"—the tendency for our minds to dart around, jumping like a monkey from branch to branch, never still, never at rest. If you stop for a moment and pay attention to the contents of your mind, you'll notice that your mind is a whirlwind of activity. We are constantly thinking about stuff, like deciding what to make for dinner, analyzing whether or not we look good in our outfit, remembering our first love, or conjuring up a smart retort to the person who slighted us last week. You never need to ask your mind to start thinking or feeling something (McDonald, 2015). It is always active, like a mental perpetual motion machine. One of the ways meditation works is by allowing us to subdue this internal cacophony and achieve what is called *calm abiding*, a form of intensive concentration that lets us focus on whatever we want, for as long as we want, while experiencing calmness and clarity (McDonald, 2015). Calm abiding is one of the main outcomes of focused attention meditation.

Meditation also changes the way we interact with our thoughts and feelings. This outcome is produced largely by mindfulness meditation. Dr. Shauna Shapiro is a professor at Santa Clara University and a recognized expert on mindfulness. Along with some of her colleagues, Dr. Shapiro explains that mindfulness stimulates a change in perspective that involves our experiences becoming the target of our attention (Shapiro, Carlson, Aston, & Freedman, 2006). Put another way, through mindfulness we transform our subjective experiences into the objects of observation. This is called *reperceiving*. As we develop our skill at recognizing the objects of our own consciousness we begin to understand that they don't define us. We are not the contents of our minds. We realize that we must be distinct from the thoughts and feelings that occupy our minds because we are able to observe them, the same way a scientist might observe other people. This recognition lays the foundation for an ability to decouple ourselves from the contents of consciousness and to watch them instead of being consumed by them. This ability, in turn, leads to more objectivity, clarity, and tranquility, and helps us disrupt unconstructive habits, like the way Erica disrupted her tendency to get upset with her mom. The detachment we develop from our thoughts and feelings does not numb us or make us indifferent to our experiences. In fact, the opposite occurs. By learning to not be enmeshed with the contents of consciousness, we become more attuned to our natural and spontaneous on-going experiences. Calm abiding and reperceiving are both keys to understanding how meditation gives us a boost.

IT DOESN'T TAKE MUCH

The beneficial effects of meditation intensify with practice. For example, when people first start meditating, the more frequently they practice the better they feel (Fredrickson, Cohn, Coffey, Pek, & Finkel, 2008), and the longer we practice meditation the better we get at controlling our attention (Ortner, Kilner, & Zelazo, 2007). Also, the positive impact of meditation is strong. In fact, the effect that meditation has on healthy people is about as strong as the impact that counseling has on people in therapy (Sedlmeier et al., 2012).

It doesn't take long for our skills to improve. The Dalai Lama suggests that we can learn to effectively tame our mental monkeys and hold our concentration in just 6 months (Dalai Lama & Hopkins, 2002). But beneficial changes occur even faster than that. Research shows that after just three 20-minute sessions of meditation our performance on mental tasks improves (Zeidan, Johnson, Diamond, David, & Goolkasian, 2010), and after just 11 hours of meditation distributed over the course of 1 month, changes occur in the white-matter of our brains (Tang et al., 2010). Even a single session of meditation can produce boosting effects. For example, research has shown that after just one 15-minute meditation session, people recover more effectively and suffer less distress after being exposed to a stressor (van Hoof & Baas, 2013).

You don't need to take off on a week-long retreat if you want to start making meditation a part of your life. Short meditation sessions can be highly effective. In fact, the Dalai Lama suggests that as they are learning to develop their powers of concentration, beginners should meditate for just 5 minutes at a time (Dalai Lama & Hopkins, 2002). Who doesn't have 5 minutes?

MEDITATION FILLS THE ReNU BUCKETS

There is evidence that the different forms of mediation have different neurophysiological effects (Lippelt et al., 2014). For example, focused attention mediation impacts brain activation in areas of the prefrontal cortex that are involved in the deliberate regulation of thought and behavior, whereas open monitoring meditation affects activation in the left inferior frontal gyrus which is involved in the inhibition of automatic or impulsive behavior (Fox et al., 2016). However, despite these differences, in this section we will consider both forms of meditation together. We will do this for a number of reasons. First, elaborating on the subtle neurological differences between the two forms of meditation is too detailed for our purposes. Second, although the different approaches of meditation have different emphases, most meditation practices ultimately include both forms (Sedlmeier et al., 2012). Third, the overall effects of the different forms of meditation on psychological outcomes are similar (Sedlmeier et al., 2012). And fourth, there are some brain regions that are affected by both forms of meditation, such as the insula, which is involved with the awareness of bodily signals (Fox et al., 2016). Indeed, it has been suggested that because they all share the common goals of regulating attention and achieving detachment from thoughts, there are brain networks that are common to all forms of meditation (Sperduti, Martinelli, & Piolino, 2012). For these reasons, we will focus on the overall benefits of meditation.

By offering us a dedicated period of relaxed concentration during which we are free from our obligations, meditation gives us the opportunity to replenish our depleted resources and fill the rebuild bucket. For example, the resource of self-control is like a muscle that can be depleted, and many studies have shown that if we deplete our self-control in one task, our performance on subsequent tasks that require self-control is compromised (Hagger, Wood, Stiff, & Chatzisarantis, 2010). However, researchers in Switzerland have demonstrated that if we meditate after engaging in a task that depletes our self-control, our performance on subsequent tasks that draw on the same resource is not compromised at all (Friese, Messner, & Schaffner, 2012). Meditation replenishes our self-control. Also, our obligations tend to drain our energy and tire us out, thus depleting our physical resources. But research shows that meditation reduces our level of fatigue, and that meditating is more effective at reducing fatigue than activities that are merely relaxing, such as listening to an audio book (Zeidan, Johnson, Diamond, et al., 2010).

Not only does meditation rebuild our resources, but it also allows us to develop new resources. Research has shown that meditation improves our ability to concentrate. In one study people were shown numerous color words written in contrasting colors (e.g., the word "blue" written in green ink) and were asked to say the color of the ink shown in each word. This task, called the Stroop task, is tough. People find it hard to concentrate on the color of the ink and tend to incorrectly blurt out the word instead. However, the researchers found that meditators make fewer errors on this task, and can correctly report the color of the ink more often than non-meditators (Moore & Malinowski, 2009). This is because meditation improves attentional resources.

Numerous other resources are impacted by introducing meditation into our lives. Meditation makes us more flexible in our thinking (Greenberg, Reiner, & Meiran, 2012), improves our ability to regulate our emotions (Vago & Silbersweig, 2012), and improves our memory (Mrazek, Franklin, Tarchin Phillips, Baird, & Schooler, 2013). There is even evidence that meditation slightly increases our level of intelligence (Tang et al., 2007). If you want to fill the rebuild bucket, meditate.

Meditation also fills the nourish bucket. It helps us satisfy our physical needs by promoting better sleep. A study out of Canada found that after taking part in an 8-week mindfulness-based meditation program, people's sleep improved along every measure of sleep quality examined, including sleep latency, sleep duration, and sleep efficiency (Carlson & Garland, 2005). Meditation can even improve the sleep of chronic insomniacs. When people who meet the diagnostic criteria for an insomnia disorder start meditating they become less aroused at bedtime, the severity of their insomnia decreases, and the amount of time they spend awake in bed drops by about 45 minutes (Ong et al., 2014). And all these benefits can accrue quickly. Research has found that sleep quality improves after just 10 days of meditation (Hülsheger, Feinholdt, & Nübold, 2015).

Meditation also helps to satisfy our psychological needs. It helps to satisfy our need for relatedness because, as Erica learned, when we meditate and promote mindfulness, the quality of our relationships improves. Once Erica began meditating, the weekly visits to her mother's house felt less like a chore and more like precious quality time. This happens because meditation increases our ability to handle relationship stress, interact effectively with others, and increase our overall relationship satisfaction (Davis & Hayes, 2011). In fact, one review of the outcomes of meditation found that its strongest effects involve the positive changes it has on relationships (Sedlmeier et al., 2012). Meditation also satisfies our need for autonomy because it's an activity we choose voluntarily (Ivtzan et al., 2016). And it can also fulfill our need for competence because it's an activity we can continually improve at (van Hoof & Baas, 2013). Meditation is an efficient way to satisfy many of our needs.

One of the reasons meditation fosters recovery is because it helps us relax, which partially fills the unhook bucket. You will recall from our opening chapter that relaxing experiences reduce our allostatic load and allow our physiological systems to return to their baseline levels of activation. A number of studies have shown that meditation fosters relaxation by lowering our stress and anxiety levels (Shapiro, Brown, & Biegel, 2007), reducing tension (Zeidan, Johnson, Gordon, & Goolkasian, 2010) and increasing the amount of serenity we experience (van Hoof & Baas, 2013). Overall, meditation is an effective way to relax. In fact, meditation is more effective at helping us relax than many other activities we engage in to promote relaxation such as listening to a radio program (van Hoof & Baas, 2013). In order to relax people often plop on the couch and watch TV after a long day of facing their obligations. Research suggests that if we want to relax as effectively as possible it might be a better idea to grab a meditation pillow before we grab a remote control.

Although meditation helps us relax, research shows that, contrary to popular opinion, the benefits of meditation are not due only to its relaxing effects (Sedlmeier et al., 2012). One of the other reasons meditation fosters recovery is because it encourages psychological detachment. As a result, meditation completely fills the unhook bucket. Practicing mindfulness, which is cultivated by meditation, has been found by researchers to foster psychological detachment among employees (Hülsheger et al., 2014). In fact, numerous studies have shown that meditation reduces people's tendency to ruminate. In one study, Australian researchers showed that after 10 days of meditation people didn't ruminate as much, even if they had never meditated before (Chambers, Lo, & Allen, 2008).

When it comes to mentally disengaging from our obligations, meditation is more effective than relaxation. A group of American researchers trained people either to meditate or to relax and looked at the effects of the different forms of training on various outcomes, including positive mood states and detachment. They found that although both forms of training made people feel better, only meditation fostered psychological detachment (Jain et al., 2007). So, meditation fills the unhook bucket in a way that relaxation can't, and is therefore an invaluable asset for transforming our downtime into uptime.

MEDITATION AND BOOSTING

People often meditate precisely because they want to decompress and find a way to recover from the many demands placed upon them in their topsy-turvy lives. If you mediate for this reason, you won't be disappointed. Research shows that meditation is a great way to get a boost.

Psychological Well-Being

As we've seen, meditation helps us de-stress and feel more serene. One of the reasons this happens is because when we meditate, upsetting things don't upset us as much. Meditation reduces our emotional reactivity in the face of distressing events (Ortner et al., 2007). But there are other ways in which meditation promotes our psychological well-being. Research shows that meditation reduces the level of anxiety and depression we experience (Hofmann, Sawyer, Witt, & Oh, 2010). In general, meditation reduces negative mood states such as fatigue, confusion, and tension (Zeidan, Johnson, Gordon, & Goolkasian, 2010), and increases positive mood states such as contentment, joy, and pride (Fredrickson et al., 2008). When we meditate we also enjoy a higher level of self-acceptance, we feel we have more of a purpose in life, and our level of life satisfaction goes up (Fredrickson et al., 2008). Overall, meditation increases our psychological well-being (Ortner et al., 2007). Fostering well-being is one of the most common reasons people decide to start meditating, and research shows that it is an effective method for achieving this goal.

Physical Health

Meditation promotes physical health too. For example, after 5 days of meditation, when people are exposed to a stressor they produce less of the stress hormone cortisol (Tang et al., 2007). Meditation also reduces our blood pressure (Kok, Waugh, & Fredrickson, 2013), and just three sessions of meditation lowers our heart rate (Zeidan et al., 2010).

It's also beneficial for our telomeres. What are telomeres you ask? They are the caps you find at the tips of chromosomes, like the protective plastic covers at the end of shoelaces (Epel, Daubenmier, Tedlie Moskowitz, Folkman, & Blackburn, 2009). The length of our telomeres is an indication of how healthy we are. Telomeres shorten as we get older, and stressful events accelerate the rate at which they contract (Epel et al., 2009). Shorter telomeres are also associated with earlier death (Cawthon, Smith, O'Brien, Sivatchenko, & Kerber, 2003). However, research has shown that meditation prevents telomere shrinkage. Compared to people who don't meditate, those who do have longer telomeres and fewer short telomeres (Alda et al., 2016). This preventative effect is thought to occur as a result of meditation's ability to reduce the impact that stress has on us (Epel et al., 2009).

Meditation also has beneficial consequences for our immune systems. For example, after an 8-week meditation program people demonstrate a stronger immune response after receiving an influenza vaccine (Davidson et al., 2003). Improved immune system functioning has also been found among cancer patients who participated in a mindfulness meditation program (Carlson, Speca, Faris, & Patel, 2007). Researchers have suggested that meditation strengthens our immune systems because it stimulates the secretion of neurohormones that have health-promoting effects (Lee, Kim, & Ryu, 2005), and because it generates positive emotions and allows us to better regulate our behavior in the face of stress (Kok et al., 2013). Ultimately, research demonstrates that if we meditate, we are healthier (Grossman, Niemann, Schmidt, & Walach, 2004).

Enhancement

Given that meditation undermines the performance-diminishing effects of stress, and fosters the development of resources we need to handle our obligations, it serves to reason that our performance will be enhanced through meditation. Indeed, research shows that meditation improves our performance on many tasks. For starters, there is research showing that meditation makes us more creative (Colzato, Ozturk, & Hommel, 2012). After 2 weeks of meditation, undergraduate students show enhanced reading comprehension (Mrazek et al., 2013). And in a recent paper that summarized the effects of mindfulness interventions in the workplace, the authors reported that, across a wide variety of occupations, the development of mindfulness has a positive effect on job performance (Lomas et al., 2017).

Because meditation replenishes and builds attentional resources, it enhances our performance on tasks that require attention. Specifically, meditation improves our performance on tasks that involve vigilance, concentration, or dividing our attention (Chiesa, Calati, & Serretti, 2011). For example, compared to non-meditators, people who meditate on a regular basis can identify more changes in scenes depicted on a computer screen, and can do so more rapidly. They can switch their perspectives more quickly, and don't get sidetracked by distracting but erroneous information that can interfere with their performance on tasks requiring visual attention (Hodgins & Adair, 2010). In short, the training of attention that occurs during meditation leads to more effective, more flexible, and more efficient performance in tasks involving visual processing (Hodgins & Adair, 2010) as well as other tasks that draw on attentional resources.

Meditation and mindfulness also improve our decision making by making us more adaptive, less impulsive, and reducing the impact of biases that can affect our judgment (Sun, Yao, Wei, & Yu, 2015). When we meditate we become less reactive and develop an enhanced ability to focus on our tasks, allowing us to respond to situations, particularly those that are stressful, in a more constructive way (Davis & Hayes, 2011). In one study, musicians either participated in a meditation program, or didn't, and then performed solo at a concert. Among those who hadn't meditated, increased performance anxiety compromised their musical performance. However, among those who had meditated, increased anxiety did not compromise their performance (Lin, Chang, Zemon, & Midlarsky, 2008). Meditators were still able to focus on the task at hand by reperceiving and distancing themselves from their anxiety. Overall, there is a lot of evidence that meditation enhances our performance in many ways.

ADDING MEDITATION TO YOUR UPTIME

Now that you are undoubtedly convinced of the wisdom of including meditation in your uptime, let's consider how to meditate. As noted earlier, it is best to start with focused attention meditation and develop your concentration skills before advancing to open monitoring meditation. The pointers below will get you started. These recommendations are a mixture of techniques adapted from books on meditation such as Kathleen McDonald's (2015) *How to Meditate*, The Dalai Lama and Hopkins' (2002) *How to Practice*, Philip Kapleau's (1989) *The Three Pillars of Zen*, and Alan Wallace's (2006) *The Attention Revolution*. You can find the references for these books in the reference section of this chapter if you'd like to read further. Note that although you can certainly begin learning how to meditate on your own, your meditation practice will be greatly enhanced if you find a teacher to help you learn the ropes and hone your skills (McDonald, 2015).

Practicing Focused Attention Meditation

1. Decide for how long you will meditate.
2. Sit comfortably. You may choose to sit in a traditional lotus posture on the floor, which is facilitated by putting an extra cushion under your bottom, but any comfortable position will work. You can even sit in a chair or lie on your back with your head on a pillow. Be sure to keep your body comfortably straight.
3. Keep your eyes open. If you're sitting, gaze comfortably downward towards the area in front of you without focusing on anything specific. Keep your head straight.
4. Do a body scan. Start at the top of your head and continue down to your toes pausing at each body part to detect any tension. Relax that part of the body and let the tension dissolve.
5. Direct your attention to your breathing. Focus on the openings of your nostrils or the expansion and contraction of your abdomen as you breathe in and out.
6. Don't try to control your breathing. Just breathe naturally. You may find that your breaths become naturally deeper and "fuller" as your practice evolves.
7. Count each inhalation and exhalation as one breath. Count up to 10 and then start over.
8. Thoughts, sounds, and sights will enter your mind. Don't concern yourself with them. This is normal and expected. Don't get discouraged when you are distracted. Instead, be encouraged that you noticed a distraction. Anytime something distracts you just refocus on your breathing, and resume counting.
9. If you lose your count, start again at one.
10. Relax, but remain alert. You want to keep your mind sharp. Don't let it get dull. Don't daydream, drift away, or fall asleep. Don't become absentminded. Stay intensely focused and attentive.
11. Your concentration should be taut, but not tense. Focused, but not strained.
12. When your time is up, don't get up quickly. Instead, sway side to side a few times as a way of gently ending your meditation session.
13. Meditate regularly. Your ability to focus your mind takes practice. Don't be disheartened if it takes a little time. Your objective is not to be perfect. It is to improve, slowly and steadily. Over time you will find that it takes less and less effort to successfully maintain your concentration.

Practicing Open Monitoring Meditation

1. Do the same preparatory activities used in focused attention meditation (items 1–4).
2. Focus your attention on your conscious awareness, "watching" your thoughts, feelings, and reactions.
3. As you notice each content of consciousness don't hold onto it and don't try to push it away. Don't grasp at it, and don't reject it. Clinging to, or suppressing, the contents of our minds gives them power over us. Just "watching" them gives us power over them. Try to observe the contents of consciousness coming and going like waves rising and falling on a shoreline. As something arises in your mind, just mentally smile at it and let it dissolve on its own. Don't embrace it, and don't fight it.
4. Watch the contents of your consciousness with an attitude of acceptance. You should not evaluate some contents as good and others as bad. Observe all contents non-judgmentally, uncritically open to whatever arises.
5. As with focused attention meditation, your goal is not to stop all thinking. Your objective in open monitoring meditation is to simply observe and become more familiar with the contents of your own mind. Eventually, you will naturally develop the ability to distance yourself from these contents.
6. Like focused attention meditation, getting better at open monitoring meditation takes time. Don't get discouraged if you still find yourself enmeshed in your thoughts after a stint of time. Even if you simply learn to recognize the chaos of your monkey mind, you've made progress.
7. In time, as you tame your mental monkey and learn its habits, it will calm down. And when the monkey does jump to another branch you will easily notice it. As your skills evolve, reperceiving gets easier.

SUMMARY

Although meditation has esoteric roots, the scientific study of meditation focuses on its neurological underpinnings and the way it benefits us cognitively and emotionally. And research shows that meditation has significant boosting properties. As Erica, the lady who opened this chapter, learned, meditation can refresh and revitalize us, and change difficult circumstances into enjoyable ones.

Once you have achieved some success in focusing and taming your monkey mind by meditating in a quiet place, you can begin trying to achieve a heightened level of concentration anytime and anywhere—while jogging, brushing your teeth, making dinner, or performing your daily obligations (McDonald, 2015). Mindfulness is a state of consciousness, and meditation is just a scaffolding to help you achieve it (Shapiro et al., 2006). Eventually, as your skills develop, you can quickly and effortlessly attain a state of calm abiding or mindfulness whenever you need it. This means you can boost during your morning shower, while eating lunch, or during an afternoon coffee break. Enjoy the boosting power of taking control of your own mind.

Boosting Bites

Begin with focused attention meditation.

As your powers of concentration develop, move on to open monitoring meditation.

Cycle between the two forms of meditation and incorporate both into your routine.

Start with short meditation sessions, just a few times per week.

Gradually increase the duration and frequency of your meditation sessions.

Once your powers of concentration and observation improve, practice mindfulness outside of meditation sessions.

UPTIME ACTION PLAN

Step 1. Create a place to meditate. The place should be quiet and peaceful. Prepare the area by making sure you have what you need, such as pillows, possibly a chair, and a clock that can sound a gentle, non-startling alarm or play soft music.

Step 2. Determine the best times to meditate. Consider your typical weekly schedule and figure out when would be the ideal times to fit in some meditation. Make a note of the best times in the spaces below. If you have trouble finding time, schedule it for as soon as you wake up in the morning.

Step 3. Begin practicing focused attention meditation as outlined above. Feel free to learn more about this form of meditation by reading a book, watching an online video, or perusing the blog posts of experts on the topic.

Step 4. Start with 5-minute meditation sessions. As you develop your skills you will find meditating to be increasingly relaxing, enjoyable, and fulfilling and may want to extend the duration and/or frequency of your sessions.

Step 5. Once you feel that you have improved in concentrating your mind, start practicing open monitoring meditation as outlined above. Again, feel free to research the topic more fully.

Step 6. Continue extending the duration and/or frequency of your meditation sessions. Intensify your practice in accordance with what feels comfortable and natural. You may eventually find yourself meditating every day.

REFERENCES

Alda, M., Puebla-Guedea, M., Rodero, B., Demarzo, M., Monero-Marin, J., Roca, M., & Garcia-Campayo, J. (2016). Zen meditation, length of telomeres, and the role of experiential avoidance and compassion. *Mindfulness, 7*, 651–659.

Carlson, L. E., & Garland, S. N. (2005). Impact of mindfulness-based stress reduction (MBSR) on sleep, mood, stress, and fatigue symptoms of cancer outpatients. *International Journal of Behavioral Medicine, 12*, 278–285.

Carlson, L. E., Speca, M., Faris, P., & Patel, K. D. (2007). One year pre-post intervention follow-up of psychological, immune, endocrine and blood pressure outcomes of mindfulness-based stress reduction (MBSR) in breast and prostate cancer outpatients. *Brain, Behavior, and Immunity, 21*, 1038–1049.

Cawthon, R. M., Smith, K. R., O'Brien, E., Sivatchenko, A., & Kerber, R. A. (2003). Association between telomere length in blood and mortality in people aged 60 years or older. *Lancet, 361*, 393–395.

Chambers, R., Lo, B. C. Y., & Allen, N. B. (2008). The impact of intensive mindfulness training on attentional control, cognitive style, and affect. *Cognitive Therapy and Research, 32*, 303–322.

Chiesa, A., Calati, R., & Serretti, A. (2011). Does mindfulness training improve cognitive abilities? A systematic review of neuropsychological findings. *Clinical Psychology Review, 31*, 449–464.

Colzato, L. S., Ozturk, A., & Hommel, B. (2012). Meditate to create: The impact of focused-attention and open-monitoring training on convergent and divergent thinking. *Frontiers in Psychology, 3*. doi:10.3389/fpsyg.2012.00116

Dalai Lama & Hopkins, J. (2002). *How to practice: The way to a meaningful life.* New York, NY: Pocket Books.

Davidson, R. J., Kabat-Zinn, J., Schumacher, J., Rosenkranz, M., Muller, D., Santorelli, S. F., ... Sherdian, J. F. (2003). Alterations in brain and immune function produced by mindfulness meditation. *Psychosomatic Medicine, 65*, 564–570.

Davis, D. M., & Hayes, J. A. (2011). What are the benefits of mindfulness? A practice review of psychotherapy-related research. *Psychotherapy, 48*, 198–208.

Eberth, J., & Sedlmeier, P. (2012). The effects of mindfulness meditation: A meta-analysis. *Mindfulness, 3*, 174–189.

Epel, E., Daubenmier, J., Tedlie Moskowitz, J. Folkman, S., & Blackburn, E. (2009). Can meditation slow rate of cellular aging? Cognitive stress, mindfulness, and telomeres. *Annals of the New York Academy of Sciences, 1172*, 34–53.

Fox, K. C. R., Dixon, M. L., Nijeboer, S., Girn, M., Floman, J. L., Lifshitz, M., ... Christoff, K. (2016). Functional neuroanatomy of meditation: A review and meta-analysis of 78 functional neuroimaging investigations. *Neuroscience and Biobehavioral Reviews, 65*, 208–228.

Fredrickson, B. L., Cohn, M. A., Coffey, K. A., Pek, J., & Finkel, S. M. (2008). Open hearts build lives: Positive emotions, induced through loving-kindness meditation, build consequential personal resources. *Journal of Personality and Social Psychology, 95*, 1045–1062.

Friese, M., Messner, C., & Schaffner, Y. (2012). Mindfulness meditation counteracts self-control depletion. *Consciousness and Cognition, 21*, 1016–1022.

Greenberg, J., Reiner, K., & Meiran, N. (2012). "Mind the trap": Mindfulness practice reduces cognitive rigidity. *PLoS One, 7.* doi:10.1371/journal.pone.0036206

Grossman, P., Niemann, L., Schmidt, S., & Walach, H. (2004). Mindfulness-based stress reduction and health benefits: A meta-analysis. *Journal of Psychosomatic Research, 57,* 35–43.

Hagger, M., Wood, C., Stiff, C., & Chatzisarantis, N. L. D. (2010). Ego depletion and the strength model of self-control: A meta-analysis. *Psychological Bulletin, 136,* 495–525.

Hodgins, H. S., & Adair, K. C. (2010). Attentional processes and meditation. *Consciousness and Cognition, 19,* 872–878.

Hofmann, S. G., Sawyer, A. T., Witt, A. A., & Oh, D. (2010). The effects of mindfulness-based therapy on anxiety and depression: A meta-analytic review. *Journal of Consulting and Clinical Psychology, 78,* 169–183.

Hülsheger, U. R., Feinholdt, A., & Nübold, A. (2015). A low-dose mindfulness intervention and recovery from work: Effects of psychological detachment, sleep quality, and sleep duration. *Journal of Occupational and Organizational Psychology, 88,* 464–489.

Hülsheger, U. R., Lang, J. W. B., Depenbrock, F., Fehrmann, C., Zijlstra, F. R. H., & Alberts, H. J. E. M. (2014). The power of presence: The role of mindfulness at work for daily levels and change trajectories of psychological detachment and sleep quality. *Journal of Applied Psychology, 99,* 1113–1128.

Ivtzan, I., Young, T., Martman, J., Jeffrey, A., Lomas, T., Hart, R., & Eiroa-Orosa, F. J. (2016). Integrating mindfulness into positive psychology: A randomized controlled trial of an online positive mindfulness program. *Mindfulness, 7,* 1396–1407.

Jain, S., Shapiro, S., Swanick, S., Roesch, S. C., Mills, P. J., Bell, I., & Schwartz, G. E. R. (2007). A randomized controlled trial of mindfulness meditation versus relaxation training: Effects on distress, positive states of mind, rumination, and distraction. *Annals of Behavioral Medicine, 33,* 11–21.

Kapleau, P. (1989). *The three pillars of Zen.* New York, NY: Doubleday.

Kok, B. E., Waugh, C. E., & Fredrickson, B. L. (2013). Meditation and health: The search for mechanisms of action. *Social and Personality Psychology Compass, 7,* 27–39.

Lee, M. S., Kim, M. K., & Ryu, H. (2005). Qi-training (Qigong) enhanced immune functions: What is the underlying mechanism? *International Journal of Neuroscience, 115,* 1099–1104.

Lin, P., Chang, J., Zemon, V., & Midlarsky, E. (2008). Silent illumination: A study on Chan (Zen) meditation, anxiety, and musical performance quality. *Psychology of Music, 36,* 139–155.

Lippelt, D., Hommel, B., & Colzato, L. S. (2014). Focused attention, open monitoring, and loving kindness meditation: Effects on attention, conflict monitoring, and creativity—a review. *Frontiers in Psychology, 5.* doi:10.3389/fpsyg.2014.01083

Lomas, T., Medina, J. C., Ivtzan, I., Rupprecht, S., Hart, R., & Eiroa-Orosa, F. J. (2017). The impact of mindfulness on well-being and performance in the workplace: An inclusive systematic review of the empirical literature. *European Journal of Work and Organizational Psychology, 26*, 492–513.

Lutz, A., Slagter, H. A., Dunne, J. D., & Davidson, R. J. (2008). Attention regulation and monitoring in meditation. *Trends in Cognitive Sciences, 12*, 163–169.

McDonald, K. (2015). *How to meditate: A practical guide* (2nd ed.). Somerville, MA. Wisdom.

Moore, A., & Malinowski, P. (2009). Meditation, mindfulness, and cognitive flexibility. *Consciousness and Cognition, 18*, 176–186.

Morin, A. (2016, June 8). Why mindfulness is the key to performing at your peak. *Forbes*. Retrieved from https://www.forbes.com/sites/amymorin/2016/06/08/why-mindfulness-is-the-key-to-performing-at-your-peak/#2bf879e56cb3

Mrazek, M. D., Franklin, M. S., Tarchin Phillips, D., Baird, B., & Schooler, J. W. (2013). Mindfulness training improves working memory capacity and GRE performance while reducing mind wandering. *Psychological Science, 24*, 776–781.

Ong, J., Manber, R., Segal, Z., Xia, Y., Shapiro, S., & Wyatt, J. K. (2014). A randomized controlled trial of mindfulness meditation for chronic insomnia. *Sleep, 37*, 1553–1563.

Ortner, C. N. M., Kilner, S. J., & Zelazo, P. D. (2007). Mindfulness meditation and reduced emotional interference on a cognitive task. *Motivation and Emotion, 31*, 271–283.

Sedlmeier, P., Eberth, J., Schwarz, M., Zimmermann, D., Haarig, F., Jaeger, S., & Kunze, S. (2012). The psychological effects of meditation: A meta-analysis. *Psychological Bulletin, 138*, 1139–1171.

Shapiro, S. L., Brown, K. W., & Biegel, G. M. (2007). Teaching self-care to caregivers: Effects of mindfulness-based stress reduction on the mental health of therapists in training. *Training in Education in Professional Psychology, 1*, 105–115.

Shapiro, S. L., Carlson, L. E., Astin, J. A., & Freedman, B. (2006). Mechanisms of mindfulness. *Journal of Clinical Psychology, 62*, 373–386.

Sperduti, M., Martinelli, P., & Piolino, P. (2012). A neurocognitive model of meditation based on activation likelihood estimation (ALE) meta-analysis. *Consciousness and Cognition, 21*, 269–276.

Sun, S., Yao, Z., Wei, J., & Yu, R. (2015). Calm and smart? A selective review of meditation effects on decision making. *Frontiers in Psychology, 6*. doi: 10.3389/fpsyg.2015.01059

Tang, Y., Lu, Q., Geng, X., Stein, E. A., Yang, Y., & Posner, M. I. (2010). Short-term meditation induces white matter changes in the anterior cingulate. *Proceedings of the National Academy of Sciences of the United States of America, 107*, 15649–15652.

Tang, Y., Ma, Y., Wang, J., Fan, Y., Feng, S., Lu, Q., ... Posner, M. I. (2007). Short-term meditation training improves attention and self-regulation. *Proceedings of the National Academy of Sciences of the United States of America, 104*, 17152–17156.

Vago, D. R., & Silbersweig, D. A. (2012). Self-awareness, self-regulation, and self-transcendence (S-ART): A framework for understanding the neurobiological mechanisms of mindfulness. *Frontiers in Human Neuroscience, 6*. doi:10.3389/fnhum.2012.00296

van Hooff, M. L. M., & Baas, M. (2013). Recovering by means of meditation: The role of recovery experiences and intrinsic motivation. *Applied Psychology: An International Review, 62*, 185–210.

Wallace, B. A. (2006). *The Attention Revolution: Unlocking the power of the focused mind.* Somerville, MA: Wisdom.

Walsh, R., & Shapiro, S. L. (2006). The meeting of meditative disciplines and Western psychology: A mutually enriching dialogue. *American Psychologist, 61*, 227–239.

Zeidan, F., Johnson, S. K., Diamond, B. J., David, Z., & Goolkasin, P. (2010). Mindfulness meditation improves cognition: Evidence of brief mental training. *Consciousness and Cognition, 19*, 597–605.

Zeidan, F., Johnson, S. K., Gordon, N. S., & Goolkasian, P. (2010). Effects of brief and sham mindfulness meditation on mood and cardiovascular variables. *The Journal of Alternative and Complementary Medicine, 16*, 867–873.

Zeng, X., Chiu, C. P. K., Oei, T. P. S., & Leung, F. Y. K. (2015). The effect of loving-kindness meditation on positive emotions: A meta-analytic review. *Frontiers in Psychology, 6*. doi:10.3389/fpsyg.2015.01693

CHAPTER 7

FAMILY AND FRIENDS

Building Bonds That Boost

Instead of watching NFL football, Sean spends his Sunday afternoons doing power yoga with his kids. During class his 15-year-old son and 11-year-old daughter are on mats on either side of him contorting their bodies into intricate and sometimes absurd poses. And then it happens. They simultaneously glance over at one another and laugh.

"We don't have to be talking," says the 48-year-old father of three. "Just having your children in the same room, participating in something that you all enjoy and connecting at that level is really a unique opportunity."

It's those unspoken bonding moments between a father and his children that make the stresses and demands of Sean's job as a vice-president of a large shipping company melt away. At work he has hundreds of employees to manage, but at home around his wife and children he can release those responsibilities and just focus on being himself.

Family has always been top priority for Sean. He not only sets aside time to do the one-hour yoga class each Sunday, but also squeezes in time with kids during the week by setting his alarm an hour early. This extra hour allows him to make his children's breakfast and grab some quality family time before heading off to work.

"Spending time with the kids keeps you grounded and connects you with who you are as an individual. They bring purpose to my life."

Boost: The Science of Recharging Yourself in an Age of Unrelenting Demands, pp. 107–127
Copyright © 2018 by Information Age Publishing
All rights of reproduction in any form reserved.

HOW OTHER PEOPLE HELP US RECOVER

As we noted in our opening chapter, building relationships and feeling connected to other people is a fundamental human need (Baumeister & Leary, 1995). The relationships we form and nurture with others are a vital ingredient in allowing us to thrive. And the quality of our relationships has long-term effects on us. For example, if you grew up in a family with separated or divorced parents who didn't speak to each other, you're now three times more vulnerable to the common cold than people who grew up in intact families (Murphy, Cohen, Janicki-Deverts, & Doyle, 2017). Our relationships can support us, heal us, and help us recover, but only when they are of sufficient quality.

When our obligations stress us out and wear us down our friends and family can be a tremendous source of rejuvenation. And we seem to have an intuitive sense of this built into us. For example, stress makes us want to affiliate with other people. In a classic experiment in social psychology researchers told participants in a "low stress" condition that they would be participating in a benign procedure that involved receiving mild electrical shocks that felt like a little tickle. Participants in the "high stress" condition were told that they would be receiving strong electrical shocks that would be exceedingly painful, but wouldn't cause any permanent damage. Yikes! They then asked the people in both conditions whether they preferred to wait in adjoining rooms either alone or with others while the experimenters prepared the laboratory to begin the study. Compared to people in the "low stress" condition, almost twice as many people in the "high stress" condition chose to wait with other participants (Schachter, 1959). This study hinted at the fact that one of the strategies people use to cope with stress is affiliating with other people. Spending time with friends and family in our uptime can counteract the stress and pressures we face in our obligations and give us a boost.

Indeed, research shows that interacting with others during our uptime helps recharge our batteries. A German study showed that after a day of fulfilling our obligations, if we engage in social activities during our evening leisure time by, for example, dropping in on a friend, at bedtime we find ourselves in a better mood, feeling less tense and more recovered (Sonnentag, 2001). A follow-up study found that compared to employees who engage in relatively little social interaction in their leisure time, those who spend more time participating in social activities in their free time feel less burned out when they return to work (Fritz & Sonnentag, 2005). When Sean does yoga with his kids or spends time with them at breakfast it rejuvenates, refreshes, and revitalizes him.

Even very small doses of social interaction can give us a boost. For instance, micro-breaks are relatively short respites we take while engaged in our obligations (Trougakos & Hideg, 2009). Examples of micro-breaks include getting a drink at the water cooler or checking your inbox for new messages (Fritz, Lam, & Spreitzer, 2011). American researchers found that when people take micro-breaks that are social in nature by, for example, taking a few minutes to send a text to a friend, they help themselves recover and enjoy a better mood at the end of the day (Kim, Park, & Niu, 2017). Engaging in social activities gives us a boost.

FRIENDS, FAMILY, AND THE ReNU BUCKETS

Participating in social activities helps to promote recovery for a number of reasons. First, when we are leisurely hanging out with friends and family we generally don't draw on the same resources we use when facing our obligations (Sonnentag, 2001). This, of course, allows us to fill the rebuild bucket. One of the things that we can do during social activity in our leisure time, which we generally don't do during our obligation time, is play. Regardless of whether we partake in games with formal rules, wrestle with our kids, or engage in lighthearted verbal jousting with old friends, when we play it gives our obligation-related resources a rest, and relieves our stress by letting us escape from our daily grind (Van Vleet & Feeney, 2015). The laughter and playful interactions that occur when Sean does yoga with his children are a significant source of boosting.

Other people can also help us replenish and build new resources. For example, just thinking about our family members increases our self-regulation resources (Stillman, Tice, Fincham, & Lambert, 2009). And when the people we interact with give us positive feedback and validate us, it replenishes our depleted levels of self-control (Schmeichel & Vohs, 2009). Also, the support and encouragement others provide can build and rebuild our self-worth and confidence which are important resources that can help us handle stress when we return to our obligations (Pietromonaco & Collins, 2017).

Many of the benefits we derive from friends and family come from the social support they provide. Such support can enlarge the pool of resources we have available to us and compensate for resources we may lack (Halbesleben, 2006). This support can take a number of forms. The people we know can provide us with informational support by giving us advice or guidance on how to handle difficulties, emotional support by reassuring us when things are tough, esteem support by enhancing our confidence in our abilities, and tangible support by supplying us with material assistance when needed (Brock & Lawrence, 2009). The social support we get can reduce the impact of our stressful obligations by helping us find solutions to our problems, by putting the problems in perspective and making them seem less important, or by taking our minds off the problems for a while (Cohen, 2004). There is a lot of research demonstrating that social support helps us effectively deal with the stress in our lives, which promotes recovery. For example, when we have sufficient social support we experience less psychological distress and are physically healthier (Taylor, 2011).

The support we get from other people also helps to fill the nourish bucket. When we spend time, socialize, have fun, and share experiences with people on a regular basis we satisfy our need for relatedness (Mueller & Lovell, 2015). When other people encourage us, and we know that they will be there when we need them, it gives us the courage to explore new challenges independently, which satisfies our need for autonomy (Feeney & Thrush, 2010). And as we improve and become skilled at these new challenges it satisfies our need for competence (Feeney & Thrush, 2010). Research shows that a high-quality relationship with our partner even helps us sleep better (Troxel, 2010).

Other people can also help us fill the unhook bucket. When we engage in activities with others in our uptime it helps to reduce the physiological activation caused by stress, and distracts us from our obligations. For example, research shows that when we spend some of our leisure time jointly participating in activities with our romantic partners it produces relaxation and psychological detachment (Hahn, Binnewies, & Haun, 2012). In sum, our friends and family can help us fill all of the ReNU buckets on our way to getting a boost.

NOT EVERY RELATIONSHIP WILL HELP YOU BOOST

Research shows that there are two overall aspects of our relationships that we benefit from. The first is the sheer size of our network. Recall from the chapter on volunteering that the more roles we occupy, the better off we are psychologically and physically. More generally, the more socially integrated we are, meaning the more activities we engage in with others and the more groups we belong to, the better off we are (Cohen, 2004). For example, the more groups we belong to the more self-esteem we have (Jetten et al., 2015). So, expanding the number of activities and groups we participate in during our uptime can help to give us a boost.

The second important aspect of our relationships involves something we've already discussed—the stress-reducing effect of the social support we receive from other people (Cohen, 2004). However, not everyone we know gives us support that helps to reduce our stress levels. Each of us has people in our network who add to our stress and drain us. We can all think of spending leisure time with a continually overbearing father, a friend who is always jealous, or a constantly critical partner who make feeling rejuvenated virtually impossible. But at least such people are consistent in how they behave. Friends and family who are unpredictable in their level of support are particularly stressful to us. One day they are kind and encouraging, and the next day they are harsh and unsupportive. These erratic, volatile relationships, called ambivalent ties, can sometimes be constructive but at other times are upsetting (Uchino, Holt-Lunstad, Uno, & Flinders, 2001). We all know such people. Most of the people in our networks are supportive, but close to half can be ambivalent (Campo et al., 2009). Research shows that having a high proportion of ambivalent ties in our social networks is especially unhealthy, even compared to relationships that are primarily negative (Uchino, 2013). For example, remember the telomeres we discussed in the last chapter and how their length is an indication of health? Research has shown that when women have a lot of ambivalent ties in their social network they have shorter telomeres (Uchino et al., 2012). Because they are unpredictable, ambivalent relationships cause us stress and offer ineffective social support (Uchino et al., 2001). In general, poor quality relationships make it harder for us to recover (Feeney & Collins, 2015). To transform our downtime into uptime it is important that we spend our leisure time with people who give us energy instead of depleting it.

Spending time with the wrong people will leave the ReNU buckets drained. For example, if we fight with our partners in our leisure time it forces us to continue to draw on the same self-regulation resources we use during our obligation time, which hinders recovery. Research shows that when we have conflicts with our partners in our leisure time it inhibits boosting and leaves us feeling tired and exhausted when we return to our obligations (Hahn et al., 2012). If your partner is in a cranky mood, maybe it's a good idea to go to a movie with a friend instead of hanging out at home.

Similarly, when we spend leisure time with people who are dismissive or critical of us, or make us feel inadequate, it leaves our nourish bucket depleted. When people are a source of strain instead of support we do not feel close to them, and they weaken our motivation, curtail how hard we strive to attain goals, and thwart our development, thus undermining our psychological needs for relatedness, autonomy and competence (Feeney & Collins, 2015).

Others can also prevent us from filling the unhook bucket. Clearly, spending our leisure time with difficult, demanding, or disparaging people doesn't help us relax, because we have to be on guard. When others are taxing, we are definitely not relaxing. Other people can also prevent us from psychologically detaching. For example, when our partners fail to establish boundaries between work and leisure time, it compromises our own psychological detachment (Hahn & Dormann, 2013). When our partners, family members, or friends think about and talk to us about their obligations during our leisure time they draw us into doing the same thing. This produces what is called co-rumination, which is when two people mutually encourage each other to excessively discuss their problems (Rose, 2002). Just like individual rumination, co-rumination prevents us from mentally disengaging from our obligations. It also increases how stressed and burned-out we feel (Boren, 2014). If your friends and family want to talk about their obligations during their leisure time, that's their business. However, you can encourage them to stop, or choose to spend your uptime with other people who are more conducive to boosting.

We want to spend our uptime with people who let us unwind, make us feel good, and nurture us. Research on friendship has shown that high-quality friendships have some common qualities. Good friends are supportive, trustworthy and genuine, emotionally available, share common interests with us, help us out when needed, and are easy and enjoyable to be around (Hall, 2012). Ideal family members have similar characteristics. People who help us recover are responsive, meaning they make us feel understood, validated, and cared for (Reis & Clark, 2013). It is only when we spend our free time in the company of people with these qualities that our ReNU buckets get filled and we get a boost. Do these qualities characterize the people with whom you tend to spend your leisure time?

Psychological Well-Being

Spending uptime with responsive, supportive people enhances our psychological well-being. In fact, high-quality relationships are essential for promoting well-being (Dunkel Schetter, 2017). For example, enjoying supportive ties with others leads to higher satisfaction with life and reduces depression (Uchino et al., 2001). When people offer us responsive support it reduces the negative emotions produced by stress, such as anger, and increases positive emotions, such as gratitude and love (Pietromonaco & Collins, 2017). Effective social support also speeds up how quickly we recover from stress (Feeney & Collins, 2017). Spending quality leisure time absorbed in activities with our partners makes us feel more vigorous and jovial (Hahn et al., 2012). Because good relationships help us cope with stress and promote our growth they allow us to thrive by fostering happiness, making us feel that our lives have purpose, enhancing our psychological well-being, and promoting social well-being in the form of deep, meaningful connections (Feeney & Collins, 2017).

Research shows that other people intensify our experiences. For example, chocolate tastes better when we eat it with someone else (Boothby, Clark, & Bargh, 2014), and fun is more fun when experienced with other people

(Reis, O'Keefe, & Lane, 2017). So, one of the reasons friends and family give us a boost is because when we share positive uptime experiences with them it intensifies the positive emotions, happiness, and life satisfaction those experiences produce (Lambert et al., 2012). However, this intensification only happens when we share experiences with people we feel close to (Boothby, Smith, Clark, & Bargh, 2016). This little detail gives us another clue about the specific people in our network who might be best at helping us recover from our obligations.

Physical Health

There is an overwhelming amount of evidence that high-quality relationships make us physically healthy. Consider the research on romantic partners. Good intimate relationships protect us from heart disease (Smith & Baucom, 2017). When the quality of our marriages is high we enjoy better health, and live longer (Robles, Slatcher, Trombello, & McGinn, 2014). And when we enjoy an increase in intimacy with our partners one day, we have fewer health complaints the following day, including less back pain, headaches, or upset stomachs (Stadler, Snyder, Horn, Shrout, & Bolger, 2012).

Friends and acquaintances matter too. When we face conflict or stress, having adequate social support protects us from getting sick. The same protective effect occurs when we get lots of hugs from the people we know (Cohen, Janicki-Deverts, Turner, & Doyle, 2015). Also, research has shown that managers who have social networks with supportive friends that allow them to openly discuss their concerns, have lower levels of unhealthy blood lipids, such as low-density lipoprotein, otherwise known as "the bad cholesterol" (Bernin, Theorell, & Sandberg, 2001). Social support also influences our cardiovascular system by lowering our blood pressure. It affects our neuroendocrine function by reducing the amount of the stress hormone cortisol coursing through our bodies. And, as suggested above, it enhances our immune system (Uchino, 2006). Not only are relationships necessary for physical health, the quality of our connections with others is actually a better predictor of how long we will live than whether we smoke or drink alcohol (Holt-Lunstad, Robles, & Sbarra, 2017)!

Enhancement

Friends and family also help us perform more effectively when we return to our weekly tasks. A study in Germany found that compared to employees who engage in less social activity during their leisure time on weekends, those who participate in more social activity have higher job performance when they return to work (Fritz & Sonnentag, 2005). This occurs partly because when we have a supportive, responsive network our confidence improves, we believe we are more likely to achieve our goals, and therefore accept challenges that can lead to higher performance (Feeney, 2004). Indeed, research shows that when our spouses are supportive we make more progress in achieving our goals (Jakubiak & Feeney, 2016).

In the United Kingdom, researchers studied high-level golfers and found that not only was social support related to enhanced golf performance, but that it also eliminated the harmful effect of stress on performance. When people are highly stressed their performance tends to drop off. However, when the golfers in this study reported receiving a lot of social support their performance wasn't compromised, even when they were highly stressed by upcoming competitions (Rees & Freeman, 2009).

The people we know enhance us in other ways too. For example, the informational support we get from our network makes us more creative (Madjar, 2008). Friends and family also make our tasks seem less onerous. In one study when people were asked to guess how steep a hill was, their estimates of the gradient were lower when they guessed in the presence of a close friend (Schnall, Harber, Stefanucci, & Proffitt, 2008). Essentially, having a friend beside them made people think it would be easier to climb the hill. Overall, our friends and family can help us perform better and make tasks seem less challenging.

IS SOCIALIZING THE RIGHT CHOICE?

Spending time with friends and family only produces boosting benefits when we want to socialize. If we have just spent all day interacting with demanding clients, customers, or colleagues, we may want to just spend some time alone. A number of studies have shown that if we are required to socialize when we don't really want to, or don't enjoy the time we're spending with others, it does not help us recover. One study found that when flight attendants spend their evening leisure time engaged in social activities they have higher levels of depression at bedtime (Sonnentag & Natter, 2004). Apparently, socializing in the evening can interfere with recuperation among people who have already spent their whole day inter-acting with others. Research has also shown that socializing on our lunch breaks only reduces our fatigue if we voluntarily choose to socialize. When we don't have a choice, socializing on lunch breaks make us more tired (Trougakos, Hideg, Cheng, & Beal, 2014). Recovery is promoted when we're happy while engaged in social activities in our leisure time. If we're not happy while socializing, recovery is compromised (Oerlemans, Bakker,

& Demerouti, 2014). In essence, interacting with people helps us recover if we want to be around them and enjoy their company. However, if the need for affiliation part of our nourish bucket is already full, or we feel that other ReNU buckets require attention, socializing in our leisure time may further deplete us. When this is the case, we may be better off spending some time alone.

SOLITUDE AND BOOSTING

As we've discussed, spending time with others is a fundamental human need. But an excessive amount of social activity can be oppressive (Long, Seburn, Averill, & More, 2003). Sometimes we just need to spend some time by ourselves. Solitude is an opportunity for self-renewal (Long et al., 2003). When we are alone we can unwind, decompress, and take a break from the demands placed upon us (Cacioppo, Grippo, London, Goossens, & Cacioppo, 2015).

Solitude is often confused with loneliness, and indeed, when solitude is unwanted and produces loneliness, it is unhealthy (Cacioppo et al., 2015). However, when solitude is freely and willingly chosen it can be emancipatory, which is why so many people crave more time alone (Long & Averill, 2003). Voluntary solitude liberates us not only from our obligations but also from the social conventions that demand our attention and can drain our resources. When we're alone we can let our minds wander and allow ourselves to relax and detach completely from our obligations and other people. In solitude we can do whatever we like, which satisfies our need for autonomy. Solitude can also promote problem solving and creativity (Long et al., 2003).

In the chapter on the boosting benefits of nature, we learned that natural environments are restorative. A handful of studies have shown that the recuperative power of such environments is enhanced when we are by ourselves. For example, in one study people were asked to envision themselves in a forest either alone or with a friend and rate the recuperative value of the experience. People rated the recuperative value as higher when they envisioned themselves alone, as long as they felt safe in the environment (Staats & Hartig, 2004). Similarly, in another study researchers found that people felt more revitalized when they walked through a park alone, compared to when they walked with a friend (Johansson, Hartig, & Staats, 2011). These studies highlight one way in which other people do not intensify our experiences. Other people can't intensify solitude.

People differ in their preference for solitude (Burger, 1995). For some people being alone is bliss. For others, isolation is intolerable torture. But for most people, occasional, voluntary solitude offers a refreshing escape from daily demands that makes a valuable contribution toward getting a boost. What are your ReNU buckets telling you? Could you use some social activity, or might you prefer to have some time to yourself?

FURRY FRIENDS

Friends and family can help us feel rejuvenated, but there is one final group we should consider in our effort to understand how relationships give us a boost—animals. For many people, dogs, cats, horses and other beasts are a source of tremendous affection, companionship, and recovery. Although there are still many unanswered research questions when it comes to human-animal interactions, there is evidence that our relationships with our pets can give us a boost (Herzog, 2011).

Pets help us recover from stress. A number of studies have shown that stroking a pet decreases our blood pressure and heart rate (Wells, 2009). In fact, sometimes pets are better at helping us deal with stress than humans are. American researchers measured the heart rate and blood pressure of pet owners participating in stressful tasks with either their pet, friend, or spouse in the room with them. Compared to when just their friends or spouses were in the room, people's cardiovascular systems reacted less to the stressful tasks, and recovered faster, when their pets were with them (Allen, Blascovich, & Mendes, 2002). So, if you have had a stressful day, you might want to hug your dog before you kiss your spouse.

Our relationships with our pets can also increase our life satisfaction, happiness, and reduce the amount of negative emotions we experience (El-Alayli, Lystad, Webb, Hollingsworth, & Ciolli, 2006). In a paper that summarized the benefits of animals on human health and well-being, Deborah Wells from the Animal Behavior Center at Queen's University Belfast in Ireland explained that pets can increase our resources by, for example, boosting our self-esteem. Taking care of pets can help to satisfy our psychological needs by promoting feelings of autonomy and competence. They can also help to satisfy our need for relatedness through the close bonds we develop with them, but can additionally stimulate social interaction by, for example, serving as a conversation starter while being taken for a walk or resting with us in a park. In addition to their effect on our positive emotions, pets can enhance our psychological well-being by reducing negative states such as loneliness and depression. Our furry friends also make us healthy. Research has shown that people who have pets visit the doctor less frequently, have lower risk factors for coronary heart disease, and have a higher likelihood of survival after a heart attack.

It might seem a little odd, but our pets can actually provide us with social support. Our furry friends are non-judgmental, and are always there for us when we need them (Wells, 2009). In fact, when we crave totally positive interactions, pets can be the source of social support we prefer (Allen, 2003). Perhaps there is a reason we call a dog man's best friend. At the very least, it's valuable to know that when we try to recover from the stress of our obligations, humans are not the only species we can turn to for help.

SUMMARY

The relationships we have with others offer us an opportunity to refresh, recharge and reinvigorate ourselves. The structure of our social networks and the social support we get from others can fill all of the ReNU buckets and give us a boost. It is important to note, however, that not everyone in our network provides us with the same level of support, and some people will deplete us further instead of helping us recover. As a result, different people can be more or less helpful in providing us with an opportunity to boost. Also, despite the benefits of socializing, sometimes what we need the most is some time alone to collect our thoughts, decompress, and refuel. Well, maybe not completely alone. Our pets are an additional source of social support that can successfully help us recover from our obligations. Spending time engaged with them is another effective way to transform our downtime into uptime.

Boosting Bites

Family and friends can provide us with various kinds of resources that can help us boost—informational, emotional, esteem, and tangible resources.

The more socially integrated we are, the better off we are.

Ambivalent ties are particularly stressful.

Socializing only offers us boosting benefits when we desire and enjoy being with others.

Solitude is an effective way to recharge our batteries.

Pets can provide us with social support and help rejuvenate us.

UPTIME ACTION PLAN

Step 1. Assess how extensive your social network is. The size of our social networks affects how well we can boost. Sometimes we don't have people in our existing network who "get us" and can offer adequate support. For example, to receive adequate support and help her boost, a teenage, single mom may need to socialize with other similar mothers who won't judge or patronize her (Gottlieb, 2000). In the space below indicate the various formal and informal groups you belong to and the diverse sets of people with whom you spend your leisure time. Your goal is to get a sense of how varied your social network is.

_____

_____

_____

_____

_____

_____

_____

_____

Step 2. Examine the results of Step 1. If that step leads you to believe that you would benefit from interacting with an enlarged network of contacts, consider expanding your network. What new groups, individuals, or activities might help you associate with people who can help you boost? Do a web search on people with similar interests, concerns, or obligations as you and consider if there are any online groups you might want to join. The research on the benefits of online social networks is still inconclusive, however there is evidence that they can produce the same advantages as off-line social networks (Holt-Lunstad & Smith, 2012). In the space below write down new groups, individuals, or activities you might want to include in your network. Then, initiate contact.

_____

_____

_____

_____

_____

_____

Step 3. Analyze the quality of your existing relationships. In the space below write down the 10 people with whom you spend most of your leisure time. In your head, assess whether your interactions with each of them is mostly positive, mostly negative, or ambivalent, meaning they are sometimes supportive but frequently upsetting. We recommend doing this second part in your head to avoid the possibility of someone finding your written assessment and being insulted.

Name	Positive	Negative	Ambivalent

When you find yourself needing a boost, spend less of your leisure time with people with whom you have a negative or ambivalent relationship.

Step 4. One of the principles of effective social support is the matching hypothesis, which refers to the fact that we find the various forms of social support most beneficial when the resources provided by the support match the demands we are facing (Cutrona & Russell, 1990). For example, when we feel like we need to be comforted, emotional support is ideal, and when we need to figure out how to solve a problem, informational support is best. Consider the various forms of social support below and indicate in the table who in your existing network you can count on to provide you the different forms of support.

Informational Support: When people give us advice, information, news, guidance, or suggestions

Emotional Support: When people comfort us, or help us feel secure in times of distress

Esteem Support: When people make us feel confident that we can handle and solve problems

Tangible Support: When people give us direct or indirect instrumental help (e.g., moving)

Informational	Emotional	Esteem	Tangible	Name

Your objective in this analysis is not to try to maximize the quality of your leisure time by only socializing with people who are best at providing the resources you seek. The reason for this is twofold: First, even minimal amounts of support are beneficial to us, so there is no need to try to maximize the level of support we get from others (Shor, Roelfs, & Yogev, 2013). And second, research shows that such maximizing efforts are detrimental to well-being (Newman, Schug, Yuki, Yamada, & Nezlek, 2017). Rather, you simply want to put yourself in a position to make more informed decisions about who you might elect to spend your leisure time with given the particular pressures of your obligations at any given time. Who tends to give you the kind of support you need today?

REFERENCES

Allen, K. (2003). Are pets a healthy pleasure? The influence of pets on blood pressure. *Current Directions in Psychological Science, 12*, 236–239.

Allen, K., Blascovich, J., & Mendes, W. B. (2002). Cardiovascular reactivity and the presence of pets, friends, and spouses: The truth about cats and dogs. *Psychosomatic Medicine, 64*, 727–739.

Baumeister, R. F., & Leary, M. R. (1995). The need to belong: Desire for interpersonal attachments as a fundamental human motivation. *Psychological Bulletin, 117*, 497–529.

Bernin, P., Theorell, T., & Sandberg, C. G. (2001). Biological correlates of social support and pressure at work in managers. *Integrative Physiological and Behavioral Science, 36*, 121–136.

Boothby, E. J., Clark, M. S., & Bargh, J. A. (2014). Shared experiences are amplified. *Psychological Science, 25*, 2209–2216.

Boothby, E. J., Smith, L. K., Clark, M. S., & Bargh, J. A. (2016). Psychological distance moderates the amplification of shared experience. *Personality and Social Psychology Bulletin, 42*, 1431–1444.

Boren, J. P. (2014). The relationships between co-rumination, social support, stress, and burnout among working adults. *Management Communication Quarterly, 28*, 3–25.

Brock, R. L., & Lawrence, E. (2009). Too much of a good thing: Underprovision versus overprovision of partner support. *Journal of Family Psychology, 23*, 181–192.

Burger, J. M. (1995). Individual differences in preference for solitude. *Journal of Research in Personality, 29*, 85–108.

Cacioppo, S., Grippo, A. J., London, S., Goossens, L., & Cacioppo, J. T. (2015). Loneliness: Clinical import and interventions. *Perspectives on Psychological Science, 10*, 238–249.

Campo, R. A., Uchino, B. N., Vaughn, A., Reblin, M., Smith, T. W., & Holt-Lunstad, J. (2009). The assessment of positivity and negativity in social networks: The reliability and validity of the social relationships index. *Journal of Community Psychology, 37*, 471–486.

Cohen, S. (2004). Social relationships and health. *American Psychologist, 59*, 676–684.

Cohen, S., Janicki-Deverts, D., Turner, R. B., & Doyle, W. J. (2015). Does hugging provide stress-buffering social support? A study of susceptibility to upper respiratory infection and illness. *Psychological Science, 26*, 135–147.

Cutrona, C. E., & Russell, D. (1990). Type of social support and specific stress: Toward a theory of optimal matching. In I. G. Sarason, B. R. Sarason, & G. R. Pierce (Eds.), *Social support: An interactional view* (pp. 319–366). New York, NY: Wiley.

Dunkel Schetter, C. (2017). Moving research on health and close relationships forward: A challenge and an obligation: Introduction to the special issue. *American Psychologist, 72*, 511–516.

El-Alayli, A., Lystad, A. L., Webb, S. R., Hollingsworth, S. L., & Ciolli, J. L. (2006). Reigning cat and dogs: A pet-enhancement bias and its link to pet attachment, pet-self similarity, self-enhancement, and well-being. *Basic and Applied Social Psychology, 28*, 131–143.

Feeney, B. C. (2004). A secure base: Responsive support of goal strivings and exploration in adult intimate relationships. *Journal of Personality and Social Psychology, 87*, 631–648.

Feeney, B. C., & Collins, N. L. (2015). A new look at social support: A theoretical perspective on thriving through relationships. *Personality and Social Psychology Review, 19*, 113–147.

Feeney, B. C., & Thrush, R. L. (2010). Relationship influences on exploration in adulthood: The characteristics and function of a secure base. *Journal of Personality and Social Psychology, 98*, 57–76.

Fritz, C., Lam, C. F., & Spreitzer, G. M. (2011). It's the little things that matter: An examination of knowledge workers' energy management. *Academy of Management Perspectives, 25*, 28–39.

Fritz, C., & Sonnentag, S. (2005). Recovery, health, and job performance: Effects of weekend experiences. *Journal of Occupational Health Psychology, 10*, 187–199.

Gottlieb, B. H. (2000). Selecting and planning support interventions. In S. Cohen, L. G. Underwood, & B. H. Gottlieb (Eds.), *Social support measurement and interventions: A guide for health and social scientists* (pp. 195–220). New York, NY: Oxford University Press.

Hahn, V. C., Binnewies, C., & Haun, S. (2012). The role of partners for employees' recovery during the weekend. *Journal of Vocational Behavior, 80*, 288–298.

Hahn, V. C., & Dormann, C. (2013). The role of partners and children for employees' psychological detachment from work and well-being. *Journal of Applied Psychology, 98*, 26–36.

Halbesleben, J. R. B. (2006). Sources of social support and burnout: A meta-analytic test of the Conservation of Resources Model. *Journal of Applied Psychology, 91*, 1134–1145.

Hall, J. A. (2012). Friendship standards: The dimensions of ideal expectations. *Journal of Social and Personal Relationships. 29*, 884–907.

Herzog, H. (2011). The impact of pets on human health and psychological well-being: Fact, fiction or hypothesis? *Current Directions in Psychological Science, 20*, 236–239.

Holt-Lunstad, J., & Smith, T. B. (2012). Social relationships and mortality. *Social and Personality Psychology Compass, 6*, 41–53.

Holt-Lunstad, J., Robles, T. F., & Sbarra, D. A. (2017). Advancing social connection as a public health priority in the United States. *American Psychologist, 72*, 517–530.

Jakubiak, B. K., & Feeney, B. C. (2016). Daily goal progress is facilitated by spousal support and promotes psychological, physical, and relational well-being throughout adulthood. *Journal of Personality and Social Psychology, 111*, 317–340.

Jetten, J., Branscombe, N. R., Haslam, A., Haslam, C., Cruwys, T., Jones, J., ... Zhang, A. (2015). Having a lot of a good thing: Multiple important group memberships as a source of self-esteem. *PLOS ONE.* doi:10.1371/journal.pone.0124609

Johansson, M., Hartig, T., & Staats, H. (2011). Psychological benefits of walking: Moderation by company and outdoor environment. *Applied Psychology: Health and Well-Being, 3*, 261–280.

Kim, S., Park, Y., & Niu, Q. (2017). Micro-break activities at work to recover from daily work demands. *Journal of Organizational Behavior, 38*, 28–44.

Lambert, N. M., Gwinn, A. M., Baumeister, R. F., Strachman, A., Washburn, I. J., Gable, S. L., & Fincham, F. D. (2012). A boost to positive affect: The perks of sharing positive experiences. *Journal of Social and Personal Relationships, 30*, 24–43.

Long, C. R., & Averill, J. R. (2003). Solitude: An exploration of benefits of being alone. *Journal for the Theory of Social Behavior, 33*, 21–44.

Long, C. R., Seburn, M., Averill, J. R., & More, T. A. (2003). Solitude experiences: Varieties, settings, and individual differences. *Personality and Social Psychology Bulletin, 29*, 578–583.

Madjar, N. (2008). Emotional and informational support from different sources and employee creativity. *Journal of Occupational and Organizational Psychology, 81*, 83–100.

Mueller, M. B., & Lovell, G. P. (2015). Theoretical constituents of relatedness need satisfaction in senior executives. *Human Resource Development Quarterly, 26*, 209–229.

Murphy, M. M., Cohen, S., Janicki-Deverts, D., & Doyle, W. J. (2017). Offspring of parents who were separated and not speaking to one another have reduced resistance to the common cold. *Proceedings of the National Academy of Sciences of the United States of America, 114*, 6515–6520.

Newman, D. B., Schug, J., Yuki, M., Yamada, J., & Nezlek, J. B. (2017). The negative consequences of maximizing in friendship selection. *Journal of Personality and Social Psychology*. Advance online publication. doi:10.1037/pspp0000141

Oerlemans, W. G. M., Bakker, A. B., & Demerouti, E. (2014). How feeling happy during off-job activities helps successful recovery from work: A day reconstruction study. *Work & Stress, 28*, 198–216.

Pietromonaco, P. R., & Collins, N. L. (2017). Interpersonal mechanisms linking close relationships to health. *American Psychologist, 72*, 531–542.

Rees, T., & Freeman, P. (2009). Social support moderates the relationship between stressors and task performance through self-efficacy. *Journal of Social and Clinical Psychology, 28*, 244–263.

Reis, H. T., & Clark, M. S. (2013). Responsiveness. In J. Simpson & L. Campbell (Eds.), *The Oxford handbook of close relationships* (pp. 400–423). Oxford, UK: Oxford University Press.

Reis, H. T., O'Keefe, S. D., & Lane, R. (2017). Fun is more fun when others are involved. The *Journal of Positive Psychology, 12*, 547–557.

Robles, T. F., Slatcher, R. B., Trombello, J. M., & McGinn, M. M. (2014). Marital quality and health: A meta-analytic review. *Psychological Bulletin, 140*, 140v187.

Rose, A. J. (2002). Co-rumination in the friendships of girls and boys. *Child Development, 73*, 1830–1843.

Schachter, S. (1959). *The psychology of affiliation*. Stanford, CA: Stanford University Press.

Schmeichel, B. J., & Vohs, K. (2009). Self-affirmation and self-control: Affirming core values counteracts ego depletion. *Journal of Personality and Social Psychology, 96*, 770–782.

Schnall, S., Harber, K. D., Stefanucci, J. K., & Proffitt, D. R. (2008). Social support and the perception of geographical slant. *Journal of Experimental Social Psychology, 44*, 1246–1255.

Shor, E., Roelfs, D. J., & Yogev, T. (2013). The strength of family ties: A meta-analysis and meta-regression of self-reported social support and mortality. *Social Networks, 35*, 626–638.

Smith, T. W., & Baucom, B. R. W. (2017). Intimate relationships, individual adjustment, and coronary heart disease: Implications of overlapping associations in psychosocial risk. *American Psychologist, 72*, 578–589.

Sonnentag, S. (2001). Work, recovery activities, and individual well-being: A diary study. *Journal of Occupational and Health Psychology, 6*, 196–210.

Sonnentag, S., & Natter, E. (2004). Flight attendants' daily recovery from work: Is there no place like home? *International Journal of Stress Management, 11*, 366–391.

Staats, H., & Hartig, T. (2004). Alone of with a friend: A social context for psychological restoration and environmental preferences. *Journal of Environmental Psychology, 24*, 199–211.

Stadler, G., Snyder, K. A., Horn, A. B., Shrout, P. E., & Bolger, N. P. (2012). Close relationships and health in daily life: A review and empirical data on intimacy and somatic symptoms. *Psychosomatic Medicine, 74*, 398–409.

Stillman, T. F., Tice, D. M., Fincham, F. D., & Lambert, N. M. (2009). The psychological presence of family improves self-control. *Journal of Social and Clinical Psychology, 28*, 498–529.

Taylor, S. E. (2011). Social support: A review. In H. S. Friedman (Ed.), *The Oxford Handbook of Health Psychology* (pp. 189–214). Oxford, UK: Oxford University Press.

Trougakos, J. P., & Hideg, I. (2009). Momentary work recovery: The role of within-day work breaks. In S. Sonnentag, P. L. Perreré, & D. C. Ganster (Eds.), *Current perspectives on job stress recovery* (pp. 37–84). Bingley, UK: Emerald.

Trougakos, J. P., Hideg, I., Cheng, B., & Beal, D. J. (2014). Lunch breaks unpacked: The role of autonomy as a moderator of recovery during lunch. *Academy of Management Journal, 57*, 405–421.

Troxel, W. M. (2010). It's more than sex: Exploring the dyadic nature of sleep and implications for health. *Psychosomatic Medicine, 72*, 578–586.

Uchino, B. N. (2006). Social support and health: A review of physiological processes potentially underlying links to disease outcomes. *Journal of Behavioral Medicine, 29*, 377–387.

Uchino, B. N. (2013). Understanding the links between social ties and health: On building stronger bridges with relationship science. *Journal of Social and Personal Relationships, 30*, 155–162.

Uchino, B. N., Cawthon, R. M., Smith, T. W., Light, K. C., McKenzie, J., Carlisle, M., … Bowen, K. (2012). Social relationships and health: Is feeling positive, negative, or both (ambivalent) about your social ties related to telomeres? *Health Psychology, 31*, 789–796.

Uchino, B. N., Holt-Lunstad, J., Uno, D., & Flinders, J. B. (2001). Heterogeneity in the social networks of young and older adults: Prediction of mental health and cardiovascular reactivity during acute stress. *Journal of Behavioral Medicine, 24*, 361–382.

Van Vleet, M., & Feeney, B. C. (2015). Play behavior and playfulness in adulthood. *Social and Personality Psychology Compass, 9*, 630–643.

Wells, D. L. (2009). The effect of animals on human health and well-being. *Journal of Social Issues, 65*, 523–543.

CHAPTER 8

EXERCISE

How Movement Makes
You Feel Marvelous

It was the morning of Emily's (not her real name) wedding day but before she could walk down the aisle in the church she felt compelled to jog along the trail in the park.

"I had to go for a run," says the 38-year-old. "Whenever there is a big event, I make sure to go for a run beforehand. It's not something I fit in, it's a requirement."

For this product and solutions manager and mother of three, exercise is the secret to her success.

It gives her an edge when it comes to work by helping to clear her mind, kick-start her creativity and heighten her focus. When Emily has a problem to tackle or a presentation to prepare for, she laces up her running shoes and hits the trails.

"I find I do my best problem solving while I run," she says. "When I get back, I grab a paper and pen and jot it all down. I feel organized and ready to go."

Running also helps her to re-energize and improves her mood when she is feeling tired and stressed.

"When I am at my busiest is when I need exercise the most."

Emily's life is often hectic with almost every minute of the day spoken for. However, she still manages to weave exercise into her daily regime. When she isn't running, Emily is doing yoga during her lunch break,

---

playing ultimate Frisbee with her husband in the evenings, joining her kids on bike rides on weekends and coaching their sports teams. It sounds exhausting, but incorporating bouts of exercise into her routine is how she is able to lead such a full life.

WE NEED EXERCISE

We can make a strong argument that exercise is a fundamental human need. If we think of needs as conditions that promote health and well-being when satisfied, and when not satisfied lead to sickness and ill-being, exercise fits the bill (Ryan & Deci, 2000). When we exercise we feel better physically and mentally, and when we don't exercise we not only miss out on these positive outcomes, but suffer completely opposite outcomes. Exercise is necessary for us to flourish (Bloodworth, McNamee, & Bailey, 2012). Emily doesn't run, throw frisbees, and assume the downward dog pose because she has to. She does it because it helps her live better, enhancing her performance and improving her mood. It helps her boost.

The American Heart Association recommends at least 30 minutes of moderate-intensity aerobic exercise a minimum of 5 days a week, or at least 25 minutes of vigorous aerobic activity a minimum of 3 days a week, in addition to muscle strengthening activity twice a week (American Heart Association, 2016). However, many people don't get enough exercise. According to the World Health Organization, about a quarter of adults are insufficiently active, and this level of inactivity is one of the leading causes of premature death (World Health Organization, 2017).

One of the reasons inactivity is associated with mortality is because of the direct relationships between exercise and physical health. The Centers for Disease Control and Prevention (2015) notes that physical activity reduces our risk of cardiovascular disease, type 2 diabetes, metabolic syndrome, and both colon and breast cancer. However, another reason exercise helps us live longer is because it counteracts the effects of stress and helps us recover from our obligations. By helping us fill the ReNU buckets, physical activities like swimming, jogging, and mountain climbing reduce our allostatic load and prevent the long-term negative consequences of stress, including premature death.

Research shows that exercise gives us a boost. A study of Dutch teachers found that when the teachers participated in physical activities, like sports or cycling, during their evening leisure time, they felt more recovered at bedtime (Sonnentag, 2001). Our obligations tire us out, but research shows that exercise revitalizes us and makes us feel less tired. In one German study researchers asked participants to rate their mood after participating in physical activities. They found that even low intensity activities, like going for a walk, made people feel less fatigued (Kanning & Schlicht, 2010). Another study in Germany found that as long as employees get enough sleep, exercise on one day makes them feel less exhausted the following day (Nägel & Sonnentag, 2013). As part of a U.K. study, researchers asked employees who exercise on their lunch breaks, about the benefits they get from it. The employees reported that it gives them a break from their obligations and re-energizes them. One employee said that "doing exercise at lunchtime just gives me a sense of feeling rejuvenated for the afternoon" (Coulson, McKenna, & Field, 2008, p. 189). Similarly, when we participate in physical activities like sports, or dancing, or just taking a stroll in the evening, we feel more vigorous when we wake up the next morning (ten Brumelhuis & Bakker, 2012). Overall, the research is clear. Physical activity helps to recharge our batteries and gives us a boost.

DON'T OVERREACT

Exercise has a way of calming the body and mind, which allows us to handle our obligations better. In the British study cited above, when people were asked about how exercising on their lunch breaks affected them at work one respondent said that exercise "makes a problem that you may have had in work, or whatever, beforehand seem less of a problem when you get back" (Coulson et al., 2008, p. 188).

Indeed, one of the reasons exercise helps us boost is because it improves our ability to handle the stress caused by our obligations. For example, caring for a sick or debilitated relative can be stressful and take a lot out of us. In fact, research shows that compared to people who don't care for others, those who serve as caregivers for elderly relatives suffer higher levels of depression and stress, and have lower levels of well-being and physical health (Pinquart & Sörensen, 2003). Exercise can help to improve this state of affairs. In one U.S. study, wives caring for husbands with dementia participated in a 6-month exercise program designed to help ease their burden of care. The program involved customized exercise goals that took into account the women's level of fitness, and they were encouraged to set goals of at least 30 minutes of low-to-moderate aerobic exercise, a minimum of three times per week. Compared to a control group that was simply given written materials about physical activity, at the end of the 6-month intervention the caregivers who participated in the exercise program reported having less stress in their lives and tended to have lower levels of depression (Connell & Janevic, 2009). Exercise gave them a boost.

In a similar study, women providing care for relatives with dementia participated in a year-long exercise program that primarily involved brisk walking. At the start and end of the study the participants rated their sleep quality and had their blood pressure monitored while they discussed the stress of being a caregiver. This was done to measure their cardiovascular reactivity—how much their cardiovascular systems reacted in the face of stress—a heightened level of which is known to lead to poor health outcomes. After participating in the exercise program, the women were sleeping better and had lower cardiovascular reactivity, demonstrating that the stress of caregiving wasn't affecting them as much (King, Baumann, O'Sullivan, Wilcox, & Castro, 2002).

As this study suggests, exercise gives us a boost partly because it reduces how intensely we react to stress. As we discussed in the introductory chapter, stress causes activation of the body's autonomic nervous system and hypothalamo-pituitary-adrenal axis. When these systems are activated it causes physiological reactions such as an increased heart rate and blood pressure, things we know are associated with anxiety and, if prolonged, poor long-term health. Physical activity reduces the magnitude of these physiological reactions, minimizing the psychological experience of stress and allowing us to recover from stressful episodes more quickly (Huang, Webb, Zourdos, & Acevedo, 2013).

German researchers enrolled 50 healthy men in a 12-week running program to see what effect it would have on their physiological reactivity. Before and after the study the researchers tested the men's reactivity by exposing them to stressful tasks that involved being evaluated while giving a speech and doing difficult mathematical calculations. After participating in the exercise program, the men produced lower levels of the stress hormone cortisol when exposed to the stressors. They also experienced a smaller increase in heart rate, and their heart rate returned to normal levels faster (Klaperski, von Dawans, Heinrichs, & Fuchs, 2014). In short, exercise diminished the degree to which the men reacted to stress, and increased how quickly they recovered from it.

There are, in fact, many studies demonstrating that exercise reduces the extent to which our physiological systems react to stress, and improves how rapidly we recover from stressful experiences (Forcier et al., 2006). Exercise keeps our stress level in check, making us feel better psychologically and physically, and helping us recover from our obligations.

SINGLE SHOTS OF EXERCISE ARE BOOSTING

The studies described in the last section all involved prolonged periods of exercise lasting many weeks, months, or even a year. Does this mean that in order to promote recovery we need to implement lengthy exercise programs? Is it possible to benefit from less extensive periods of physical activity? Indeed, it is. In fact, research has shown that even a single session of exercise, called acute exercise, provides boosting benefits. For example, researchers in Germany obtained a baseline measure of the amount of cortisol in men's saliva and then asked the participants to either exercise on a treadmill or do simple, light stretching for one 30-minute session. They then had both groups do mental arithmetic problems which were made increasingly difficult and stressful by continually reducing the amount of time the men had to complete them. When the researchers measured the amount of cortisol the men produced in response to the stressful task, they found that, compared to the baseline cortisol levels established earlier, the men who had spent time on the treadmill displayed smaller increases in their cortisol levels than those who had simply stretched (Zschucke, Renneberg, Dimeo, Wüstenberg, & Ströhle, 2015). In short, a single dose of physical activity reduced the men's stress reactivity.

The same beneficial effect happens with our blood pressure. Researchers in the U.K. analyzed 15 studies that had explored whether a single dose of aerobic exercise can reduce the spike in blood pressure that typically occur in response to stress. They concluded that, in fact, acute exercise is successful at inhibiting stress-induced blood pressure increases. They also suggested that at least 30 minutes of physical exertion at moderate intensity is needed to produce the effect (Hamer, Taylor, & Steptoe, 2006). However, other research has suggested that we can boost in even less time.

In a study specifically designed to determine how much time people need to exercise in order to derive emotional benefits, American research-ers found that people feel more vigorous and less tired after just 10 minutes of moderate-intensity exercise on a stationary bicycle (Hansen, Stevens, & Coast, 2001). So, the available research shows that even if you don't exer-cise regularly, after a stressful day of facing your obligations, a single, short bout of physical activity can help to restore you and make you feel better. Jumping rope, getting on a bike, or going line dancing represent effective strategies for relieving the symptoms of stress and negative emotions that our obligations can produce (Basso & Suzuki, 2017).

STRESSED OUT? WORK OUT!

Paradoxically, although exercise helps us handle the stress in our lives and recover from our obligations, when we are stressed we are actually *less* likely to exercise. Most of the research on this topic shows that when we experience stress during our obligation time, we are less likely to engage in physical activity during our leisure time (Sonnentag, Venz, & Casper, 2017). Here's an example. Researchers in Germany asked police employees to fill in surveys assessing the amount of job stress they experienced and how much time they spent engaged in sports over the course of five consecutive work days. They found that on days the employees had more stress at work, they were less likely to participate in sports during their leisure time. This occurred despite the fact that the employees believed that physical activities would be more restorative, and in fact, were more restorative, than low-effort activities, such as watching television (Sonnentag & Jelden, 2009).

The reality is people working more stressful jobs exercise less than people working less stressful jobs. And during weeks that are more stressful, people exercise less than during weeks that are not as stressful (Sonnentag et al., 2017). Essentially, we are less likely to exercise during times when we need it the most. When we would most benefit from the stress-buffering effects of jogging, kayaking, or going for a hike, we are less likely to engage in any sort of physical activity. This happens because the stress and strain we experience during our obligations drains us of the resources, such as energy and self-control, we need to begin exercising in our leisure time (Englert & Rummel, 2016; Sonnentag & Jelden, 2009). Ironically, however, exercise replenishes our resources. The next time you have a stressful day, buck the trend and make a point of working out.

FILL THE ReNU BUCKETS WITH EXERCISE

One of the ways exercise rejuvenates us is by helping us restore our depleted resources and filling the rebuild bucket. When we break a sweat on an elliptical machine or try to score in a pick-up hockey game, we avoid using the same resources we use during our obligations. This gives those resources a break and an opportunity to rebuild. Research shows that when our resource levels are high enough, the stress and demands of our obligations take less of a toll on us. For example, when we lack the resources of hopefulness, optimism and resiliency, the demands of our obligations make us feel burned out. But when we have sufficient levels of these resources it keeps burnout at bay (Cheung, Tang, & Tang, 2011). Physical activity keeps our resources fully stocked. Exercise not only replenishes our depleted resources but also allows us to build, or reinforce, other resources. One study found that exercise after work increased people's resilience and optimism, and enhanced their ability to think of ways to achieve goals that were important to them, which is part of what makes us hopeful. Having these resources, in turn, made people feel less exhausted the next day (Nägel & Sonnentag, 2013). Exercise also improves our ability to regulate our behavior (Oaten & Cheng, 2006), increases our confidence (Netz, Wu, Becker, & Tenenbaum, 2005), and enhances our self-esteem (McAuley, Blissmer, Katula, Duncan, & Mihalko, 2000). All of these are resources that give us a boost.

Exercise also fills the nourish bucket. As we discussed in the sleep chapter, exercise helps us get a good night's sleep. In fact, when sedentary people who suffer from insomnia start exercising, they fall asleep faster, stay asleep longer, spend a higher percentage of their time in bed actually sleeping, and report overall better sleep quality (Reid et al., 2010). They also have more vitality and energy. Given that sleep is such an important part of boosting, adding some physical activity to your weekly schedule is a smart way to promote better recovery.

Exercise also helps us satisfy our psychological needs. When we can finally swim 10 lengths at the pool without losing our breath, we satisfy our need for competence. When we freely choose to hit the gym and decide for ourselves which machines to get on, we satisfy our need for autonomy. When we chat and experience feelings of connection with the people in our spin class, we satisfy our need for relatedness (Teixeira, Carraça, Markland, Silva, & Ryan, 2012). Indeed, Canadian researchers have shown that when we participate in exercise programs it promotes the satisfaction of our psychological needs (Wilson, Longley, Muon, Rodgers, & Murray, 2006; Wilson, Rodgers, Blanchard, & Gessell, 2003).

A specific way exercise helps us satisfy our need for relatedness is by protecting our relationships. When our obligations cause us stress we often have difficulty regulating our behavior at home and are more likely to lose our tempers or lash out the people close to us. This can drive a wedge between us and the people who help us satisfy our needs. But research shows that exercise in our leisure time can break this pattern. When we exercise we restore our self-regulation resources and are nicer to others, thus protecting our relationships (Barber, Taylor, Burton, & Bailey, 2017). This helps to satisfy our need for relatedness.

Physical activity also helps us fill the unhook bucket. By counteracting the stress caused by our obligations, exercise can help us relax. After jogging, riding a stationary bike, or swimming, people often feel more relaxed and calm (Kanning & Schlicht, 2010). In fact, this is a common reason people choose to exercise in the first place. Also, when we're actively trying to keep a basketball away from an opponent, or concentrating on where to throw a football so it isn't intercepted, we tend not to think about our obligations and are able to psychologically detach. Research has shown that when we exercise after a long day of facing our obligations, we feel better in the evening partly because of the psychological detachment we achieve (Feuerhahn, Sonnentag, & Woll, 2014). We also feel more vigorous the day after we exercise because of the relaxation and psychological detachment it promotes (ten Brummelhuis & Bakker, 2012).

EXERCISE GIVES US A BOOST

By restoring the resources we require, satisfying the needs that allow us to thrive, and allowing us to successfully unwind from the demands of our obligations, exercise gives us a boost.

Psychological Well-Being

Exercise affects our psychological well-being in two ways. First, it increases the level of positive emotions and positive states we enjoy. Research shows that physical activity increases how happy and contented we feel (Kanning & Schlicht, 2010). In a review of 105 studies that tested the effect of aerobic exercise on positive emotions, American researchers found that exercise consistently improves our mood (Reed & Buck, 2009). On the days we spend more of our leisure time exercising we feel stronger, more excited, and more alert (Feuerhahn et al., 2014). Exercise also increases our life satisfaction and overall level of well-being (Hecht & Boies, 2009; Netz et al., 2005).

The second way exercise enhances psychological well-being is that it reduces the negative emotions and states that we prefer to avoid. For instance, exercise reduces the amount of tension and anger we feel (Berger & Motl, 2000). The power of exercise to minimize negative states is actually quite remarkable. In one study, researchers wanted to see how effectively exercise would compare to drugs in reducing people's level of depression. They assigned sedentary people who suffered from depression, but weren't receiving any treatment for it, to either an exercise condition or a drug condition. The people assigned to the exercise condition spent 30 minutes, three times a week, walking or jogging on a treadmill while maintaining a heart rate that was 70–85% of their maximum capacity. They kept this up for 16 weeks. Those assigned to the drug condition were given Zoloft—a commonly prescribed antidepressant medication—for the same 16-week period. At the end of the study, participants in the exercise group had reduced their levels of depression *by virtually the same amount* as the people who had been taking the antidepressant drug (Blumenthal et al., 2007). Amazing! We can promote psychological health and well-being through exercise. Who knew?

One thing we do know is how hard it is for so many of us to maintain an exercise program. Fifty per cent of people who start an exercise program drop out within the first six months (Linke, Gallo, & Norman, 2011). An effective way to ensure that we stay on track is to focus on the immediate well-being benefits of exercise instead of the long-term health benefits (Otto & Smits, 2011). Rather than waiting weeks, months, or decades to reap the physical rewards of activity, we should try concentrating on the short-term and immediate emotional rewards—the pleasant way exercise makes us feel. These positive benefits are an instant payoff that can increase how eager you'll be to break a sweat when you're feeling run down.

That being said, if you have no intention of adhering to a long-term exercise program, you may be encouraged to know that a single dose of exercise can promote psychological well-being. For example, one 15-minute session of moderate-intensity cycling puts us in a better mood (Hogan, Mata, & Carstensen, 2013). In addition to enhancing our positive emotions, acute exercise decreases our negative emotions, and these desirable effects can last up to a full day (Basso & Suzuki, 2017). For these reasons, acute exercise is one of the most effective techniques available for improving our moods (Basso & Suzuki, 2017).

Physical Health

It will come as no surprise to know that exercise promotes physical health, and that a lack of exercise compromises it. Researchers have estimated that physical inactivity accounts for 6% of coronary heart disease, 7% of type 2 diabetes, 10% of breast cancer and colon cancer, and 9% of premature death (Lee et al., 2012). Exercise eliminates this additional risk. Researchers in Germany did a comprehensive survey of the studies that examined the relationship between physical activity and a number of non-communicable diseases and disorders, including obesity, heart disease, type 2 diabetes, Alzheimer's disease and dementia. They found that exercise had a protective effect for every condition they surveyed (Reiner, Niermann, Jekauc, & Woll, 2013). Physical activity can also alleviate arthritis, sexual dysfunction, and low-back pain (Penedo & Dahn, 2005).

As we have discussed, one of the reasons exercise promotes physical health is because it reduces how much our physiological systems react, and increases how quickly they recover, in the face of stress. Further evidence for the value of these exercise-induced biological changes comes from research showing that when we encounter stress, those of us who exercise suffer fewer physical health problems (Gerber & Puhse, 2009). Essentially, exercise is a stress-buffer that fosters health.

Somewhat ironically, when we exercise it actually increases the level of the stress hormone cortisol in our bodies. However, the more we exercise, the better our bodies get at blocking the damaging effects that cortisol has on us. So, in essence, the "good" physical stress produced by exercise makes us better at fighting the "bad" psychological stress caused by our obligations (Heijnen, Hommel, Kibele, & Colzato, 2016).

Enhancement

Many studies have shown that exercise enhances our mental abilities and subsequent performance on numerous tasks. For example, regular physical activity improves our cognitive flexibility and our ability to switch between different tasks, increases how quickly we process information and how effectively we control our attention, and helps us put the brakes on unwanted responses (Guiney & Machado, 2013). Call center employees perform better when they exercise frequently (Moradi, Nima, Rapp Ricciardi, Archer, & Garcia, 2014), and simply walking makes us more creative (Oppezzo & Schwartz, 2014). Emily, the manager who opened this chapter, noted that running helps her clear her mind, kick-start her creativity and heighten her focus. Research supports Emily's experience. On the days employees exercise during their lunch breaks they are better at managing their time, mentally sharper, get along better with their colleagues, and are more effective at handling their work responsibilities (Coulson et al., 2008).

Do you know what "inchoate" means? Could you use it in a sentence? In one study college students were asked to spend 20 minutes either doing puzzles or engaging in vigorous step aerobics. They were then asked to learn a set of difficult words and demonstrate that they understood the words by correctly using them in a sentence. Compared to the inactive students who just did puzzles, those who exercised demonstrated a much higher level of comprehension by using the words correctly. In fact, they performed about twice as well as the sedentary students (Salis, 2013). Inchoate means "not fully formed," or "just begun." If you jump rope for a few minutes right now, you'll be twice as likely to properly use "inchoate" in a sentence next week.

Why does exercise seem to make us smarter? It's partly because physical activity increases the level of brain-derived neurotrophic factor (BDNF) circulating in our heads. BDNF has been called Miracle-Gro for the brain (Ratey & Hagerman, 2008). It is a protein that promotes neurogenesis, which is the growth of new brain cells, and neuroplasticity, which is when brain cells build new connections among themselves (Heijnen et al., 2016). Exercise also stimulates the production of new blood vessels in the brain, which gives brain cells more fuel to process information (Voss, Vivar, Kramer, & van Praag, 2013).

Even a single dose of physical activity can enhance us. For example, just one 15-minute session on a stationary bicycle improves our reaction times (Hogan et al., 2013). American researchers statistically combined studies that had looked at the effects of a single session of exercise on how well we perform cognitive tasks, such as those requiring attention or problem solving. They concluded that just one bout of physical activity consistently improves our performance on such tasks, with the strongest effects occurring 11–20 minutes after exercising (Chang, Labban, Gapin, & Etnier, 2012).

One of the things that is most affected by exercise, including acute exercise, is our executive function. Executive function is like the master control center in the brain. It is involved in regulating attention, problem solving, and mental flexibility, and therefore is highly involved in planning and organizing mental activities. Research shows that the biggest benefits from acute exercise involve executive function (Basso & Suzuki, 2017). No wonder we get a performance boost when we exercise, even once. A single bout of physical activity enhances the mental abilities we use in planning, organizing, and executing our obligations. This explains why when Emily goes for a run, she returns home with solutions to her problems and a clear plan on how to reach her goals.

BOLSTERED BOOSTING

As you contemplate how to best leverage the power of exercise to get a boost, consider how physical activity can complement other ideas for recovery you have learned about in this book. For example, exercise can make a great transition ritual (Otto & Smits, 2011). Devoting a specific amount of time each day to a workout can serve as an effective way to psychologically leave your obligations behind and demarcate the transition into uptime.

Try incorporating some nature into your exercise routine. This is called green exercise, and it is beneficial because studies show that nature can intensify the boosting power of physical activity. For example, in a study designed to test the restorative potential of green exercise, researchers in Norway found that compared to a group people who exercised indoors, those who exercised in a forested area had higher levels of positive emotions and lower diastolic blood pressure (Calogiuri et al., 2016). Essentially, when we exposure ourselves to nature while exercising, we reap the boosting power of both, synergistically and simultaneously.

Consider cutting the virtual cord when you're working out. When we stay virtually connected to others it reduces how intensely we exercise. An American study found that when we talk or text while running on a treadmill, we don't run as quickly (Rebold, Lepp, Sanders, & Barkley, 2015). However, this study also found that we tend to enjoy ourselves more if we stay connected to others while working out. Social contact can intensify the effect of exercise. Researchers in the U.K. found that our bodies release more endorphins, which promotes well-being, when we work out with other people (Cohen, Ejsmond-Frey, Knight, & Dunbar, 2010). This heightened well-being can also make us enjoy exercise more. Enjoying our workouts is important. Not only does enjoyment increase the likelihood that we will exercise in the first place, but research shows that physical activity only helps us recover when we are intrinsically motivated and want to exercise (ten Brummelhuis & Trougakos, 2014). So, if staying connected, or exercising with others, helps you enjoy the activity and makes you want to exercise, go ahead and do it, but pay closer attention to the quality of your workout.

SUMMARY

Exercise fills all of the ReNU buckets, notably the nourish bucket because physical activity is, itself, a fundamental human need. As Emily, the manager and mother who opened this chapter, knew, exercise promotes psychological well-being, physical health, and enhancement. Although there are guidelines for how much overall exercise we should get, science has not yet established minimal recommendations for the amount of exercise we need to recover from our obligations. That being said, research shows that even a small amount of exercise helps us recharge our batteries. So, incorporating a bike ride to work, a lunchtime squash game, or an evening spin class into your schedule is a smart move if you want to feel, and be, at your best. Regardless of whether your ideas on how to incorporate exercise into your routine are clearly established, or inchoate, you will definitely get a boost by including some physical activity in your uptime.

Boosting Bites

Exercise helps us recover from our obligations.

Single shots of exercise can give us a boost.

At a physiological level, physical activity makes us more resilient and less prone to the effects of stress.

Paradoxically, we are less likely to exercise when we experience stress.

Exercising for immediate mood enhancement may keep us more motivated than exercising for long-term physical health benefits.

Combining exercise with other boosting activities can intensify how effectively we recover.

UPTIME ACTION PLAN

Step 1. Incorporate some exercise into your life. Moderate-intensity exercise, such as brisk walking, is safe for most people (Centers for Disease Control and Prevention, 2015). Regardless, you should consult a physician before beginning any exercise program.

Step 2. Consider if exercise is the best choice for you. For most people, physical activity is a tremendously valuable component of boosting. However, exercise may not be the best choice if your daily obligations are highly physical. Remember that boosting occurs when we fill the ReNU buckets. If physical activity has already filled part of your nourish bucket, focusing on a different activity or a different bucket may be advisable. Pay attention to the buckets.

Step 3. Decide when you can fit some exercise into your week. You don't have to go to a gym. Jumping rope in your basement, jogging up and down a flight of stairs, or working out to an online video in your living room are as effective for boosting as participating in a formal exercise program at a fitness club. Before you decide when to schedule some activity, consider Step 4.

Step 4. If you find it difficult to carve out enough time for lengthy workouts, consider interval training. Interval training is a form of exercise that involves brief, intermittent bursts of high-intensity activity, interspersed with periods of rest or low-intensity activity (Gibala, Little, MacDonald, & Hawley, 2012). A great advantage of interval training is that it allows us to obtain the same benefits of traditional exercise programs in a fraction of the time, even as little as 10 minutes (Gillen et al., 2016). Despite the minimal time investment, interval training enhances our cognitive performance, and there is preliminary evidence that interval training is as effective as traditional exercise at enriching our emotions after we exercise (Stork, Banfield, Gibala, & Martin Ginis, 2017). With this in mind, now consider when you can fit some exercise into your week. Record your thoughts in the spaces below.

Monday_____   Tuesday _____

Wednesday_____   Thursday _____

Friday _____   Saturday_____

Sunday _____

Step 5. Be reasonable. If you're 40 pounds overweight and haven't exercised in 20 years, starting an exercise program by ramping your heart rate to 90% of its maximum capacity is probably not the best idea. Start slowly (Centers for Disease Control and Prevention, 2015).

Step 6. Interval training can be rather intense, which is likely not everyone's cup of tea (Hardcastle, Ray, Beale, & Hagger, 2014). It is important to enjoy your workout and do what feels good. For example, research shows that people enjoy exercising more when they listen to music while working out (Rebold et al., 2015). In the space below indicate what you can do to ensure your exercise is fun and enjoyable.

_____

_____

_____

_____

_____

_____

Step 7. Use "surgical strikes" to help you boost. Remember that we tend to exercise less when we're stressed. Counteract this tendency and make a point of breaking a sweat on the days you feel most anxious and strained. Let the boost you experience after working out motivate you to do the same thing the next time you feel stressed.

REFERENCES

American Heart Association. (2016). *American Heart Association recommendations for physical activity in adults*. Retrieved from: http://www.heart.org/HEARTORG/HealthyLiving/PhysicalActivity/FitnessBasics/American-Heart-Association-Recommendations-for-Physical-Activity-in-Adults_UCM_307976_Article.jsp#.WgXIBKIZMwV

Barber, L. K., Taylor, S. G., Burton, J. P., & Bailey, S. F. (2017). A self-regulatory perspective of work-to-home undermining spillover/crossover: Examining the roles of sleep and exercise. *Journal of Applied Psychology, 102*, 753–763.

Basso, J. C., & Suzuki, W. A. (2017). The effects of acute exercise on mood, cognition, neurophysiology, and neurochemical pathways: A review. *Brain Plasticity, 2*, 127–152.

Berger, B. G., & Motl, R. W. (2000). Exercise and mood: A selective review and synthesis of research employing the profile of mood states. *Journal of Applied Sport Psychology, 12*, 69–92.

Bloodworth, A., McNamee, M., & Bailey, R. (2012). Sport, physical activity, and well-being: An objectivist account. *Sport, Education and Society, 17*, 497–514.

Blumenthal, J. A., Babyak, M. A., Doraiswamy, P. M., Watkins, L., Hoffman, B. M., Barbour, K. A., ... Sherwood, A. (2007). Exercise and pharmacotherapy in the treatment of major depressive disorder. *Psychosomatic Medicine, 69*, 587–596.

Calogiuri, G., Evensen, K., Weydahl, A., Andersson, K., Patil, G., Ihlebæk, C., & Raanaas, R. K. (2016). Green exercise as a workplace intervention to reduce job stress. Results from a pilot study. *Work, 53*, 99–111.

Centers for Disease Control and Prevention. (2015). *Physical activity and health*. Retrieved from https://www.cdc.gov/physicalactivity/basics/pa-health/index.htm#ReduceCancer

Chang, Y. K., Labban, J. D., Gapin, J. I., & Etnier, J. L. (2012). The effects of acute exercise on cognitive performance. *Brain Research, 1453*, 87–101.

Cheung, F., Tang, C. S., & Tang, S. (2011). Psychological capital as a moderator between emotional labor, burnout, and job satisfaction among school teachers in China. *International Journal of Stress Management, 18*, 348–371.

Cohen, E. E. A., Ejsmond-Frey, R., Knight, N., & Dunbar, R. I. M. (2010). Rowers' high: Behavioral synchrony is correlated with elevated pain thresholds. *Biology Letters, 6*, 106–108.

Connell, C. M., & Janevic, M. R. (2009). Effects of a telephone-based exercise intervention for dementia caregivers wives. *Journal of Applied Gerontology, 28*, 171–194.

Coulson, J. C., McKenna, J., & Field, M. (2008). Exercising at work and self-reported work performance. *International Journal of Workplace Health Management, 1*, 176–197.

Englert, C., & Rummel, J. (2016). I want to keep exercising but I don't. The negative impact of momentary lack of self-control on exercise adherence. *Psychology of Sports and Exercise, 26*, 24–31.

Feuerhahn, N., Sonnentag, S., & Woll, A. (2014). Exercise after work, psychological mediators, and affect: A day-level study. *European Journal of Work and Organizational Psychology, 23*, 62–79.

Forcier, K., Stroud, L. R., Papandonatos, G. D., Hitsman, B., Reiches, M., Krishnamoorthy, J., & Niaura, R. (2006). Links between physical fitness and cardiovascular reactivity and recovery to psychological stressors: A meta-analysis. *Health Psychology, 25*, 723–739.

Gerber, M., & Puhse, U. (2009). Do exercise and fitness protect against stress-induced health complaints? A review of the literature. *Scandinavian Journal of Public Health, 37*, 801–819.

Gibala, M. J., Little, J. P., MacDonald, M. J., & Hawley, J. A. (2012). Physiological adaptations to low-volume, high-intensity interval training in health and disease. *Journal of Physiology, 590*, 1077–1084.

Gillen, J. B., Martin, B. J., MacInnis, M. J., Skelly, L. E., Tarnopolsky, M. A., & Gibala, M. J. (2016). Twelve weeks of sprint interval training improves indices of cardiometabolic health similar to traditional endurance training despite a five-fold lower exercise volume and time commitment. *PLOS ONE, 11*. doi:10.1371/journal.pone.0154075

Guiney, H., & Machado, L. (2013). Benefits of regular aerobic exercise for executive functioning in healthy populations. *Psychonomic Bulletin and Review, 20*, 73–86.

Hamer, M., Taylor, A., & Steptoe, A. (2006). The effect of acute aerobic exercise on stress related blood pressure responses: A systematic review and meta-analysis. *Biological Psychology, 71*, 183–190.

Hansen, C. J., Stevens, L. C., & Coast, R. (2001). Exercise duration and mood state: How much is enough to feel better? *Health Psychology, 20*, 267–275.

Hardcastle, S., Ray, H., Beale, L., & Hagger, M. S. (2014). Why sprint interval training is inappropriate for a largely sedentary population. *Frontiers in Psychology, 5*. doi:10.3389/fpsyg.2014.01505

Hecht, T. D., & Boies, K. (2009). Structure and correlates of spillover from nonwork to work: An examination of nonwork activities, well-being, and work outcomes. *Journal of Occupational Health Psychology, 14*, 414–426.

Heijnen, S., Hommel, B., Kibele, A., & Colzato, L. S. (2016). Neuromodulation of aerobic exercise: A review. *Frontiers in Psychology, 6*. doi:10.3389/fpsyg.2015.01890

Hogan, C. L., Mata, J., & Carstensen, L. L. (2013). Exercise holds immediate benefits for affect and cognition in younger and older adults. *Psychology and Aging, 28*, 587–594.

Huang, C., Webb, H. E., Zourdos, M. C., & Acevedo, E. O. (2013). Cardiovascular reactivity, stress, and physical activity. *Frontiers in Physiology, 4*. doi:10.3389/fphys.2013.00314

Kanning, M., & Schlicht, W. (2010). Be active and become happy: An ecological momentary assessment of physical activity and mood. *Journal of Sport & Exercise Psychology, 32*, 253–261.

King, A. C., Baumann, K., O'Sullivan, P., Wilcox, S., & Castro, C. (2002). Effects of moderate-intensity exercise on physiological, behavioral, and emotional responses to family caregiving: A randomized controlled trial. *Journal of Gerontology: Medical Sciences, 57A*, M26–M36.

Klaperski, S., von Dawans, B, Heinrichs, M., & Fuchs, R. (2014). Effects of a 12-week endurance training program on the physiological response to psychosocial stress in men: A randomized controlled trial. *Journal of Behavioral Medicine, 37*, 1118–1133.

Lee, I., Shiroma, E. J., Lobelo, F., Puska, P., Blair, S. N., & Katzmarzyk, P. T. (2012). Effect of physical inactivity on major non-communicable diseases worldwide: An analysis of burden of disease and life expectancy. *Lancet, 380*, 219–229.

Linke, S. E., Gallo, L. C., & Norman, G. J. (2011). Attrition and adherence rates of sustained vs. intermittent exercise interventions. *Annals of Behavioral Medicine, 42*, 197–209.

McAuley, E., Blissmer, B., Katula, J., Duncan, T. E., & Mihalko, S. L. (2000). Physical activity, self-esteem, and self-efficacy relationships in older adults: A randomized controlled trial. *Annals of Behavioral Medicine, 22*, 131–139.

Moradi, S., Nima, A. A., Rapp Ricciardi, M., Archer, T., & Garcia, D. (2014). Exercise, character strengths, well-being, and learning climate in the prediction of performance over a 6-month period at a call center. *Frontiers in Psychology, 5*. doi:10.3389/fpsyg.2014.00497

Nägel, I. J., & Sonnentag, S. (2013). Exercise and sleep predict personal resources in employees' daily lives. *Applied Psychology: Health and Well-Being, 5*, 348–368.

Netz, Y., Wu, M., Becker, B. J., & Tenenbaum, G. (2005). Physical activity and psychological well-being in advanced age: A meta-analysis of intervention studies, *20*, 272–284.

Oaten, M., & Cheng, K. (2006). Longitudinal gains in self-regulation from regular physical exercise. *British Journal of Health Psychology, 11*, 717–733.

Oppezzo, M., & Schwartz, D. L. (2014). Give your ideas some legs: The positive effect of walking on creative thinking. *Journal of Experimental Psychology: Learning, Memory, and Cognition, 40*, 1142–1152.

Otto, M. W., & Smits, J. A. J. (2011). *Exercise for mood and anxiety: Proven strategies for overcoming depression and enhancing well-being.* New York, NY: Oxford University Press.

Penedo, F. J., & Dahn, J. R. (2005). Exercise and well-being: A review of mental and physical health benefits associated with physical activity. *Current Opinion in Psychiatry, 18*, 189–193.

Pinquart, M., & Sörensen, S. (2003). Differences between caregivers and noncaregivers in psychological health and physical health: A meta-analysis. *Psychology and Aging, 18*, 250–267.

Ratey, J. J., & Hagerman, E. (2008). *Spark: The revolutionary new science of exercise and the brain.* New York, NY: Little, Brown and Company.

Rebold, M. J., Lepp, A., Sanders, G. J., & Barkley, J. E. (2015). The impact of cell phone use on the intensity and liking of a bout of treadmill exercise. *PLoS ONE, 10*. doi:10.1371/journal.pone0125029

Reed, J., Buck, S. (2009). The effect of regular aerobic exercise on positive-activated affect: A meta-analysis. *Psychology of Sport and Exercise, 10*, 581–594.

Reid, K. J., Glazer Baron, K., Lu, B., Naylor, E., Wolfe, L., & Zee, P. C. (2010). Aerobic exercise improves self-reported sleep and quality of life in older adults with insomnia. *Sleep Medicine, 11*, 934–940.

Reiner, M., Niermann, C., Jekauc, D., & Woll, A. (2013). Long-term health benefits of physical activity: A systematic review of longitudinal studies. *BMC Public Health, 13*. doi:10.1186/1471-2458/13/813

Ryan, R. M., & Deci, E. L. (2000). Self-determination theory and the facilitation of intrinsic motivation, social development, and well-being. *American Psychologist, 55*, 68–78.

Salis, A. S. (2013). Proactive and reactive effects of vigorous exercise on learning and vocabulary comprehension. *Perceptual & Motor Skills: Motor Skills & Ergonomics, 116*, 918–928.

Sonnentag, S. (2001). Work, recovery activities and individual well-being: A diary study. *Journal of Occupational Health Psychology, 6*, 196–210.

Sonnentag, S., & Jelden, S. (2009). Job stressors and the pursuit of sport activities: A day-level perspective. *Journal of Occupational Health Psychology, 14*, 165–181.

Sonnentag, S., Venz, L., & Casper, A. (2017). Advances in recovery research: What have we learned? What should be done next? *Journal of Occupational Health Psychology, 22*, 365–380.

Stork, M. J., Banfield, L. E., Gibala, M. J., & Martin Ginis, K. A. (2017). A scoping review of the psychological responses to interval exercise: Is interval exercise a viable alternative to traditional exercise? *Health Psychology Review, 11*, 324–344.

Teixeira, P. J., Carraça, E. V., Markland, D., Silva, M. N., & Ryan, R. M. (2012). Exercise, physical activity, and self-determination theory: A systematic review. *International Journal of Behavioral Nutrition and Physical Activity, 9*, 78–108.

ten Brumelhuis, L. L., & Bakker, A. B. (2012). Staying engaged during the week: The effect of off-job activities on next day work engagement. *Journal of Occupational Health Psychology, 17*, 445–455.

ten Brummelhuis, L. L., & Trougakos, J. P. (2014). The recovery potential of intrinsically versus extrinsically motivated off-job activities. *Journal of Occupational and Organizational Psychology, 87*, 177–199.

Voss, M. W., Vivar, C., Kramer, A. F., & van Praag, H. (2013). Bridging animal and human models of exercise-induced brain plasticity. *Trends in Cognitive Sciences, 17*, 525–544

Wilson, P. M., Longley, K., Muon, S., Rodgers, W. M., & Murray, T. C. (2006). Examining the contributions of perceived psychological need satisfaction to wellbeing in exercise. *Journal of Applied Biobehavioral Research, 11*, 243–264.

Wilson, P. M., Rodgers, W. M., Blanchard, C. M., & Gessell, J. (2003). The relationship between psychological needs, self-determined motivation, exercise attitudes, and physical fitness. *Journal of Applied Social Psychology, 33*, 2373–2392.

World Health Organization. (2017). *Global health observatory (GHO) data. Prevalence of insufficient physical activity.* Retrieved from http://www.who.int/gho/ncd/risk_factors/physical_activity_text/en/

Zschucke, E., Renneberg, B., Dimeo, F., Wüstenberg, T., & Ströhle, A. (2015). The stress-buffering effect of acute exercise: Evidence for HPA axis negative feedback. *Psychoneuroendocrinology, 51*, 414–425.

CHAPTER 9

HOBBIES

Recover by Following Your Passion

It's the bottom of the ninth. Jeff's team already has two outs. Another strike and it's over for the season. The batter winds up and swings. Jeff jumps off the couch in excitement, gripping the game controller as he watches the ball float across the screen. It's a homerun! Playing in the major leagues, even if it is just a video game, is the perfect escape for this 36-year-old father of two. After enduring an onslaught of demands and other stressors that come with being a senior manager in communications and fundraising, Jeff tucks his two young boys into bed and heads down to the basement where with the push of a button he becomes the general manager of a professional baseball team.

"It's a release from reality for me," he says. "Playing a videogame is consequence free so it helps me to relax and turn off the daily pressures of work."

On the job, Jeff is always on stage. He has to be engaging, friendly and welcoming to every person he meets so unwinding in the company of electronics allows him to give his social skills a break. Gaming also provides Jeff with the opportunity to focus on achieving a new goal – winning the virtual World Series.

"It brings a level of joy when my team does well," he says. "I have been playing video games since I was in high school, so I have gained in skill."

Within minutes of turning on the game, all of Jeff's focus is directed towards his team. He is making trades to improve his roster and determin-

---

Boost: The Science of Recharging Yourself in an Age of Unrelenting Demands, pp. 147–166
147

ing which line-up will increase his odds of beating the computer. Video games take his mind off of the responsibilities of everyday life and these distracting effects last right until his head hits the pillow.

THE WONDERFUL WORLD OF HOBBIES

Hobbies are the quintessential leisure activity. When we pursue our hobbies, we are the masters of our own domain. Unlike our obligations which make demands of us and force us to conform to others' wishes, our hobbies allow us to pursue whatever activities we find appealing. Within the boundaries of our hobby's practices, we can do what we want, when we want, how we want, and with whom we want. And if we get tired of a particular hobby, there are innumerable others to enjoy, and we are completely free to choose whichever ones suit our fancy.

Hobbies come in many forms. Wikipedia breaks hobbies down into those pursued indoors, such as baking, or outdoors, such as scuba diving, and categorizes many as involving either collection, such as antiquing and collecting hockey cards, competition, such as poker and horseback riding, or observation, such as bird watching and astrology (List of hobbies, n.d.).

Some hobbies require special skills and knowledge and can be so consuming that they take on the character of an alternate career. For example, an amateur photographer can spend inordinate amounts of time perfecting her craft and eventually be asked to shoot friends' weddings and Christmas photos. Other hobbies are less substantial and are just fun and pleasurable, such as scrapbooking, painting, or doing crossword puzzles (Stebbins, 2011). However, what all hobbies have in common is that they are enjoyable leisure activities that people voluntarily choose when they are free from their obligations (Pressman et al., 2009).

Although hobbies share this commonality, they also differ in many ways and will therefore fill the various parts of the three ReNU buckets to different degrees. For example, if you successfully scale the face of a mountain while rock climbing you are likely to feel accomplished, which will satisfy your need for competence. Whereas if you spend evenings at your book club discussing the plotline of a new novel with a group of friends, you are more likely to satisfy your need for relatedness. So, although all hobbies share the feature of being freely chosen, and therefore satisfy our need for autonomy, particular hobbies will fill certain parts of the ReNU buckets more than others. This gives us a clue as to which hobbies might be most restorative at different times. If your self-esteem took a beating at work this week, a hobby that restores your confidence will most replenish you. If you felt lonely and isolated while studying for final exams, a hobby that lets you socialize with others will best help you boost.

What hobbies occupy most of our time? In the world's largest survey on rest, people reported that reading was the most restful leisure time activity (Hammond & Lewis, 2016), and according to the U.S. Bureau of Labor Statistics, reading is one of the activities people spend a good chunk of their leisure time on (United States Department of Labor, 2016). However, the most common hobby in many parts of the world is watching television. While Americans spend 19 minutes a day reading (United States Department of Labor, 2016), they watch on average 145 hours, or *6 days*, of TV a month (Perez, 2013). A close runner up is video games. Americans spend six and a half hours a month playing video games (Perez, 2013). These include console-based games, such as Xbox or PlayStation, but also casual computer games that can be played in a Web browser on a computer or phone (Reinecke, 2009a). It turns out when Jeff is trying to win the virtual World Series, he's in good company.

HOBBIES RECHARGE OUR BATTERIES

Hobbies offer us a great opportunity to get a boost. As enjoyable leisure activities, hobbies serve as "breathers" or "restorers" that help us recover (Pressman et al., 2009, p. 725). Notably, hobbies serve as an effective counterbalance to the strain and potential dissatisfaction we experience during our obligations (Dik & Hansen, 2008). In fact, research shows that hobbies can mitigate the effects of stress (Pressman et al., 2009). American researchers demonstrated that when we partake in more leisure time activities, including hobbies, stress takes less of a toll on us psychologically and physically (Pressman et al., 2009). Essentially, hobbies serve as a buffer against the negative physical and psychological effects of our obligation-related stressors (Iwasaki & Mannell, 2000).

More generally, research shows that when we engage in hobbies it helps us recover (Garrick et al., as cited in Demerouti, Bakker, Guerts, & Taris, 2009). American researchers studied the leisure habits of members of the clergy and found that those who regularly engaged in hobbies suffered less burnout (Stanton-Rich & Iso-Ahola, 1998). Similarly, a collaborative study between Australian and Dutch researchers found that the more employees engage in hobbies during their leisure time, the less fatigued and more recovered they feel (Winwood, Bakker, & Winefield, 2007). Many hobbies, such as painting, writing, and dancing, are highly creative endeavors, and research shows that participating in creative activities in our uptime gives us a boost. For instance, American researchers found that when employed adults spent more time engaged in creative endeavors on the weekend they feel more recovered on Monday (Eschleman, Mathieu, & Cooper, 2017).

It's important to note that these benefits aren't limited to people who can produce works of art, write a novel, or perform on stage. We can achieve a boost through creativity from small and spontaneous acts of originality (Ivcevic, 2007), which is what our hobbies encourage. We demonstrate creativity when we assemble a playlist of our favorite music, improvise a deke in a game of flag football, or decide which species to group together in a fish tank. Most hobbies provide opportunities for small acts of creativity.

While we may be attracted to certain hobbies because they allow us to express some creativity, we may be attracted to other types of hobbies because they pique our curiosity. When we investigate new recipes from far-away lands, explore how to best care for the plants in our gardens, or read online reviews to learn what others think about our favorite musical artists, our curiosity is aroused. And curiosity helps us recover. Researchers from Spain and Chile found that when college students participated in activities that piqued their curiosity during the day, at nighttime they felt less exhausted by their studies (Garrosa, Blanco-Donoso, Carmona-Cobo, & Moreno-Jiménez, 2017).

While feeding our creative soul and satisfying our curiosity are behind many of our hobby choices, the most popular hobbies involve entertainment media. And the good news is these types of hobbies recharge our batteries too. Regardless of whether we watch traditional TV or stream videos on another device, media used for entertainment is strongly related to recovery (Reiger, Reinecke, Frischlich, & Bente, 2014). For instance, when we feel depleted, watching movies can refresh us and increase our energy and vitality (Reiger et al., 2014). Video games can also help us boost. In fact, research shows that people often play computer games when they are tired or stressed during their obligations and are looking for opportunities to recover (Reinecke, 2009b). For Jeff, video games provided him with a much-needed break from the responsibilities he had at his job and at home. Almost 50% of employed adults report playing computer games at work. Among these game players, the more fatigued they are on the job, the more likely they are to take a break and play computer games, and the more recovery they experience as a result (Reinecke, 2009a).

Media such as TV, videos, and computer games seem to play a vital role in our attempts to recover from exhaustion (Reinecke, 2009b). And they're effective. A German study found that after people were depleted by completing a draining work task, entertainment media gave them a boost by making them feel more energetic, vigorous and full of pep (Reinecke, Klatt, & Krämer, 2011). Overall, hobbies provide an enjoyable way to recharge our batteries.

INTENTIONAL INEFFICIENCY

In our efficiency- and productivity-obsessed world, hobbies give us room to leisurely float through activities, paying no mind to obligation-related metrics, outcomes, or standards. Like a feather in the wind, hobbies allow our interests and passions to take us in whatever direction they want, oblivious to time or external demands. Although hobbies are often goal-directed activities, they paradoxically give us free space within which to figuratively do nothing, while doing something. When we're sitting in a boat, patiently waiting for a fish to bite our lure, we can enjoy the warm sun on our face and the gentle bobbing of the waves beneath us as we essentially do nothing while outwardly engaged in a respectable pursuit. When we walk through the woods looking for birds that we haven't yet photographed, we can allow our minds to wander or shoot the breeze with fellow bird-watchers, casually filling time within the larger context of a shared activity. Although many hobbies involve effort, concentration, and discipline, they also often give us the freedom to drift, letting our momentary fascinations direct our attention, thoughts and actions.

Part of the boosting potential of hobbies is that they allow us to counter the pressures of our daily obligations by letting us engage in intentional inefficiency. Intentional inefficiency is when we deliberately choose to let ourselves be disorganized instead of structured, unproductive instead of industrious, and improvisational instead of methodical. Intentional inefficiency is a conscious attempt to balance the state of being goal-oriented and focused on achievement, with the opposite state of being playful and focused on enjoyment (Wright, Wright, Sadlo, & Stew, 2014). Within the boundaries of our hobbies, we give ourselves a boost by relinquishing the standards and constraints of our obligations and acting in whatever way feels natural, spontaneous, and free.

When we resist the temptation to check the time, we are being intentionally inefficient. When we avoid the habit of establishing a deadline to finish a task, we are being intentionally inefficient. And when we venture into an activity with no idea of what we will do once we start, or where we will end up when we finish, we are being intentionally inefficient. Intentional inefficiency fills all of the ReNU buckets and is a particularly valuable tactic for getting a boost.

We don't need to indulge in a hobby to practice intentional inefficiency. For example, taking an unscheduled day trip to a nearby town and exploring aimlessly is an equally effective approach. However, hobbies give us an opportunity to engineer intentional inefficiency into our busy lives.

In the sections that follow, we concentrate on hobbies that have received the most research attention. Although it would be interesting to know more details about the boosting power of craft brewing, whittling, and wingsuit flying (possibly the scariest hobby in the world), there is little to no relevant research on these specific activities. In fact, casual forms of leisure, such as hobbies, are virtually ignored by researchers who investigate leisure or recovery (Best, 2010; Demerouti et al., 2009). Therefore, our discussion will focus on topics that have a direct bearing on hobbies, in addition to the specific hobbies on which some research has been done, notably TV and video games. These will serve as effective examples of the boosting power of hobbies in general.

FILLING THE ReNU BUCKETS WITH HOBBIES

Hobbies can help us recover from our obligations by replenishing exhausted resources and filling the rebuild bucket (Pressman et al., 2009). However, in order for that to happen we need to ensure that our hobbies don't make use of the same resources we use to fulfill our obligations. For example, we saw earlier that participating in creative activities in our leisure time makes us feel recovered. However, this only happens for people whose jobs don't require much creativity. For people whose jobs already involve innovation, originality, or thinking creatively, participating in explicitly creative activities during leisure time either has no effect, or a negative effect, on how recovered they feel when they return to their obligations (Eschleman et al., 2017). Although hobbies are creative endeavors, they vary in the amount of the creativity involved. For example, producing works of art is a highly creative activity that will draw more intensely on creativity resources than devising ways to display a collection of action figures. Ultimately, to get a boost it is important that our hobbies draw on resources that are different from those we use during our obligation time.

As we will discuss further later, hobbies promote our psychological well-being. And this has a beneficial effect on our level of resources. The enjoyment we derive from our hobbies and the positive emotions such as joy and contentment we experience when engaged in them allows us to fill the rebuild bucket because positive emotions help us cultivate personal resources (Fredrickson 2001). When we are in a good mood, we tend to playfully experiment with new ideas, techniques, and actions. For example, if you are happily engrossed in constructing model airplanes, you are likely to think up new designs, test out different kinds of materials and methods of construction, and consult with people who have similar interests. All of this broadens our repertoire of thoughts and behaviors and helps to build enduring physical, social, intellectual and psychological resources (Fredrickson, 2001). For instance, research shows that positive emotions promote the development of resilience (Cohn, Fredrickson, Brown, Mikels,

& Conway, 2009), self-acceptance, hope, and social support (Fredrickson, Cohn, Coffey, Pek, & Finkel, 2008).

And it doesn't stop there. These positive emotions spurred by our hobbies can also replenish our resources related to controlling ourselves. As we discussed in the sleep chapter, one of the resources that gets depleted by our obligations is self-regulation. Self-regulation resources allow us to override our immediate impulses and control our thoughts and behavior. When we exert effort to control ourselves during obligations, our self-regulation resources get depleted, and our self-control is compromised. When we tell people that they are "getting on our last nerve" or we find ourselves needing a moment to compose ourselves before having a tough conversation, it is often because we need to refill the rebuild bucket with more self-regulation resources.

Researchers have found that positive emotions replenish self-regulation resources. In a series of studies, American researchers depleted people's self-regulation resources by having them perform a variety of tasks that required self-control, such as resisting the temptation to eat freshly-baked cookies. They then put half of the participants in a good mood by, for example, giving them a small gift. The other half of the participants didn't have their mood adjusted. All of the participants then had to complete a second activity that required self-regulation, such as persisting on a difficult or unpleasant task. When they examined the results, the researchers found that participants who had been kept in a neutral mood didn't persist for very long on the second task, demonstrating the exhaustion of self-regulation. However, the participants who had been put into a good mood showed no reduction in their self-regulation. In fact, they persisted on the tasks for just as long as people whose self-regulation resources hadn't initially been exhausted by performing any draining activities (Tice, Baumeister, Shmueli, & Muraven, 2007). Good moods replenish resources. When we participate in stamp collecting, amateur theater, or bee keeping, one of the reasons we get a boost is because the positive emotions we feel as a result of enjoying the hobby replenishes our ability to self-regulate our thoughts and actions.

Another reason hobbies give us a boost is because we find them interesting. Interesting activities also replenish our self-regulation resources. In one study, American researchers first depleted people's self-regulation resources by having them complete the draining Stroop task, which you may recall from the meditation chapter involves presenting people with lots of color words written in contrasting colors (e.g., the word "orange" written in purple ink) and asking them to say the color of the ink in which each word is written. They then had people engage in a task that either involved solving mysteries, which aroused their interest, or a boring, word-underlining task, that didn't. They subsequently asked the participants to spend as much time as they wanted solving word puzzles, another draining task that requires self-regulation in order to persevere. When the researchers compared how long the two groups of participants spent working on the word puzzles, they found that those who had had their interest piqued by solving mysteries persisted longer, demonstrating that the interesting task had replenished the participants' self-regulation resources (Thoman, Smith, & Silvia, 2011). The same thing happens when we participate in a hobby. Because we find them interesting they replenish our ability to exert self-control.

In addition to self-regulation, hobbies can affect other resources as well. Hobbies such as creating works of art (Kaimal & Ray, 2017) and learning to cook (Reicks, Trofholz, Stang, & Laska, 2014) can enhance our confidence. And spending our leisure time playing video games can increase our self-esteem (Ryan, Rigby, & Przybylski, 2006). Whenever Jeff's virtual baseball team beats the computer, he feels proud about his ability to select the right players and out-perform his opponent. Although these may seem like small, perhaps even insignificant successes, they still give him a sense of accomplishment.

Hobbies are enjoyable leisure activities that we engage in voluntarily when we are free from our obligations (Pressman et al., 2009). As such, they satisfy our need for autonomy and help to fill the nourish bucket. The fact that we freely choose to partake in hobbies is vital because, as we've seen in previous chapters, whether or not we voluntarily choose to engage in specific leisure activities is an essential part of their boosting effect. As was stated in the friends and family chapter, socializing isn't boosting unless we want to socialize. And as we noted in the exercise chapter, physical activity makes us feel recovered only when we want to exercise. Similarly, if you spend your leisure time in the kitchen because you love to prepare meals and want to cook, you will find it restorative. However, if you cook reluctantly and throw spaghetti into a pot just because you have to feed your family, cooking will drain your resources rather than give you a boost.

Not only do we freely choose to engage in our hobbies, we choose them eagerly, which is part of what gives them their boosting power. Research shows that when we spend our leisure time participating in activities we want to engage in, we feel more recovered the next day (Volman, Bakker, & Xanthoploulou, 2013). This was further demonstrated by Canadian researchers who found that when we engage in low-effort activities, like reading a book or watching TV, it has a more pronounced effect on how recovered we feel the next morning if we were intrinsically motived to partake in the activities (ten Brummelhuis & Trougakos, 2014).

This little detail highlights why trying to boost by focusing on activities, instead of the ReNU buckets, can backfire. Many activities can be boosting or draining depending on whether we choose them freely, and satisfy our need for autonomy, or engage in them grudgingly. Even chores we often don't like to do, such as housework, can have recovery potential if they are freely chosen (ten Brummelhuis & Trougakos 2014). Have you ever noticed how attractive housework becomes when you have a more disagreeable task that needs to get done? Autonomy is also supported by our hobbies because we choose for ourselves *how* to engage with them. For example, video games allow us to influence the progress of the game and provide numerous opportunities to exert control, further satisfying our need for autonomy (Reinecke, 2009b)

Hobbies also allow us to satisfy our other psychological needs. Our need for competence is satisfied because hobbies allow us to master new challenges (Sonnentag, Venz, & Casper, 2017). For instance, as we rise to the challenges presented to us in video games we satisfy our need for competence (Reinecke, 2009a). Similarly, American researchers found that participating in creative endeavors during leisure time is associated with feelings of mastery (Eschleman, Madsen, Alarcon, & Barelka, 2014). And as we noted earlier, most hobbies give us opportunities to display creativity. When we learn how to cross-stitch, build a picturesque scene in our aquarium, or finally figure out how to lay out our new scrapbook, it gives us a sense of accomplishment that satisfies our need for competence.

TV and videos can also satisfy this need. TV is often considered a passive hobby that involves little concentration (Kubey & Csikszentmihalyi, 1990). And there's no denying that this does sometimes characterize the television-watching experience. But people watch TV for numerous reasons, including to learn new things and grow (Weaver, 2003). When we intensely watch a video or TV show in order to earnestly learn about the workings of the universe, figure out how to do home repairs, or better understand a global conflict, we are active processors of information and the growth in our knowledge base makes us feel more competent. Similarly, research shows that watching meaningful movies broadens our horizons and promotes our development, which additionally satisfies our need for competence (Reiger et al., 2014).

Hobbies can also fulfill our need for relatedness. Many hobbies, such as knitting circles, book clubs, and ballroom dancing are inherently social and let us build and enjoy connections with other people. Hobbies involving entertainment media can also help to satisfy this need. For example, a common reason people watch videos is to create an opportunity to spend time with their families (Winn, 2009). And online interactive video games offer us opportunities to mingle and build relationships with other people, again satisfying our need for relatedness (Ryan et al., 2006).

We should note that hobbies can also promote the satisfaction of physical needs, such as sleep. People who participate in a greater number of leisure activities that include hobbies sleep better than those who engage in fewer such activities (Pressman et al., 2009). Being an audiophile is a particularly useful hobby for achieving restful slumber. Research shows that listening to music is effective at enhancing the quality of our sleep (de Niet, Tiemens, Kloos, & Hutschemaekers, 2009).

Hobbies also fill both parts of the unhook bucket. First, as enjoyable leisure activities, hobbies can foster relaxation (Pressman et al., 2009). American researchers found that when we participate in creative endeavors during our leisure time we feel more relaxed (Eschleman et al., 2014). Finnish researchers have shown that receptive hobbies, such as watching live theater, also foster relaxation (Tuisku, Virtanen, de Bloom, & Kinnunen, 2016). We can also relax successfully by watching TV (Reiger et al., 2014), playing computer games (Reinecke, 2009a), or listening to music (van Goethem & Sloboda, 2011). In fact, when people are asked how listening to music helps them modify their mood the most common response is that it helps them relax (van Goethem & Sloboda, 2011). On that note, if you are looking to boost through music it might interest you to know that the most relaxing music has a moderate tempo of about 60 beats per minute, a simple rhythm that is easily repeatable, and little variation in loudness (Tan, Yowler, Super, & Fratianne, 2012)

Second, hobbies help us psychologically detach (Sonnentag et al., 2017). Because we get absorbed in them, hobbies prevent rumination and help us forget about our obligations. Research shows that because of the attention they require and immersion they produce, video games produce psychological detachment (Reinecke, 2009a). Similarly, watching enjoyable movies absorbs us and allows us to psychologically detach from our weekly obligations (Reiger et al., 2014). In general, we are more likely to psychologically detach when we participate in activities that we want to engage in (Volman et al., 2013). Hobbies fit the bill.

HOBBIES GIVE US A BOOST

Psychological Well-Being

It goes without saying that we like our hobbies. As such, they make us feel good and foster psychological well-being. American researchers found that people who reported participating in a greater number of leisure activities, including hobbies, had higher levels of positive emotions such as well-being and calm, and lower levels of negative emotions such as depression and anger. They also had higher levels of life satisfaction (Pressman et al., 2009).

Research on specific hobbies supports this general finding. For example, watching TV can foster positive emotions and keep negative emotions at bay by offering us a means of diversion (Schreier, 2006). Similarly, video games can increase our positive emotions and decrease our negative emotions (Przybylski, Weinstein, Murayama, Lynch, & Ryan, 2012). Listening to music also improves our mood (Radstaack et al., 2014) and makes us happy (van Goethem & Sloboda, 2011). Creating works of art increases our positive emotions and decreases our negative emotions too (Kaimal & Ray, 2017). For example, research has shown that when we spend time drawing it improves our mood and decreases our anxiety (Bell & Robbins, 2007). And singing in a choir has a comparable effect (Fancourt et al., 2016). Cooking as a hobby can also influence our well-being. Researchers in New Zealand found that young people who can cook report being happier, have more energy, and feel more fresh and rested than those who can't cook (Utter, Denny, Lucassen, & Dyson, 2016). More generally, when we spend time pursuing creative endeavors, the next day we enjoy more positive emotions. We also experience higher levels of flourishing, which includes feeling competent, optimistic, and that our lives have purpose and meaning (Conner, DeYoung, & Silva, 2018). Overall, hobbies are an effective tonic for fostering psychological well-being.

Physical Health

Hobbies can also promote our physical health. Earlier in the chapter we noted that hobbies help us recover from stress. One reason this happens is because the positive emotions produced by our hobbies counteract the negative emotions sometimes elicited by our obligations. This is called the undoing hypothesis (Fredrickson, 2001). Research has shown that positive emotions undo the negative effects of stress and anxiety and hasten cardiovascular recovery (Fredrickson, 2001). So, the pleasure and joy we derive from our hobbies help us recover from our obligations by returning us to a healthier, non-stressed state. In a similar vein, a 5-year-long study of people caring for relatives with Alzheimer's found that caregivers who spent more time engaged in pleasant leisure activities, including hobbies such as listening to music, watching TV, or reading, had lower diastolic blood pressure than caregivers who spent less time pursuing such activities (Mausbach et al., 2017).

People who participate in a greater number of leisure activities that include hobbies have lower levels of cortisol in their bodies (Pressman et al., 2009) and enjoy other beneficial health effects. For example, a study out of Taiwan found that when nurses listened to music for 30 minutes it reduced their cortisol levels, heart rate, and mean arterial blood pressure (Lai & Li, 2011). Similarly, British researchers showed that when cancer patients, or those who care for them, sing in a choir it reduces the cortisol in their bodies, and increases the level of cytokines, which are molecules that enhance our immune system (Fancourt et al., 2016). Watching comedies on television or another device can also reduce stress and improve the functioning of our immune system (Schreier, 2006).

Hobbies can even extend our lives. Researchers in Japan found that women who had surgery for breast cancer lived longer if they had a hobby, and the more hobbies they had the longer they survived (Tominaga et al., 1998). The researchers surmised that hobbies such as painting, dancing, or gardening might give patients strength, mitigate the stress of having a disease, and potentially increase social contact, which could prolong life. And the benefits of hobbies occur across our lifespan. Researchers from the University of Pittsburgh found that older people who spent more time participating in hobbies were subsequently less likely to develop dementia (Hughes, Chang, Bilt, & Ganguli, 2010). Overall, one of the ways hobbies give us a boost is by promoting our physical health.

Enhancement

Hobbies can also enhance us and make us better at our obligations. By giving us an enjoyable breather that allows us to restore and build resources, hobbies put us in a position to return to our obligations refreshed and more effective. For example, one study found that when Dutch employees participated in activities they wanted to engage in during their evening leisure time they felt more recovered in the morning and performed better at work (Volman et al., 2013). Because hobbies are activities we want to engage in, they similarly foster recovery and performance.

In another study, American researchers found that listening to music enhanced people's performance by leading them to respond more quickly and accurately on two different tasks (Angel, Polzella, & Elvers, 2010). However, consistent with one of the main themes of this chapter, the ability of music to improve our performance is contingent on whether or not we want to listen to music (Nantias & Schellenberg, 1999). As we saw earlier, music influences our moods, and when we voluntarily choose to listen to music our mood will be enhanced. The effect of music on performance is not due to the inherent properties of music, but on its ability to influence how we feel, which in turn, affects our performance (Schellenberg, 2012)

Video games can also enhance our performance. In one German study, participants had their resources drained by performing a repetitive task in which they spent 20 minutes monotonously highlighting particular combinations of letters within a text. They then either played a simple "drag and drop" video game or just waited for the next phase of the study to begin. Five minutes later, both groups performed a series of demanding mathematical problems. The results showed that compared to participants who had simply spent time waiting around, those who had played the video game solved more mathematical problems correctly (Reinecke et al., 2011). Essentially, playing the video game counteracted the effect of the draining initial task and gave participants a performance boost.

In a review of the effects that video games have on our information-processing abilities, American researchers reported that playing video games has beneficial effects on our visual processing skills such as the ability to notice changes in the environment, motor skills such as our hand-eye coordination, and our spatial imagery skills such as the ability to read a map (Powers, Brooks, Aldrich, Palladino, & Alfieri, 2013). A similar review by Chinese researchers found that when adults start playing video games that contain lots of action, their attention and memory improves (Wang et al., 2016). And it doesn't take long for these positive effects to occur. Video games can restore us and improve our performance after just 5 minutes of play (Reinecke & Trepte, 2006).

In another example of how hobbies enhance our performance, research has shown that participating in creative activities during our leisure time is associated with more creativity during our obligation time. American researchers asked duty captains in the United States Air Force to report the extent to which they engaged in creative activities during their personal time. The researchers then asked the captains' subordinates and co-workers to rate how creative the captains were in executing their responsibilities. For example, they asked how often the captains came up with creative solutions to problems. The researchers found that the captains who participated in more creative activities during their leisure time displayed greater creativity on the job (Eschleman et al., 2014). The authors concluded that creativity during leisure time promoted the captains' recovery, which stimulated more creativity during obligation time. Countering the possibility that creative captains are simply more creative in general, the researchers performed a separate study that produced similar results, even after taking people's general level of creativity into account (Eschleman et al., 2014). For people, like captains, whose weekly obligations are not intensely creative, engaging in creative activities during leisure time is restorative and boosting. In sum, hobbies can enhance our performance.

THE WHOLE STORY

Hobbies help us recover from our obligations, but any beneficial activity done in excess can become problematic. For example, exercise gives us a boost, but excessive exercise can become an addiction (Berczik et al., 2012) and be depleting. Sleep is necessary for recovery, but too much sleep is associated with premature death (Cohen-Mansfield & Perach, 2012). Hobbies are no different. Although computer games can give us a boost, excessively long periods of computer gaming can be draining and compromise our level of resources (Reinecke, 2009a). Light or moderate intentional television viewing may promote well-being, but heavy viewing that just fills time and substitutes for engaged living, doesn't (Schreier, 2006). Boosting is not promoted by being a couch potato. This general principle applies to any hobby that becomes an obsession, replaces engaged living, and depletes rather than fills the ReNU buckets. Spending all evening researching which movie poster to add to your collection won't promote positive family interactions and help you boost, but spending an hour doing so will. If Jeff, the communications manager who opened this chapter, plays video baseball for a short while to unwind after work, he's likely to get a boost. But if he plays all evening, every evening, he's more likely to get a divorce. As with most things, the good life is promoted by balance (Gruman, Lumley, & González-Morales, 2018). Hobbies will help you balance your life and recover from your obligations, as long as your hobbies don't become an obsession that consumes you instead of replenishing you.

SUMMARY

Although there is limited research in this area, the research that does exist provides strong evidence that hobbies are boosting. The evidence is also consistent with people's general experience with hobbies as offering an effective break from the demands, pressures and stress of their obligations. Some hobbies allow us to enjoy the benefits of other activities we've discussed. For example, gardening allows us to reap the benefits of nature (York & Wiseman, 2012), and dancing allows us to benefit from exercise (Rehfeld et al., 2017), but apart from these synergistic benefits hobbies serve as an effective and rewarding respite that in-and-of themselves fill the ReNU buckets, give us a boost, and help to transform our downtime into uptime.

Boosting Bites

Hobbies serve as an effective break from our obligations.

Hobbies buffer the negative effects of stress.

Intentional inefficiency, the deliberate attempt to be unproductive, fills all of the ReNU buckets.

To foster recovery, hobbies should draw on resources not used during our obligations.

The fact that we enjoy and freely choose our hobbies is a large part of what gives them their boosting power.

UPTIME ACTION PLAN

Step 1a. Choose a hobby. If you already have a hobby, or hobbies, that's great. If not, you should find one. To help make a good choice, consider activities to which you are naturally attracted. For example, if you walk into a book store, what section do you gravitate to first? Be sure to select a hobby that uses resources you don't draw on during your obligations. For example, as we suggested in the opening chapter, surgery involves tremendous concentration, precision, and following prescribed procedures. An effective hobby for a surgeon is something that draws on different, or opposite, skills. For instance, abstract painting, which involves imagination, looseness, and originality. Surgeons who paint in their uptime will get a boost. However, painters who do surgery in their uptime will get a jail sentence. We recommend that painters find a different hobby.

Step 1b. Consider reviving a hobby you used to practice. Many of us used to engage in a hobby but over time abandoned it. What hobbies did you used to practice? These likely represent activities you enjoyed immensely. Why not pick up that hobby again? If you used to draw, buy a new set of pencils. If you used to love flower arranging, see if classes are offered in your community. If you used to play the guitar, dust it off and re-learn some chords. In spaces below, write down some hobbies that you would find appealing and satisfying.

_____

_____

_____

_____

_____

_____

Step 2. Make time for your hobby. Carve out a dedicated timeslot to allow yourself to participate in your favorite hobbies. Devote an appropriate amount of time given your various responsibilities. In the spaces below, indicate the best time for you to indulge.

Monday_____   Tuesday _____

Wednesday_____   Thursday _____

Friday _____   Saturday_____

Sunday _____

Step 3. Practice intentional inefficiency. Within the time you allot for your hobby, allow yourself to dawdle and play. Don't worry about quality, quantity, or any other standard as you practice your hobby. Your only objective is to enjoy yourself. Allow your momentary inclinations to direct you. Have no goals, and no plans. You are not wasting time. You are boosting.

REFERENCES

Angel, L. A., Polzella, D. J., & Elvers, G. C. (2010). Background music and cognitive performance. *Perceptual and Motor Skills, 110*, 1059–1064.

Bell, C. E., & Robbins, S. J. (2007). Effect of art production on negative mood: A randomized, controlled trial. *Art Therapy: Journal of the American Art Therapy Association, 24*, 71–75.

Berczik, K., Szabo, A., Griffiths, M. D., Kurimay, T., Kun, B, Urbán, R., & Demetrovics, Z. (2012). Exercise addiction: Symptoms, diagnosis, epidemiology, and etiology. *Substance Use & Misuse, 47*, 403–417.

Best, S. (2010). *Leisure Studies: Themes & Perspectives*. Thousand Oaks, CA: SAGE.

Cohen-Mansfield, J., & Perach, R. (2012). Sleep duration, nap habits, and mortality in older persons. *Sleep, 35*, 1003–1009.

Cohn, M. A., Fredrickson, B. L., Brown, S. L., Mikels, J. A., & Conway, A. M. (2009). Happiness unpacked: Positive emotions increase life satisfaction by building resilience. *Emotion, 9*, 361–368.

Conner, T. S., DeYoung, C. G., & Silva, P. J. (2018). Everyday creative activity as a path to flourishing. *The Journal of Positive Psychology, 13*, 181–189.

Demerouti, E., Bakker, A. B., Guerts, S. A. E., & Taris, T. W. (2009). Daily recovery from work-related effort during non-work time. In S. Sonnentag, P. L. Perrewé, & Ganster, D. C. (Eds.), *Current perspectives on job-stress recovery* (pp. 85–123). Bingley, UK: Emerald.

de Niet, G. J., Tiemens, B. G., Kloos, M. W., & Hutschemaekers, G. J. M. (2009). Review of systematic reviews about the efficacy of non-pharmacological interventions to improve sleep quality in insomnia. *International Journal of Evidence-Based Healthcare, 7*, 233–242

Dik, B. J., & Hansen, J, C. (2008). Following passionate interests to well-being. *Journal of Career Assessment, 16*, 86–100.

Eschleman, K. J., Madsen, J., Alarcon, G., & Barelka, A. (2014). Benefiting from creative activity: The positive relationships between creative activity, recovery experiences, and performance-related outcomes. *Journal of Occupational and Organizational Psychology, 87*, 579–598.

Eschleman, K. J., Mathieu, M., & Cooper, J. (2017). Creating a recovery filled weekend: The moderating effect of occupation type on the relationship between non-work creative activity and state of feeling recovered at work. *Creativity Research Journal, 29*, 97–107.

Fancourt, D., Williamon, A., Carvalho, L. A., Steptoe, A., Dow, R., & Lewis, I. (2016). Singing modulates mood, stress, cortisol, cytokine and neuropeptide activity in cancer patients and carers. *Ecancermedicalscience, 10*. doi:10.3332/ecancer.2016.631

Fredrickson, B. L. (2001). The role of positive emotions in positive psychology: The broaden-and-build theory of positive emotions. *American Psychologist, 56*, 218–226.

Fredrickson, B. L., Cohn, M. A., Coffey, K. A., Pek, J., & Finkel, S. M. (2008). Open hearts build lives: Positive emotions, induced through loving-kindness meditation, build consequential personal resources. *Journal of Personality and Social Psychology, 95*, 1045–1062.

Garrosa, E., Blanco-Donoso, L. M., Carmona-Cobo, I., & Moreno-Jiménez, B. (2017). How do curiosity, meaning in life, and search for meaning predict college students' daily emotional exhaustion and engagement? *Journal of Happiness Studies, 18*, 17–40.

Gruman, J. A., Lumley, M. N., & González-Morales, M. G. (2018). Incorporating balance: Challenges and opportunities for positive psychology. *Canadian Psychology*. Advance online publication. doi:10.1037/cap0000109

Hammond, C., & Lewis, G. (2016). The rest test: Preliminary findings from a large-scale international survey on rest. In F. Callard, K. Staines, & J. Wilkes (Eds.), *The restless compendium: Interdisciplinary investigations of rest and its opposites* (pp. 59–67). Cham, Switzerland: Palgrave Macmillan

Hughes, T. F., Chang, C., Bilt, J. V., & Ganguli, M. (2010). Engagement in reading and hobbies and risk of incident dementia: The MoVIES project. *American Journal of Alzheimer's Disease & Other Dementias, 25*, 432–438.

Ivcevic, Z. (2007). Artistic and everyday creativity: An act-frequency approach. *The Journal of Creative Behavior, 41*, 271–290.

Iwasaki, Y., & Mannell, R. C. (2000). Hierarchical dimensions of leisure stress coping. *Leisure Sciences, 22*, 163–181.

Kaimal, G., & Ray, K. (2017). Free art-making in an art therapy open studio: Changes in affect and self-efficacy. *Arts & Health, 9*, 154–166.

Kubey, R., & Csikszentmihalyi, M. (1990). *Television and the quality of life: How viewing shapes everyday experience*. Hillsdale, NJ: Lawrence Erlbaum Associates.

Lai, H., & Li, Y. (2011). The effect of music on biochemical markers and self-perceived stress among first-line nurses: A randomized controlled crossover trial. *Journal of Advanced Nursing, 67*, 2414–2424.

List of hobbies, (n.d). *Wikipedia*. Retrieved from https://en.wikipedia.org/wiki/List_of_hobbies

Mausbach, B. T., Romero-Moreno, R., Bos, T., von Känel, R., Ziegler, M. G., Allison, M. A., ... Grant, I. (2017). Engagement in pleasant leisure activities and blood pressure: A 5-year longitudinal study in Alzheimer caregivers. *Psychosomatic Medicine, 79*, 735–741.

Nantais, K. M., & Schellenberg, E. G. (1999). The Mozart effect: An artifact of preference. *Psychological Science, 10*, 370–373

Perez, S. (2013, January 7). Nielsen: TV still king in media consumption; only 16 percent of TV homes have tablets. Retrieved from https://techcrunch.com/2013/01/07/nielsen-TV-still-king-in-media-consumption-only-16-percent-of-TV-homes-have-tablets/

Powers, K. L., Brooks, P. J., Aldrich, N. J., Palladino, M. A., & Alfieri, L. (2013). Effects of video-game play on information processing: A meta-analytic investigation. *Psychonomic Bulletin Review, 20*, 1055–1079.

Pressman, S. D., Matthews, K. A., Cohen, S., Martire, L. M., Scheier, M., Baum, A., & Schulz, R. (2009). Association of enjoyable leisure activities with psychological and physical well-being. *Psychosomatic Medicine, 71*, 725–732.

Przybylski, A. K., Weinstein, N., Murayama, K., Lynch, M. F., & Ryan, R. M. (2012). The ideal self at play: The appeal of video games that let you be all you can be. *Psychological Science, 23*, 69–76.

Radstaak, M., Geurts, S. A. E., Brosschot, J. F., & Kompier, M. A. J. (2014). Music and psychophysiological recovery from stress. *Psychosomatic Medicine, 76*, 529–537.

Rehfeld, K., Müller, P., Aye, M., Schmicker, M., Dordevic, M., Kaufmann, J., … Müller, N. G. (2017). Dancing or fitness sport? The effects of two training programs on hippocampal plasticity and balance abilities in healthy seniors. *Frontiers in Human Neuroscience, 11.* doi:10.3389/fnhum.2017.00305

Reicks, M., Trofholz, A. C., Stang, J. S., & Laska, M. N. (2014). Impact of cooking and home food preparation interventions among adults: Outcomes and implications for future programs. *Journal of Nutrition Education and Behavior, 46*, 259–276.

Reiger, D., Reinecke, L., Frischlich, L., & Bente, G. (2014). Media entertainment and well-being: Linking hedonic and eudaimonic entertainment experience to media-induced recovery and vitality. *Journal of Communication, 64*, 456–478.

Reinecke, L. (2009a). Games at work: The recreational use of computer games during working hours. *CyberPsychology & Behavior, 12*, 461–465.

Reinecke, L. (2009b). Games and recovery: The use of video and computer games to recuperate from stress and strain. *Journal of Media Psychology, 21*, 126–142.

Reinecke, L., Klatt, J., & Krämer, N. C. (2011). Entertaining media use and the satisfaction of recovery needs: Recovery outcomes associated with the use of interactive and noninteractive entertaining media. *Media Psychology, 14*, 192–215.

Reinecke, L., & Trepte, S. (2006). In a working mood? The effects of mood management processes on subsequent cognitive performance. *Journal of Media Psychology, 20*, 3–14.

Ryan, R., M., Rigby, C. S., & Przybylski, A. (2006). The motivational pull of video games: A self-determination theory approach. *Motivation and Emotion, 30*, 347–363.

Schellenberg, E. G. (2012). Cognitive performance after listening to music: A review of the Mozart effect. In R. MacDonald, G. Kreutz, & L. Mitchell (Eds.), *Music, health, and wellbeing* (pp. 324–338). New York, NY: Oxford University Press.

Schreier, M. (2006). (Subjective) well-being. In J. Bryant & P. Vorderer (Eds.), *Psychology of entertainment* (pp. 389–404). Mahwah, NJ: Lawrence Erlbaum Associates.

Sonnentag, S., Venz, L., & Casper, A. (2017). Advances in recovery research: What have we learned? What should be done next? *Journal of Occupational Health Psychology, 22*, 365–380.

Stanton-Rich, H. M., & Iso-Ahola, S. E. (1998). Burnout and leisure. *Journal of Applied Social Psychology, 28*, 1931–1950.

Stebbins, R. A. (2011). The semiotic self and serious leisure. *The American Sociologist, 42*, 238–248.

Tan, X., Yowler, C. J., Super, D. M., & Fratianne, R. B. (2012). The interplay of preference, familiarity, and psychophysical properties in defining relaxation music. *Journal of Music Therapy, 49*, 150–179.

ten Brummelhuis, L. L., & Trougakos, J. P. (2014). The recovery potential of intrinsically versus extrinsically motivated off-job activities. *Journal of Occupational and Organizational Psychology, 87*, 177–199.

Thoman, D. B., Smith, J. L., & Silvia, P. J. (2011). The resource replenishment function of interest. *Social Psychological and Personality Science, 2*, 592–599.

Tice, D. M., Baumeister, R. F., Shmueli, D., & Muraven, M. (2007). Restoring the self: positive affect helps improve self-regulation following ego depletion. *Journal of Experimental Social Psychology, 43*, 379–384.

Tominaga, K., Andow, J., Koyama, Y., Numao, S., Kurokawa, E., Ojima, M., & Nagai, M. (1998). Family environment, hobbies, and habits as psychosocial predictors of survival for surgically treated patients with breast cancer. *Japanese Journal of Clinical Oncology, 28*, 36–41.

Tuisku, K., Virtanen, M., de Bloom, J., & Kinnunen, U. (2016). Cultural leisure activities, recovery and work engagement among hospital employees. *Industrial Health, 54*, 254–262.

United States Department of Labor, Bureau of Labor Statistics. (2016). *American time use survey.* Retrieved from https://www.bls.gov/TUS/CHARTS/LEISURE.HTM

Utter, J., Denny, S., Lucassen, M., & Dyson, B. (2016). Adolescent cooking abilities and behaviors: Associations with nutrition and emotional well-being. *Journal of Nutrition Education and Behavior, 48*, 35–41.

van Goethem, A., & Sloboda, J. (2011). The functions of music for affect regulation. *Musicae Scientiae, 15*, 208–228.

Volman, F. E., Bakker, A. B., & Xanthopoulou, D. (2013). Recovery at home and performance at work: A diary study on self-family facilitation. *European Journal of Work and Organizational Psychology, 22*, 218–234.

Wang, P., Liu, H., Zhu, X., Meng, T., Li, H., & Zuo, X. (2016). Action video game training for healthy adults: A meta-analytic study. *Frontiers in Psychology, 7.* doi:10.3389/fpsyg.2016.00907

Weaver, J. B., III. (2003). Individual differences in television viewing motives. *Personality and Individual Differences, 35*, 1427–1437.

Winn, J. E. (2009). Videotime: Selection and structuring family social time with rented commercially prerecorded electronic media. *Journal of Broadcasting & Electronic Media, 53*, 227–241.

Winwood, P. C., Bakker, A. B., & Winefield, A. H. (2007). An investigation of the role of non-work-time behavior in buffering the effects of work strain. *Journal of Occupational and Environmental Medicine, 49*, 862–871.

Wright, J. J., Wright, S., Sadlo, G., & Stew, G. (2014). Exploring optimal experiences: A reverse theory perspective of flow and occupational science. *Journal of Occupational Science, 21*, 173–187.

York, M., & Wiseman, T. (2012). Gardening as an occupation: A critical review. *British Journal of Occupational Therapy, 75*, 76–84.

CHAPTER 10

VACATIONS DONE RIGHT

Nita had a routine. Get out of bed, drive the kids to daycare, come home, pull the blinds and go back to sleep for the day.

The 37-year-old mother of two looks back on the summer of 2011 as the summer she hit rock bottom. For weeks, Nita spent her days sleeping, getting up only to the sound of the alarm reminding her to go pick up her kids from daycare at the end of the day. She would then gather enough energy to make dinner and spend a couple of hours with her family before heading back to bed for the night.

"My husband didn't even catch on. He didn't know I wasn't working all day."

She had returned to work just 6 months earlier after being off for the birth of her second son. Motivated to prove to her colleagues that she could balance a successful career as a university professor and take care of her 1-year-old and 2-year-old boys, she hit the ground running. She managed to keep pace with the overwhelming demands of a publish-or-perish career and finish the school year before everything came to a crashing halt.

Nita had burned out.

After several weeks of spending her days in bed, she eventually confided in her husband and went to see her doctor.

"It turned out it was sheer exhaustion. I was in the habit of going on regular vacations and I had not gone on a vacation in 6 months."

It took suffering from severe burnout for Nita to realize how important vacations are to her health. Now between long weekend getaways, all-inclusive cruises and longer trips to big cities across North America, she makes sure she jets off on at least a dozen vacations a year.

"I can't check out of work unless I physically leave. I learned that the hard way."

Boost: The Science of Recharging Yourself in an Age of Unrelenting Demands, pp. 167–186

VACATIONS—THE GOOD

Not everyone has the chance to venture out on as many trips as Nita does, but even people who take an occasional vacation reap tremendous benefits. Studies that have examined the recuperative benefits of vacations have shown what many of us believe implicitly, that vacations are good for us. Vacations can fill all the ReNU buckets. They help us to replenish by giving us a break and an opportunity to rebuild our resources (Fritz & Sonnentag, 2006). They nourish our physical needs by encouraging better sleep (Strauss-Blasche, Ekmekcioglu, & Marktl, 2000). They nourish our psychological needs when they, for example, let us build new relationships (Strauss-Blasche, Reithofer, Schobersberger, Ekmekcioglu, & Marktl, 2005), freely choose how to spend our time (Davidson et al., 2010), or allow us to rise to exciting challenges and learn new things (Fritz & Sonnentag, 2006). Vacations also give us a chance to unhook by letting us relax (de Bloom, Guerts, & Kompier, 2013) and mentally detach from our obligations (Davidson et al., 2010).

Filling the ReNU buckets allows us to feel recovered so we return from vacations more invigorated, and start back into our regular routines more engaged, feeling less burned out (Kühnel & Sonnentag, 2011), and requiring less effort to get our work done (Fritz & Sonnentag, 2006). Indeed, research shows that vacations can give us a boost. They promote psychological well-being by putting us in a better mood, making us feel less tense, more energized and more satisfied (de Bloom et al., 2010). They also make us feel healthier (de Bloom et al., 2010). In fact, the more vacations you take, the longer you will live (Gump & Matthews, 2000).

If all that isn't enough for you, what if we told you vacations will also enhance you by making you smarter? Well, they may not actually raise your IQ, but they will improve your cognitive flexibility, which is your ability to think outside the box and come up with a diversity of ideas.

Jessica de Bloom, a leading recovery expert in Finland, conducted a study on vacationers who went away on summer holidays for at least two to three weeks and did interviews with them before, during, and after their trips. She and her colleagues discovered that vacationers' cognitive flexibility was much higher after returning home from a long summer holiday compared to before they left (de Bloom, Ritter, Kühnel, Reinders, & Guerts, 2014).

One might assume this happens simply because we are able to rest while away and therefore return re-energized and motivated, which can lead to an outpouring of fresh ideas. While it's true that taking a holiday allows us to replenish our mental resources so that we have the capacity to come up with new thoughts, de Bloom suspects there are a couple of other vacation benefits beyond recuperation that are likely playing a role.

The first is the exposure to different surroundings when we travel, she says. When we take a trip, especially outside of our own country, we experience different scenery, smells, tastes and people. All of our senses are being stimulated with new information, which can trigger us to think differently about things.

"People think creativity happens when you have a quiet moment, think very hard and suddenly this idea pops up. But that is not how it works. You need a lot of stimulation and input and then you get a lot of information that you can combine in different ways. This then helps you to be creative and get good ideas."

But it can't be all new experiences all the time, de Bloom adds. The ideas come from all the stimulation, but we also need to have moments of calmness so that we can process the information. This is why a work problem you may have been struggling to find a solution to for weeks finally gets solved while you are floating on your back in your hotel pool.

Cognitive flexibility is also spurred by positive emotions, which we often have an abundance of while away on vacation. The reason behind this is that when we are handling our obligations and experiencing stress from an overwhelming amount of demands we often go on autopilot and do only what is strictly necessary to fulfill our tasks. This task-oriented way of thinking limits our potential to be creative, says de Bloom.

Stressful situations can also cause an increase in negative emotions and these negative emotions can narrow our view, she adds.

"When you are feeling stressed and are walking through a forest you are less likely to see all the nice things around you. But when you aren't stressed and you go into a forest your mind will be more open and you will see the flowers, smell the air, get curious and want to explore."

Given that research reveals that extended periods of time off the job benefits workers, makes them more creative, and reduces absenteeism (Westman & Etzion, 2001), you would think employers would be jumping all over this. Well a few of them have.

Social Strata, a company in Charleston, South Carolina in the United States that creates online community software, established unlimited paid leave for its employees in 2010.

"What we had hoped would happen was that people would use it to enrich their lives and spend more time with their family," says Rosemary O'Neill, who owns the company with her husband Ted. "We wanted each of our employees to become more of a whole person, someone who brings great experience and family life back into the office."

To ensure employees aren't deterred from taking vacation because of a lack of specified days, the couple included a mandatory two-week holiday into the policy. So far, the plan has worked.

The policy allowed one new father to take 7 weeks off to spend with his baby, another employee to work flexible hours to care for an injured spouse and another to go away on a month's trip to Italy. The O'Neill's have even taken advantage of the policy and went away with their three young children on a month-long cross-country road trip a few summers ago.

"We have found our employees are now happier, more productive and more well-rounded. Taking time off brings a different perspective. You get new ideas and you get creative because you aren't sitting in a cubicle. I think it allows you to widen your horizons and bring a refreshed, renewed spirit to your work."

Just like Nita, the employees at Social Strata benefit from the boosting effects of regular vacations.

HOW LONG IS LONG ENOUGH?

Researchers have found that lengthy holidays have a place in effective recovery. But how long is long enough? De Bloom and her colleagues conducted a study where they regularly contacted people who went on an extended summer vacation and asked them about their experiences, such as how healthy they felt, how good their mood was, how satisfied they were, and how much tension and energy they were experiencing (de Bloom et al., 2013). These measures were combined to form an overall indicator of the vacationers' health and well-being. After analyzing the data, the researchers found that the vacationers' levels of health and well-being improved quickly once they went on vacation and peaked on the eighth day. When they surveyed people on the 12th and 16th days of long vacations they found that although people's levels of health and well-being were higher than they were before or after their vacations, they were not as high as on that magical eighth day. Additionally, when they compared the postvacation health and well-being of people who took holidays of different lengths, they found that their health and well-being after their trip was virtually unaffected by the duration of their vacation. Put simply, a vacation of 8 days generally produced the same health and well-being benefits as longer vacations.

It seems that vacations that allows us to disengage from our obligations for a little more than a week represent the ideal amount of time to get away from it all. It's long enough to produce a boosting effect, and has the same impact as vacations that last considerably longer. However, whatever length of trip you choose it is important to know that all the recovery you captured while away on your ideal vacation has an expiration date. Research on *vacation fade out effects* shows that once your vacation is over its benefits can last for as little as 1 day (de Bloom et al., 2013) or as long as a month

(Kühnel & Sonnentag, 2011), but on average tend to endure for only about 2 or 3 weeks (Chen & Petrick, 2013). That being said, there are ways to prolong the value you derive from your vacations.

VACATIONS—THE BAD AND THE UGLY

As fade out effects show, the complete vacation picture is not all sunshine and margaritas. Not all vacations give us a boost. One study that looked at the effects of vacations on people's health and well-being found that 60% of people report an increase in their health and well-being while on vacation, but 23% report no change, and 17% actually report a decrease (de Bloom et al., 2011). Put another way, close to half of people report either no change or a drop in how good they feel while on vacation and therefore don't enjoy a *vacation effect*. Why does this happen? One reason is that vacations can be difficult and taxing. For example, a study of Austrian employees found that about half of them engaged in stressful activities while on vacation (Strauss-Blasche et al., 2000). Vacations can also produce health problems such as gastrointenstinal disorders, expose people to dangers such as muggings, cause frustrations due to language barriers, intensify relationship problems among people forced to spend time together, and generate stress from the aggravations of travel. Additionally, some people, such as workaholics, may simply find the break from work traumatic (Eden, 1990). The first day or so on vacation seems to be the most awful. People's moods tend to be worst in the very early part of their vacations (Nawijn, 2010). Indeed, the risk of heart attacks on vacation is highest in the first 2 days (Kop, Vingerhoets, Kruithof, & Gottdiener, 2003). By contrast, people tend to feel best and enjoy the most positive emotions in the middle of their vacations (Lin, Kerstetter, Nawijn, & Mitas, 2014).

Another reason people don't always replenish on vacation concerns the main theme of this book—a failure to satisfy the ReNU elements. For example, people who have trouble rebuilding their resources on vacation by having to contend with non-work-related hassles, such as arguments with their partners, or who fail to nourish their need for competence while on vacation by not expanding their horizons in any way, return to work feeling more exhausted than those who avoid such hassles and satisfy their need to challenge themselves. Similarly, people who fail to unhook, and continue to ruminate about negative aspects of their work while on vacation, return from their trips more exhausted than those who manage to mentally disengage (Fritz & Sonnentag, 2006). Not only does a failure to satisfy the ReNU elements while on vacation produce no improvement in our well-being, it can actually reduce it. Research has found that when people don't recuperate on vacation it results in lower levels of life satisfaction and higher levels of negative mood (Strauss-Blasche et al., 2000). In short, bad vacations can backfire and leave you worse off than before you took one, so you have to take steps to ensure your vacation gives you a boost.

VACATIONS THAT BOOST

So how do we ensure our vacations give us a boost? We fill the ReNU buckets. For example, researchers have found that nourishing our need for autonomy is a big factor in whether we are able to recover while on vacation or not. As we discussed in the chapter on hobbies, satisfying our needs and doing what we enjoy during our time away from our obligations is vital to recovery. However, this can be tricky when you go on vacation with family, friends or even spouses. You and your co-vacationers may have different ideas of the best way to unwind. To avoid constantly compromising your wishes in order to keep peace, experts recommend that you discuss trip expectations beforehand to ensure everyone is on the same page. Once you are clear on what each person wants out of the holiday, you can determine how best to meet everyone's needs. If a family is traveling together, then each family member could have their own day to do what they want to do. Or if you are traveling with friends you could, for example, establish that you will eat dinner together every night, but everyone is free to do what they choose during the day.

"Many people are too focused on the idea that we go on holiday as a family and we need to spend all the time together and if we don't, we aren't a good family," says de Bloom. "But that's not true. Sometimes it's better for everyone if one person lies on the beach and the other person goes to the museum and then they meet up later."

Not only does this prevent arguments and potential resentment towards loved ones, but it also ensures everyone gets the most out of their vacation.

Changing your scenery is also a valuable ingredient in your ability to recharge your batteries while on vacation. A change of venue breaks you out of your routine, which gives your resources a break, lets you have new experiences which can satisfy your need for competence, and helps you forget about your obligations. In Nita's case, the fact that she didn't remove herself from her day-to-day stressors led to her becoming physically and emotionally exhausted.

It took Nita 3 months to fully recover from burnout and now she is more methodical about how often she travels in order to avoid vacation deprivation.

"I don't ever want to find myself in that state again."

Nita's vacation schedule is more intense than most people's. Her strategy is to have about half a dozen longer trips planned for the year with family and friends and then she fills in the gaps with several last-minute getaways with just her husband and their two boys. These "quick fix" trips as she calls them are how the couple rewards themselves after completing a significant project for work or successfully meeting an important deadline. Their recent 3-day Norwegian cruise was the grand finale to Nita completing the last edit of a textbook she had written.

"We always schedule our vacations around work deadlines. I won't compromise a deadline to go away because if I do then I won't enjoy my vacation. Our vacations are like the light at the end of the tunnel."

The couple has adjusted their lifestyle so that they always have a surplus of money each month to go towards their next last-minute holiday escape. Nita says that knowing these lengthy breaks are always just around the corner is what keeps her "hyper-productive." Essentially, she is able to focus on her career for small chunks of time because in a matter of weeks, she will get to go on vacation and give herself another boost.

"When I am on vacation I can be me. I am not a working mom, but rather just a mom, a wife and a friend."

Similarly, to Nita, Yahoo CEO Marissa Mayer is also able to focus intensely on work by splitting her year into regular vacations. Mayer, who is the youngest CEO of a Fortune 500 company, clocks as many as 130 hours per week, but makes it a priority to recharge by taking week-long vacations every 4 months.

When we're depleted, handling our obligations can feel like an overwhelming amount of work. But research shows that when people return from a successfully relaxing vacation, their everyday obligations seem to take less effort (Fritz & Sonnentag, 2006).

For Nita, vacations lighten her load and lead to increased success when she returns to work.

"I find I do more strategic work when I come back from vacation because I have had time to step away from the small picture and can see the big picture. By stepping away, you can catch things that you wouldn't have otherwise recognized. I find it helps with my productivity."

Like plenty of Canadians, Nita flees to warmer temperatures when her home near Toronto is covered in snow. Gerhard Strauss-Blasche, an Austrian recovery researcher, says there are benefits to this besides just getting a good tan. In one study he conducted, he found that vacationers who spent their holiday at a spa during its warmer months returned from their trip more recovered than those who visited during a cooler period (Strauss-Blasche, Ekmekcioglu, Leibetseder, Melchart, & Marktl, 2002). He is unclear as to why this might be but suspects the mood-enhancing effects of plenty of sunshine may be a factor.

Besides weather, Strauss-Blasche et al. (2002) also found other variables that can help you take the boosting powers of vacations to the next level. In another study, he examined a group of overweight men who participated in an organized weight-loss vacation that involved going on a hiking trek every second day. He measured their recovery for weeks after the trip and found the effect of the vacation lasted longer than previous studies he had conducted on vacationers. Rather than experiencing a fade out of the benefits a few weeks after the vacation ended, these men were still better off mentally six weeks after they returned from the trip (Strauss-Blasche, Riedmann, et al., 2004).

"This points to the possibility that what you do while on vacation makes a difference and that it's possible physical activity may prolong vacation effects."

However, what you decide to do on your vacation ultimately depends on your personality and the lifestyle you lead during your regular workweek, he adds.

If you do a lot of physical work as part of your job then it may be better for you to spend your vacation relaxing on the beach. But if you sit at a desk job all day, then an adventure-filled African Safari might be the ticket. Or if you are bored with your work then you might want to take on a challenge during your break such as mountain climbing.

"Your vacation should complement whatever your work issues are."

And we wouldn't be addressing all the ways to make the most of your vacation if we didn't mention the importance of leaving your work at home while you are enjoying your getaway. Experts say checking email while on vacation should be avoided at all costs because it can cause you to ruminate about work, which hinders recovery. Indeed, research shows that the more we check our devices for obligation-related messages while on vacation, the less recovered we feel (Kirillova & Wang, 2016). Essentially, Strauss-Blasche and others recommend what we have advocated throughout this entire book. If you want to get a boost while on vacation, you need to fill the ReNU buckets. Particularly, in this case, the unhook bucket.

However, for those who actually take comfort in checking in on work while away and find avoiding their inbox when on vacation to be a stressful test in self-discipline, it may help for them to pick a day during their break to take a quick peek. While de Bloom still insists that avoiding work while away is crucial, if you are spending your time by the pool agonizing about whether an important deal went through or if your colleagues pulled off a big presentation, then sometimes it can help to check in, relieve any concerns, and put the issue out of your mind.

Speaking of electronics, if you are anxious on vacation because you know you are going to spend days wading through a mountain of emails when you return from your trip, try e-mail triage. Every 3 or 4 days check your messages quickly. First, immediately delete any inconsequential messages. Second, respond to any messages that can be dispatched with a *simple and quick* reply. Third, mark as unread anything that requires a more substantial response, which you can address when you get back to your obligations. E-mail triage has the effect of reducing the mountain of e-mails that await you to a small pile that can be quickly and efficiently managed upon your return. Your goal in this process is to keep your head in vacation mode while eliminating e-mail angst.

Ultimately, you must create a vacation that works for you. Only people who find their vacations enjoyable, satisfying, and restorative enjoy a boosting effect (Strauss-Blasche et al., 2000). One of the classic studies of vacations found that people who were satisfied with their vacations showed a dramatic reduction in the level of burnout they experienced while on vacation, whereas those who were not satisfied showed a negligible drop in burnout levels (Westman & Eden, 1997). Satisfying the ReNU elements is what will give you a boost, but the specific elements that will give you the most satisfaction and enjoyment will depend on your personal interests and assessment of which of your ReNU buckets is low and in need of attention.

Research has revealed that passive activities, like lying on the beach relaxing and daydreaming, produce a significant vacation effect (de Bloom et al., 2013). But recuperation is also facilitated by active pursuits such as exercise and socializing (Strauss-Blasche et al., 2005). The heuristic power of the ReNU model doesn't change on vacation. You'll get a boost from participating in activities you enjoy that best allow you to fill the ReNU buckets that are most depleted from your obligations. Choosing activities that you find particularly pleasurable, and avoiding even a single unpleasant experience seems to be key to generating a vacation effect and getting a boost (de Bloom et al., 2011).

VACATIONS WITH STAYING POWER

Most people take vacations a week at a time. But think about what happens when you return from a travel vacation on a Sunday afternoon. You unlock the front door, and after rejoicing because the house didn't burn down, and nobody broke into it, you need to check your e-mail, answer a bunch of phone messages, water your plants, buy groceries, do laundry, and tidy up the mess you made before you left. You only have a few hours to do this before going to bed in anticipation of your obligations the next day and you're already tired from the return trip home. All you really want to do is take it easy, but you can't. Now you're stressed and on Monday when your colleagues ask you how your vacation was you're likely to respond with the common complaint that you "need a vacation from your vacation."

The solution to this problem is to return from holidays early enough before your vacation time expires so you give yourself sufficient time to handle all that needs to be done for you to return to your normal life. This can be a hard pill to swallow. The purpose of travel vacations is to get away from it all, so we tend to think the most successful ones involve getting away from it all for as long as possible, which means coming home late Sunday evening. But that overlooks the real purpose of a vacation, which is to recover. It's not only the amount of time we spend in leisure but also the quality of our leisure time that matters. If cutting down your time away by one day, and coming home on Saturday helps you return to your obligations more refreshed because it gives you an extra day at home to get organized, then that represents a better boost.

Research out of Austria has shown that the day of the week people return from a getaway makes a difference in how much positive emotion they experience once at home. In one study, those who returned from a three-week resort respite between Thursday and Saturday reported being in a better mood longer than those who returned on a Sunday (Strauss-Blasche, Muhry, Lehofer, Moser, & Marktl, 2004). Given that positive mood is a main component of boosting, returning from vacation early enough to allow yourself sufficient time to leisurely get back into the swing of your regular routine is an important part of transforming your downtime into uptime.

Another way to maintain the boosting effects of vacations is to avoid jumping back into work full speed. It's common for people to put in overtime at the office immediately after a vacation because they feel recharged, ready to work, and want to catch up. However, research reveals that if we clock too many hours too soon, we will quickly erase the boosting benefits that came with taking the holiday and end up more drained and right back where we started before we left for the trip (Fritz & Sonnentag, 2006).

Finally, there is one last important strategy we recommend to make the benefits of extended periods of uptime stick. We suggest that you consider taking fewer long vacations and apply those saved up vacation days towards creating more long weekends. Think about it. If fade out effects cause our vacation boosts to disappear in a matter of weeks, why not take another little break a few weeks after a vacation to maintain the benefits, and then another, and another? Research has shown that shorter vacations are as effective at reducing stress and burnout as longer vacations (Etzion, 2003). Although 8 days of vacation is ideal for promoting health and well-being, other research has revealed that long weekends are as effective at reducing exhaustion, anxiety and fatigue as longer holidays (Flaxman, Ménard, Bond, & Kinman, 2012). Taking more frequent long weekends instead of infrequent vacations allows us to get regular boosts that undermine those undesirable fade out effects.

THE STAYCATION

While travel vacations are a great way to recuperate, there are some potential travel aggravations that can work you up rather than wind you down. Traffic jams, lost luggage and jet lag are just some of the not-so-pleasant parts of travel that can reduce well-being rather than boost it and for some of us it's just not worth the hassle. Also, many of us simply don't have the discretionary funds required to fly off on regular getaways. This is where the staycation comes in. De Bloom recommends that if you are someone who tenses up at the idea of travel, it might be better to spend holidays in the comfort of your own home. Staycations are effective. Researchers have discovered that enjoying stress-free days at home produces as much recuperation as going away (Strauss-Blasche et al., 2000). But if you don't do it right, then you could reach the end of your staycation wondering where your regular obligations ended, and your break began, adds de Bloom.

"The danger when you stay at home is that you are very close to your work. It's really easy to check emails and do a bit of work and often staying at home means the housework still goes on, which can be a stressful chore for many people."

Essentially, it's more difficult to unhook when on a staycation because, as we discussed in the chapter on cutting the virtual cord, many of the cues that are associated with obligations and stress are everywhere you turn. In order to optimize your break at home, you should disconnect from your computer or phone, so you aren't tempted to squeeze in work. You should also reduce the amount of housework you take on, unless you like it. But most importantly, you should try to act like a tourist in your city, says de Bloom.

"Go sightseeing and do tourist activities. You will discover new things that you hadn't paid attention to before. If you are able to have this kind of holiday at home, then it can be very relaxing."

Particularly if you visit places that are new to you, in your own city or town you can experience the same sense of novelty and the feeling of being "somewhere else" that you have when traveling. Walking through a garden at a museum you've never attended, having lunch at a restaurant you've never been to, and lounging at a café in a part of town you rarely frequent can all make you feel as though you're away from your regular life and routine. You're not tricking yourself when doing this. You're enjoying the exact same freshness of experience you would if you had enjoyed these experiences after flying across an ocean. And, on your local excursions, don't forget to be intentionally inefficient. Hey, you're on vacation!

LEISURE SICKNESS

Although vacations have the potential to be a perfect opportunity to boost, for some people these breaks can actually make them feel sick. Do you ever find you tend to come down with a flu or a cold when you are on holiday? If so, it could mean you suffer from leisure sickness. Ad Vingerhoets, a researcher in the Netherlands who is the leading expert in this emerging area, has found that as much as three per cent of the population suffers from this phenomenon (Vingerhoets, van Huijgevoort, & Van Heck, 2002).

So, what is leisure sickness? Well it's essentially an onset of symptoms including headaches, muscle pains, fever and nausea that come on during the transition from a stretch of work to a stretch of leisure time such as vacations or weekends (Vingerhoets et al., 2002). So far researchers have been able to pin down a number of potential causes for it.

One theory is that an overload of adrenaline is behind the flu-like symptoms. When we are faced with overwhelming demands during our obligations our body produces more adrenaline, so we have the energy to take on the tasks. The problem is some of us, who are unable to disengage from our obligations before taking a holiday, may sometimes continue to produce these high levels of adrenaline even though we aren't facing the obligations and no longer need it. Having all this excess energy when we don't need it creates an "imbalance," in your body, says Vingerhoets.

"Your normal bodily functions can be disturbed by this high adrenaline causing acute immunological reactions."

Another potential cause for leisure sickness is that we are simply unaware of any physical symptoms we are experiencing until our obligations are over and we have had a chance to focus on ourselves, says Vingerhoets.

"Our brains have a limited capacity for attention, so we direct our attention to the things that are important. You don't feel pain when you don't pay attention to it. It's the same way professional athletes often don't feel pain until after the game is over because there was too much distraction while they were playing. Their attention was focused on the game and not on their body."

If you are wrapped up in a busy week, you may not notice a sore back or dull headache until the moment you sit down to start your weekend or begin packing your bags for a week-long cruise.

Researchers also suspect that the change in lifestyle that often occurs during vacations compared to during obligation time could be linked to the onset of leisure sickness. The amount of alcohol and caffeine we consume often changes on vacations and so does our sleep patterns. This can cause an imbalance and compromise our body rhythms, says Vingerhoets.

Finally, it is thought leisure sickness could be connected to the idea that our bodies are able to postpone sickness until we are ready to handle it.

This follows the same concept of how people appear to be able to hold off death until after an important personal event such as seeing a loved one for the last time or celebrating Christmas with the family. For instance, Charles Schulz, the legendary creator of the Peanuts comic strip, died just hours before he knew his final comic would be published. Similarly, some people may be able to fend off sickness when they need to be at their best. Once their tasks are complete, they let their guard down, which results in a cold or flu. Just ask Vingerhoets himself who for years found himself nursing the sniffles every Christmas and New Year's during his break from work.

"After a few years I began to wonder how this was possible and I became really aware that something was going on," he says. "This was actually the reason I started to study leisure sickness."

Although there are many possible reasons behind why some people literally find time off sickening, Vingerhoets says certain personalities are more vulnerable than others. For example, workaholics are more susceptible to leisure sickness because they are likely amped with adrenaline throughout the workweek and have trouble with the switch to vacation mode, he says. These people also tend to feel guilty when they are relaxing, and this guilt can cause stress, which in turn can activate physical symptoms.

People who are sensation seekers are also more likely to suffer from leisure sickness because of the potential lack of stimulation during their leisure time. If they thrive off of the hustle and bustle they may get from the work week, a relaxing vacation might seem boring. This boredom can then manifest itself into the flu-like symptoms of leisure sickness, says Vingerhoets.

So how do we prevent sickness from destroying all the boosting effects of vacations? Vingerhoets has found exercising on Friday night and before going on holiday has helped him fend off leisure sickness. This routine helps him to differentiate the weekdays from the weekend or vacation and lets his body know it's time to decompress. Other possible measures include changing how you sleep, reducing the amount of caffeine and alcohol you consume, and considering whether a different life pattern is warranted (Van Heck & Vingerhoets, 2007).

"Once you realize it's happening, you must do your best to create a better balance between work and nonwork."

SUMMARY

As the longest period of uptime, vacations provide us with substantial opportunities to boost. However, getting a boost on vacation is by no means guaranteed. Unless vacations help us fill the ReNU buckets we are not only unlikely to boost, but can even return from vacations feeling and being worse off than before the vacation started. Choosing pleasurable activities that allow us to rebuild our resources, nourish our needs, and unhook while on vacation is the most surefire way to guarantee that our vacations recharge our batteries and let us return to our obligations feeling better, healthier, and more effective than before we left.

Boosting Bites

Take vacations that are around 8 days long.

Come home from your vacation a little early so you have a few days to prepare before returning to your regular routine.

Save up vacations days so you can take several long weekends throughout the year to minimize fade-out effects.

Ease back into your obligations after you return from vacation.

Make sure your days spent on vacation are vastly different than your typical routine. If you work in an office, go on an adventure vacation and if you do physical labor find a trip that will help your body to recuperate.

Practice e-mail triage.

When on a staycation be a tourist in your own city. Visit an area you have never been to before or go to the local museum. Avoid your computer and phone.

UPTIME ACTION PLAN

Step 1. Before you leave on vacation, plan to minimize potential stressors. For example, before your departure pre-book any activities that you are hoping to do while away. Speak with your fellow vacationers and plan out shared and solo activities. Also, reserve a flight outside of rush hour so you are not anxious about making your flight. All of this allows you to minimize stress and get scheduling, organizing, and other obligation-type activities out of the way before you depart. This frees you up to just enjoy your vacation time. In the space below indicate the steps you will take to minimize vacation stress.

_____

_____

_____

_____

_____

_____

_____

Step 2. On vacation, fill your ReNU buckets. For example, think about which resources you use most often during your daily obligations and engage in vacation activities that will give those resources a rest. If you're a waitress and need to draw on the resource of emotional control all week while dealing with difficult customers, on vacation consider taking an acting workshop in which you can let your emotions run wild, or go on a whitewater rafting ride and scream your head off. In the space below write down which ReNU buckets you most need to fill on vacation, and which activities will give you the most pleasure.

This is how I will fill the rebuild bucket on vacation

_____

_____

_____

_____

_____

_____

This is how I will fill the nourish bucket on vacation

_____

_____

_____

_____

_____

_____

This is how I will fill the unhook bucket on vacation

_____

_____

_____

_____

_____

_____

_____

These are the activities that will give me the most pleasure on vacation

_____

_____

_____

_____

_____

_____

_____

Step 3. Reminiscing about your trip will help extend the vacation effect (Nawijn, 2011). Take pictures while you are traveling and consider making a photo album when you return. Simply flipping through the pages will help you extend the holiday bliss. The same goes for writing a journal while on vacation and re-reading it weeks after you have returned home. You can also get together with the people you travelled with, talk about the trip and even make a dish similar to what you ate while away. In the space below consider how to extend the benefits of your vacation.

_____

_____

_____

_____

_____

_____

_____

REFERENCES

Chen, C.-C., & Petrick, J. F. (2013). Health and wellness benefits of travel experiences: A literature review. *Journal of Travel Research, 52*, 709–719.

Davidson, O. B., Eden, D., Westman, M., Cohen-Charash, Y., Hammer, L. B., Kluger, A. N., … Rosenblatt, Z. (2010). Sabbatical leave: Who gains and how much? *Journal of Applied Psychology, 95*(5), 953–964,

de Bloom, J., Guerts, S. A. E., & Kompier, M. A. J. (2013). Vacation (after-) effects on employee health and well-being, and the role of vacation activities, experiences and sleep. *Journal of Happiness Studies, 14*, 613–633.

de Bloom, J., Geurts, A. E., Sonnentag, S., Taris, T., de Weerth, C., & Kompier, M. A. J. (2011). How does a vacation from work affect employee health and well-being? *Psychology and Health, 26*, 1606–1622.

de Bloom, J., Geurts, A. E., Taris, T., Sonnentag, S., de Weerth, C., & Kompier, M. A. J. (2010). Effects of vacation from work on health and well-being: Lots of fun, quickly gone. *Work & Stress, 24*, 196–216.

de Bloom, J., Ritter, S., Kühnel, J., Reinders, J., & Guerts, S. (2014). Vacation from work: A ticket to creativity? The effects of recreational travel on cognitive flexibility and originality. *Tourism Management, 44*, 164–171.

Eden, D. (1990). Acute and chronic job stress, strain, and vacation relief. *Organizational Behavior and Human Decision Processes, 45*, 175–193.

Etzion, D. (2003). Annual vacations: duration of relief from job stressors and burnout. *Anxiety, Stress, and Coping, 16*, 213–226.

Flaxman, P. E., Ménard, J., Bond, F. W., & Kinman, G. (2012). Academics' experiences of a respite from work: Effects of self-critical perfectionism and perseverative cognition on postrespite well-being. *Journal of Applied Psychology, 97*, 854–865.

Fritz, C., & Sonnentag, S. (2006). Recovery, well-being, and performance-related outcomes: The role of workload and vacation experiences. *Journal of Applied Psychology, 91*, 936–945

Gump, B. B., & Matthews, K. A. (2000). Are vacations good for your health? The 9-year mortality experience after the multiple risk factor intervention trial. *Psychosomatic Medicine, 62*, 608–612.

Kirillova, K., & Wang, D. (2016). Smartphone (dis)connectedness and vacation recovery. *Annals of Tourism Research, 61*, 157–169.

Kop, W. J., Vingerhoets, A., Kruithof, G.-J., & Gottdiener, J. S. (2003). Risk factors for myocardial infarction during vacation travel. *Psychosomatic Medicine, 65*, 396–401.

Kühnel, J., & Sonnentag, S. (2011). How long do you benefit from a vacation? A closer look at the fade-out of vacatiin effects. *Journal of Organizational Behavior, 32*, 125–143.

Lin, Y., Kerstetter, D., Nawijn, J., & Mitas, O. (2014). Changes in emotions and their interactions with personality in a vacation context. *Tourism Management, 40*, 416–424.

Nawijn, J. (2010). The holiday happiness curve: A preliminary investigation into mood during a holiday abroad. *International Journal of Tourism Research, 12*, 281–290.

Nawijn, J. (2011). Happiness through vacationing: Just a temporary boost or long-term benefits? *Journal of Happiness Studies, 12,* 651–665.

Strauss-Blasche, G., Ekmekcioglu, C., Leibetseder, V., Melchart, H., & Marktl, W. (2002). Seasonal variation in effect of spa therapy on chronic pain. *Chronobiology International, 19,* 483–495.

Strauss-Blasche, G., Ekmekcioglu, C., & Marktl, W. (2000). Does vacation enable recuperation? Changes in well-being associated with time away from work. *Occupational Medicine, 50,* 167–172.

Strauss-Blasche, G., Muhry, F., Lehofer, M., Moser, M., & Marktl W. (2004). Time course of well-being after a three-week resort-based respite from occupational and domestic demands: Carry-over, contrast and situation effects. *Journal of Leisure Research, 36,* 293–309.

Strauss-Blache, G., Reidmann, B., Schobersberger, W., Ekmekcioglu, C., Reidman, G., Waanders, R., ... Humpeler, E. (2004). Vacation at moderate and low altitude improves perceived health in individuals with metabolic syndrome. *Journal of Travel Medicine, 11,* 300–306.

Strauss-Blasche, G., Reithofer, B., Schobersberger, W., Ekmekcioglu, C., & Marktl, W. (2005). Effect of vacation on health: Moderating factors and vacation outcome. *Journal of Travel Medicine, 12,* 94–101.

Van Heck, G., & Vingerhoets, A. J. J. M. (2007). Leisure sickness: A biopsychosocial perspective. *Psihologijske Teme, 16,* 187–200.

Vingerhoets, A. J. J. M., Van Huijgevoort, M., & Van Heck, G. (2002). Leisure sickness: A pilot study on its prevalence, phenomenology, and background. *Psychotherapy and Psychosomatics, 71,* 311–317.

Westman, M., & Eden, D. (1997). Effects of respite from work on burnout: Vacation relief and fade-out. *Journal of Applied Psychology, 82,* 516–527.

Westman, M., & Etzion, D. (2001). The impact of vacation and job stress on burnout and absenteeism. *Psychology and Health, 16,* 595–606.

EPILOGUE

We all need periodic breaks from our obligations in order to recover and be at our best. Unfortunately, many of us don't recover effectively. We are regularly tired, stressed, depleted and unable to get back to prime form, even when we have some downtime and are able to get away from our weekly tasks. The reason for our constant exhaustion is that downtime is insufficient to produce recovery. In this book we've shown you how to transform your downtime into uptime in order to rejuvenate yourself, recharge your batteries, and get a boost that results in a happier, healthier and enhanced you.

An important take-away from this book is that we don't need an entire evening, weekend, or vacation to start recovering. Brief moments of recuperation are regularly available to us. We can get a boost on our lunch breaks (Trougakos, Hideg, Cheng, & Beal, 2014), coffee breaks, and even smaller breaks we take from our obligations (Tucker, 2003). We derive boosting benefits from just five minutes of meditation (Dalai Lama & Hopkins, 2002), short interactions with friendly colleagues (Kim, Park, & Niu, 2017), a 10-minute nap (Brooks & Lack, 2006), or 5 minutes of playing computer games (Reinecke & Trepte, 2006). We certainly want to make the most of our longer periods of uptime, but in our increasingly harried world it's good to know that there are shorter opportunities to give ourselves a boost whenever we feel depleted.

WE KNOW IT WORKS!

Writing this book was an enormously time-consuming and arduous under-taking, and as a result was very draining. Throughout the process, we, the authors, regularly took advantage of the material contained in the book to get a boost. When Jamie felt run down and tired in the middle of the day and writing became a difficult, frustrating chore, he frequently gave himself a boost by listening to music for a few minutes, going for a brief walk, playing with his kids, taking a short nap, streaming a YouTube video with beautiful scenes of nature, or spending a few minutes engaged in his lifelong hobby—whistling. And they all worked! Every single time he took a boosting break he returned to his writing task recharged, refreshed, and more effective. Without fail, a short boosting break always resulted in a better mood, less stress, more creativity, and higher quality output.

For Deirdre, working on the book taught her that simply being thought-ful about the way she spends the moments between tasks significantly improves not only her productivity but also her state of mind. On days when she is feeling overwhelmed from juggling the responsibilities of caring for three small children, managing a household, succeeding at her job and writing, she ensures she makes smarter choices about how to spend her breaks. Instead of using the hour while her youngest child is napping to tidy the house, she now runs on the treadmill. In fact, it was during these runs that she came up with a majority of her ideas for this book.

She also changed the way she spends the couple of hours in the evening after the kids go to bed to make sure she squeezes in a boost. Rather than sitting in front of her laptop frantically trying to type out as many para-graphs as possible before climbing the stairs to bed, she quits writing 20 minutes early, so she can read a good book snuggled up under a blanket on the couch. The cyclone of stressful thoughts that used to swirl around her head as she tried to fall asleep are now replaced with the descriptive images of a well-written fiction novel, easing her into a peaceful slumber. And although most of Deirdre's boosting happens when she is kid-free, she has also learned how to harness the benefits of turning her downtime into uptime even in the company of her children. On days when she is feeling restless, drained or stressed, she makes sure to get out into nature. So instead of taking the kids to the library or museum, she takes them on a hike to feed the birds or to the pond to throw rocks. It's fun for them and rejuvenating for her.

These are just a few of the examples of how we, the authors, have lived the ideas included in this book. We are overjoyed to be able to share them with you because we know first-hand that they are effective and will make a difference in your life.

EVERYONE NEEDS TO BOOST

Not long ago, Jamie did a workshop on boosting for a group of lawyers, a profession notorious for putting in very long hours. After Jamie had explained the advantages of getting away from work to recharge our batteries and return to work more effective, one of the lawyers put his hand up and said "But I love my work. It gives me energy. Shouldn't I keep working through the weekend instead of taking a break?" It was a reasonable question, but the available evidence suggests that the answer is "no."

Research has shown that people who are devoted to their obligations not only need an occasional break, but they actually reap more benefits from their breaks than others. For example, a study of Dutch employees found that compared to nonworkaholics, when workaholics continue working in the evening, they feel less vigorous, less happy, and less recovered at bedtime. The study also found that exercise in the evening has a stronger effect on how happy and recovered workaholics feel at bedtime compared to nonworkaholics (Bakker, Demerouti, Oerlemans, & Sonnentag, 2013). Another study found that vacations have a bigger, positive impact on the happiness, satisfaction, and overall mood of workaholics than their less work-obsessed peers (de Bloom, Radstaak, & Guerts, 2014).

People who love their work also experience stronger effects when it comes to unhooking. A German study found that employees who are highly engaged at work benefit more from psychological detachment than those who are less engaged. Specifically, compared to those who are less engaged, highly engaged employees have higher positive emotions at the end of the workweek when they psychologically detach during their leisure time (Sonnentag, Mojza, Binnewies, & Scholl, 2008). For employees who are particularly dedicated and absorbed by their work, psychological detachment from their jobs during leisure time seems to be especially valuable.

Ultimately, the available research indicates that the lawyer's intuition that he should continue to indulge in his passion for work during his leisure time because he finds it invigorating was wrong. If he loves his job, is engaged by it, and works intensely at it, he is a particularly good candidate for some uptime. Everyone needs to boost.

ENJOY THE POWER OF KNOWING HOW TO BOOST

In this book, we haven't discussed every potentially restorative endeavor. For example, we haven't discussed religious activity. Practicing a religion is an effective way to get a boost. When we go to church, or the mosque or synagogue, we pray, which is a form of meditation that can replenish our resources, we socialize with like-minded people which satisfies our need for relatedness, and we hopefully cut the virtual cord, which lets us psychologically detach. Indeed, research shows that religious environments, like monasteries, have restorative qualities (Ouellette, Kaplan, & Kaplan, 2005). So, apart from the spiritual benefits of worship, religious activity is an effective way to get a boost because it allows us to fill the ReNU buckets. It also directly promotes psychological well-being through the meaningfulness of religious participation.

We don't need to discuss every potentially restorative activity in the book. With the ReNU model in mind, you are now in a position to choose from among the innumerable leisure time activities those that are most likely to give you a boost. If the activities you select help you replenish resources, satisfy your physical and psychological needs, and let you relax and psychologically detach, you will be boosting. As we noted in the first chapter, there is no work involved in getting a boost, you just need to make smart choices. And now you understand the basis on which to make those choices, and have the tools you need to ensure that you make the best choices possible.

In the end, boosting is about living the best life you can. It is a necessary counterpoint to the draining demands of our incessant obligations. Our fast-paced, electronically-infused, media-obsessed world has led many of us to implicitly believe that we must always be busy, moving, accomplishing, and looking for the next rung on the ladder. We have become so narrowly focused on success, consumption, and industriousness that we have forgotten about the need to slow down, decompress, and enjoy life's simple pleasures during the limited amount of time we have on the planet. We've become trained to look forward in anticipation, instead of looking around in awe. We've learned to strive, but forgotten how to bask. We understand how to drive ourselves hard, but overlook the need to re-fuel. This leaves us exhausted and feeling empty. Boosting is about recapturing the meaningful moments between obligation-related matters that fill our lives with recuperative pleasure. It's about indulging in the quiet spells and exciting episodes that refresh and inspire us. It's about rebalancing lives that are out of balance. In a world obsessed with busy-ness it is about reclaiming the value of sometimes … just … doing … nothing.

Jamie has a 9-year old daughter and a 5-year old son. The little guy goes to bed a half hour before his daughter does, so she gets an extra 30 minutes each night to quietly decompress. Normally she watches TV, grabs her tablet, or plays a game with Jamie or her mother. One night, her mother was out, and Jamie and his daughter were lazily lounging on the couch.

"I'm bored," she said. "Let's do something."

Jamie responded by telling her that it's good to be bored sometimes and that the two of them should continue to just sit on the couch and do nothing.

"Nooooo!" she protested. "C'mon let's do something more fun!"

Jamie held his ground. "No," he said with a smirk. "Let's just do nothing."

The good-natured squabbling continued. As they jokingly bickered about what to do, she started pushing her father's leg trying to nudge him, metaphorically and literally, into action. Jamie pushed back. The two of them jostled, playfully engaging in a sort of tug of war. They started giggling and laughing, and Jamie had to keep telling his daughter to quiet down so she wouldn't wake her brother. They talked. They cuddled. They pondered the questions that occupy a 9-year-old mind. This continued for half an hour until it was time for his daughter to go to bed.

Two days later, Jamie once again put his son down to sleep and was alone with his daughter for the short time before it was her turn to head off to bed. As the two of them sauntered into the living room to figure out how to occupy the next 30 minutes, his daughter turned to him and coyly asked, "Daddy, can we do nothing again tonight?"

"Yes, honey," he replied. "I'd love that."

REFERENCES

Bakker, A., Demerouti, E., Oerlemans, W., & Sonnentag, S. (2013). Workaholism and daily recovery: A day reconstruction study of leisure activities. *Journal of Organizational Behavior, 34*, 87–107.

Brooks, A., & Lack, L. (2006). A brief afternoon nap following nocturnal sleep restriction: Which nap duration is most recuperative? *Sleep, 29*, 831–840.

Dalai Lama & Hopkins, J. (2002). *How to practice: The way to a meaningful life.* New York, NY: Pocket Books.

de Bloom, J., Radstaak, M., & Guerts, S. (2014). Vacation effects on behavior, cognition, and emotions of compulsive and non-compulsive workers: Do obsessive workers go 'cold turkey'? *Stress and Health, 30*, 232–243.

Kim, S., Park, Y., & Niu, Q. (2017). Micro-break activities at work to recover from daily work demands. *Journal of Organizational Behavior, 38*, 28–44.

Ouellette, P., Kaplan, R., & Kaplan, S. (2005). The monastery as a restorative environment. *Journal of Environmental Psychology, 25*, 175–188.

Reinecke, L., & Trepte, S. (2006). In a working mood? The effects of mood management processes on subsequent cognitive performance. *Journal of Media Psychology, 20*, 3–14.

Sonnentag, S., Mojza, E. J., Binnewies, C., & Scholl, A. (2008). Being engaged at work and detached at home: A week-level study on work engagement, psychological detachment, and affect. *Work & Stress, 22*, 257–276.

Trougakos, J. P., Hideg, I., Cheng, B., & Beal, D. J. (2014). Lunch breaks unpacked: The role of autonomy as a moderator of recovery during lunch. *Academy of Management Journal, 57*, 405–421.

Tucker, P. (2003). The impact of rest breaks upon accident risk, fatigue and performance: A review. *Work & Stress, 17*, 123–137.